The Right Tool for the Job!

Build your students'
understanding of the
How's and **Why's** of
modern construction
with *Construction
Technology: Today
and Tomorrow*

GLENCOE/McGRAW-HILL

Construction Technology
Today and Tomorrow

W.B.TIC. LEARNING RESOURCE CENTRE

ACADIA ... TY LIBRARY
WOLFV ... CANADA

D1430973

Student text—your blueprint for success!

Up-to-date Content Is Comprehensive, Informative, and Practical.

Filled with practical hands-on activities, **Construction Technology** provides exciting opportunities for skills building.

Construction Technology also provides comprehensive coverage of modern construction theory and development. Your students will learn how skills apply to both small- and large-scale construction projects.

Fig. 16-2. The careers available in the construction industry include a wide range of opportunities. Architects, estimators, laborers, and many other people are needed to complete a project.

Fig. 16-3. Tradespeople learn the skills they need in apprenticeship classes.

Fig. 16-9. Operating engineers need to know how to run large pieces of equipment safely. This crane operator must consider the wind and many other factors to be able to place this precast support accurately.

Fig. 16-10. This laborer is assisting a bricklayer by bringing mortar.

360   CONSTRUCTION TECHNOLOGY

CH. 16 CAREERS IN CONSTRUCTION   365

Laborers

Laborers do the supportive physical work at the construction site. Although laborers are not considered tradespeople, they are mentioned here because many laborers go on to become tradespeople. The job requires just what its title implies: hard work. Laborers work as assistants to tradespeople. Fig. 16-10. They dig, shovel, clean up, and do other jobs. They also operate motorized lifts and other equipment.

Most beginning jobs for laborers do not require training. Laborers do need to be in excellent physical condition because of the strenuous nature of the job. Laborers do a lot of standing, walking, and climbing. They must also be able to lift heavy objects. Some employers require laborers to have at least a general knowledge of construction methods and materials. A high school education is helpful but not necessary.

When it comes to meeting your needs, we've hit the nail on the head!

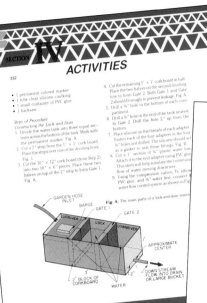

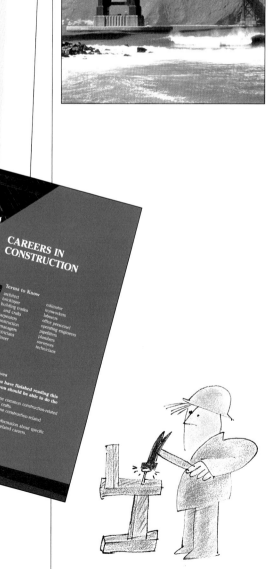

Full-color design frames unrivaled content.

- 4-color photos and illustrations build student interest.
- Readable writing style meets the needs of a wide range of student interests, ability levels, and ages.
- Exciting variety of hands-on construction activities meets the needs of students at all skill levels.
- High-interest features amplify content and boost interest.
- Text integrates basic academic skills into technology education to improve and reinforce basic skills.
- Chapters on construction careers prepare students for working world.

Exciting features break new ground for developing student interest

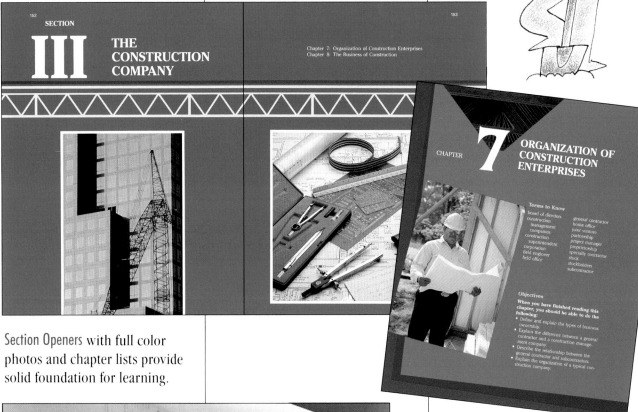

152

SECTION

III

THE CONSTRUCTION COMPANY

153

Chapter 7: Organization of Construction Enterprises
Chapter 8: The Business of Construction

CHAPTER **7** ORGANIZATION OF CONSTRUCTION ENTERPRISES

Terms to Know
board of directors
construction management companies
construction superintendent
corporation
field engineer
field office
general contractor
home office
joint venture
partnership
project manager
proprietorship
specialty contractor
stock
stockholders
subcontractor

Objectives
When you have finished reading this chapter, you should be able to do the following:
• Define and explain the types of business ownership.
• Explain the difference between a general contractor and a construction management company.
• Describe the relationship between the general contractor and subcontractors.
• Explain the organization of a typical construction company.

Section Openers with full color photos and chapter lists provide solid foundation for learning.

Chapter openers provide blueprint for learning:
- Learning Objectives help students focus on key concepts
- Terms to Know introduce students to new vocabulary.

Exciting student text was engineered with teachers in mind.

Teaching Features enliven text.

Construction Facts highlight important, relevant historical events.

Health & Safety emphasizes the *how* and *why* of safe work practices.

Did You Know provides fascinating new information to pique student's interest.

For Discussion springboards class discussion of important concepts and developments.

End of chapter material cements student understanding:

- Chapter Summary reviews main points of chapter.
- Test Your Knowledge reinforces student understanding and tests factual recall.
- Hands-on Activities help students develop basic skills in writing, logical argument, and historical perspective. Symbols for mathematics, science, language arts, and social studies help teachers integrate activities for **Basic Academic Skills.**

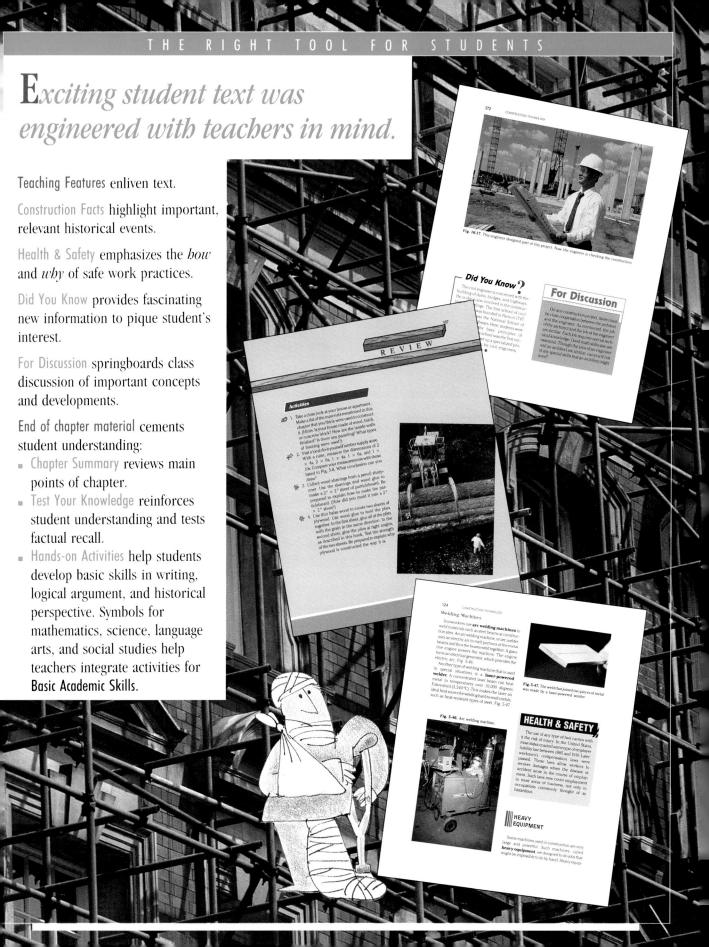

Fig. 16-17. This engineer designed part of this project. Now the engineer is checking the construction.

Did You Know?

The civil engineer is concerned with the building of dams, bridges, and highways. He or she is also involved in the construction of buildings. The first school of civil engineering was founded in Paris in 1747. It was the National School of Bridges and Highways. Here, students were taught the basic principles of construction. This school was the first such school to set up a specialized program for civil engineers.

For Discussion

On any construction project, there must be close cooperation between the architect and the engineer. As mentioned, the job of the architect and the job of the engineer are similar. Each job requires special technical knowledge. Good math skills also are essential. Though the jobs of an engineer and an architect are similar, can you think of any special skills that an architect might need?

Activities

1. Take a close look at your house or apartment. Make a list of the materials mentioned in this chapter that you think were used to construct it. (Hints: Is your house made of wood, brick, or concrete block? How are the inside walls finished? Is there any paneling? What types of flooring were used?)
2. Visit a local do-it-yourself lumber supply store. With a ruler, measure the dimensions of 2 × 4s, 2 × 6s, 1 × 4s, 1 × 6s, and 1 × 10s. Compare your measurements with those listed in Fig. 5-8. What conclusion can you draw?
3. Collect wood shavings from a pencil sharpener. Use the shavings and wood glue to make a 2" × 2" sheet of particleboard. Be prepared to explain how to make the particleboard. (How did you mold it into a 2" × 2" sheet?)
4. Use thin balsa wood to create two sheets of plywood. Use wood glue to hold the piles together. In the first sheet, glue all of the piles with the grain in the same direction. In the second sheet, glue the piles at right angles, as described in this book. Test the strength of the two sheets. Be prepared to explain why plywood is constructed the way it is.

Welding Machines

Ironworkers use **arc welding machines** to weld materials such as steel beams at construction sites. An arc welding machine, or *arc welder*, uses an electric arc to melt portions of the metal beams and thus the beams weld together. A gasoline engine powers the machine. The engine turns an electrical generator, which provides the electric arc. Fig. 5-46.

Another type of welding machine that is used in special situations is a **laser-powered welder.** A concentrated laser beam can heat metal to temperatures over 10,000 degrees Fahrenheit (5,540 °C). This makes the laser an ideal heat source for welding hard-to-melt metals, such as heat-resistant types of steel. Fig. 5-47.

Fig. 5-47. The weld that joined two pieces of metal was made by a laser-powered welder.

Fig. 5-46. Arc welding machine.

HEALTH & SAFETY

The use of any type of tool carries with it the risk of injury. In the United States, most states enacted some type of employer liability law between 1885 and 1910. Later, workmen's compensation laws were passed. These laws allow workers to recover damages when disease or accident arose in the course of employment. Such laws now cover employment in most areas of business, not only in occupations commonly thought of as hazardous.

HEAVY EQUIPMENT

Some machines used in construction are very large and powerful. Such machines, called **heavy equipment,** are designed to do jobs that might be impossible to do by hand. Heavy equip-

The only Teacher's Annotated Edition in the field—because we know there's more to teaching than basic drills and bits of information!

Saves Hours of Valuable Prep Time

Teacher's Annotated Edition helps you teach, with references, ideas for class discussion, enrichment, and student motivation overprinted directly on the student page.

The comprehensive Teacher's Manual provides plans for reinforcing basic skills, adapting to slow and fast learners, and teaching higher-order thinking skills.

A Complete Package for Today's Teacher

CH. 9 TYPES OF CONSTRUCTION PROJECTS. 213

Fig. 9-15. The Hoover Dam, also known as Boulder Dam, is a dam on the Colorado River. The lake formed behind the dam is Lake Mead.

Fig. 9-16. The area shaded light blue in this illustration represents land that will be submerged after the dam is built. People who live in this area must make arrangements to move.

RIVER BEFORE DAM
RIVER AFTER DAM

1. A great deal of soil mechanics and geology as well as engineering is involved in planning and building a dam. Ask a group of students to study and report on these.

2. Discuss the social impact that the building of a dam can have on inhabitants of the area. Consider, for example, the effect on a school district that would be split.

The construction industry as we know it is the result of thousands of years of development. Today we have heavy equipment and sophisticated tools that help us construct tall buildings and other large structures within a short period of time. Fig. 1-1.

The tools and equipment, as well as the processes construction workers use to build structures, are the result of construction technology. **Construction technology** can be described as our use of tools, materials, and processes to build structures such as buildings, highways, and dams. To say this another way, construction technology refers to all the knowledge we have gained about how to build structures to meet our needs.

BUILDINGS AND MUCH MORE

When we think of construction, we generally think first of buildings. However, construction

CH. 1 INTRODUCTION TO CONSTRUCTION 23

includes every type of structure that people build. Construction plays such a universal role in our lives because almost every type of need can be at least partially satisfied by some type of construction.

Community Development

Construction plays an important part in shaping the communities in which we live. Most communities have homes, office buildings, churches, factories, banks, stores, schools, and recreational facilities. Fig. 1-2. In the development of these structures, construction technology is helping us satisfy our needs for shelter, education, employment, and recreation, as well as many other needs. The construction of power plants and sewer and water systems meets our utility needs. The construction of broadcasting towers for radio and television stations makes communication within the community and with the rest of the world more convenient.

Agricultural Needs

Construction also provides many agricultural aids. We build wells and irrigation systems to

Fig. 1-1. The construction of a modern skyscraper draws on the full range of available tools in construction technology.

1. Discuss how the amount of labor needed to build structures has been reduced as more sophisticated tools and equipment have been developed.

Fig. 1-2. Construction contributes to community development by providing homes and facilities for community services.

2. Ask each student to list five recent construction projects in their community. Ask the student to list the need or needs met by each project.

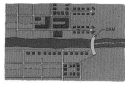

Additional materials provide finishing touches for a truly comprehensive course.

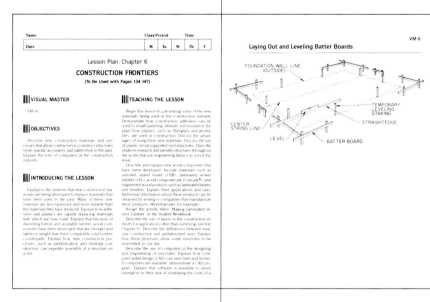

Teacher's Resource Guide
A Rich Variety of Resources

Supplementary Instructional Material includes information on mainstreaming special needs students, developing consumer awareness, leadership, entrepreneurship, and more.

Chapter Lesson Plans provide handy tips for introducing, teaching, reinforcing, and evaluating each lesson.

Two-page **Section Tests**, with answer keys, make it easy to evaluate student progress.

Reproducible Visual Masters enhance your classroom presentations.

Career Information introduces students to construction career options.

Student Workbook includes activities to expand classroom lessons and reinforce and evaluate students' mastery of concepts. Illustrated activity sheets for each section provide still more ways for students to apply learning.

Student Workbook Builds on Classroom Learning.

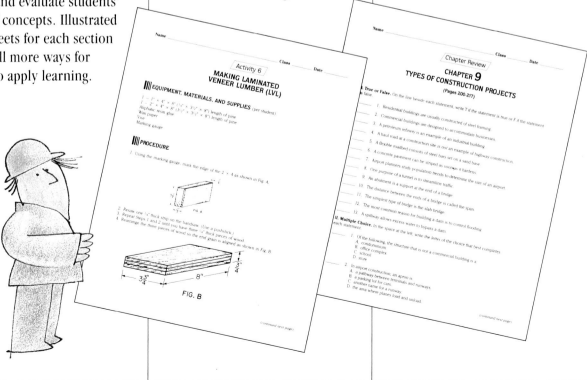

Call or write your nearest
GLENCOE/McGRAW-HILL
office to request examination copy:

NORTHEASTERN REGION
GLENCOE/McGRAW-HILL
25 Crescent St.
Stamford, CT 06906
(203) 964-9109

MID-ATLANTIC REGION
GLENCOE/McGRAW-HILL
Princeton Road, S1
Hightstown, NJ 08520
(609) 426-7356

SOUTHEASTERN REGION
GLENCOE/McGRAW-HILL
6510 Jimmy Carter Boulevard
Norcross, GA 30071
(404) 446-7431

MID-AMERICA REGION
GLENCOE/McGRAW-HILL
846 E. Algonquin Road
Schaumburg, IL 60173
(708) 397-8448
Chicago only (312) 419-1224

MID-CONTINENT REGION
GLENCOE/McGRAW-HILL
846 E. Algonquin Road
Schaumburg, IL 60173
(708) 397-8448

SOUTHWESTERN REGION
GLENCOE/McGRAW-HILL
220 E. Danieldale Road
DeSoto, TX 75115
(214) 224-1562

WESTERN REGION
GLENCOE/McGRAW-HILL
15319 Chatsworth Street
Mission Hills, CA 91345
(818) 898-1391
Includes Alaska

HAWAII
Donald Hosaka
1613 Kanalui Street
Honolulu, HI 96816
Telephone: (808) 734-6971
Telefax: 808-735-4590

DEPARTMENT OF DEFENSE DEPENDENTS
AND ALL OVERSEAS K-12 SCHOOLS
International School Sales
866 Third Avenue
New York, NY 10022-6221 USA
Telephone: (212) 702-3276
Telex: 225925 MACM UR
Telefax: 212-605-9377

The right tool for the job!

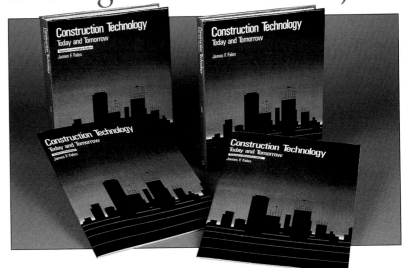

Construction Technology
Today and Tomorrow

Program Components

Student Text
ISBN 0-02-675754-0

Teacher's Annotated Edition
ISBN 0-02-675758-3

Teacher's Resource Guide
ISBN 0-02-675755-9

Student Workbook
ISBN 0-02-675756-7

GLENCOE/McGRAW-HILL
15319 Chatsworth Street
P.O. Box 9509
Mission Hills, CA 91395-9509

C-TE-012-15m 2.90

Construction Technology

Today and Tomorrow

Teacher's Annotated Edition

James F. Fales, Ed.D., CMfgE
Professor and Chairman
Department of Industrial Technology
Ohio University
Athens, Ohio

GLENCOE/McGRAW-HILL
A Macmillan/McGraw-Hill Company
Mission Hills, California

ACADIA UNIVERSITY LIBRARY
WOLFVILLE, N.S., CANADA

Copyright © 1991 by Glencoe/McGraw-Hill Educational Division. All rights reserved. Printed in the United States of America. Except as permitted under the United States Copyright Act of 1976, no part of this publication may be reproduced or distributed in any form or by any means, or stored in a database or retrieval system, without prior permission of the publisher.

Send all inquiries to:
Glencoe/McGraw-Hill
15319 Chatsworth Street
P.O. Box 9509
Mission Hills, CA 91395-9509

ISBN 0-02-675758-3 (Teacher's Annotated Edition)

1 2 3 4 5 6 7 8 9 10   95 94 93 92 91

Vaughan
TA145
.F35
1991
teacher's annotated ed
c1

Teacher's Manual

TABLE OF CONTENTS

SCOPE AND SEQUENCE

	Chapter 1 Introduction to Construction	Chapter 2 Construction and Society
Design and Engineering	— Design structures to meet agricultural needs. — Design structures to meet transportation needs. — Design structures to meet sanitation needs.	— Design safe structures that protect both humans and environment.
Management and Construction Techniques	— Building irrigation systems. — Building pipelines and roads. — Constructing aqueducts. — Processes used in the construction industry.	— Building structures that complement the environment, without destroying it.
Marketing and Finance	— Methods used to market construction projects. — Methods used to finance construction projects.	
Social and Environmental Impacts	— Effects of construction on our world. — Impact of community development. — Environmental effects of construction.	— Personal benefits of construction projects. — Social benefits of construction projects. — Impact of high cost of construction.
Equipment, Tools, and Safety	— Earthmoving equipment.	— Building structures with personal health and safety in mind.
Trends in Technology	— Trend toward more automation.	— Building construction projects while preserving the surrounding environment.

	Chapter 3 Construction Safety	Chapter 4 Construction Materials
Design and Engineering	— Designing safe structures.	— How various materials affect building designs.
Management and Construction Techniques	— Building safe structures.	— Materials used in the construction industry.
Marketing and Finance		
Social and Environmental Impacts	— Impact of loss of productivity as a result of construction accidents.	— Impact of new materials on today's construction projects.
Equipment, Tools, and Safety	— Promoting worker safety. — Promoting safety attitudes. — General safety rules. — Tool and equipment safety. — Fire safety. — First aid.	— Proper handling of construction materials
Trends in Technology	— Safety research.	— Trends toward using more fabricated materials.

Chapter 5 Construction Tools and Equipment	Chapter 6 Construction Frontiers	Chapter 7 Organization of Construction Enterprises
— Tool design.	— Engineering structures using new adhesives, plastics, and wood materials. — Prefabricated and modular designs. — Role of computers in designing and engineering new structures. — Designing and engineering structures for space habitation.	— Field engineer.
— Building structures using various hand tools, power tools, equipment, and heavy equipment.	— Constructing prefabricated structures. — Constructing modular structures. — Managing construction projects with computers. — Constructing structures in space.	— Home office. — Field office. — Project manager. — Construction supervisor. — Contractors and subcontractors.
	— Using computer to keep track of finances.	— Business administration. — Project accounting.
— Impact of tools and equipment on our society.	— Impact of new construction-related technologies on our society.	
— Types of hand tools used in construction. — Types of power tools used in construction. — Types of heavy equipment used in construction.	— Laser tools. — Computers.	— Role of safety in a construction organization.
	— Trends toward using computer in designing and modifying structures.	— Trends in management and labor relations.

	Chapter 8 The Business of Construction	Chapter 9 Types of Construction Projects
Design and Engineering		— Designing and engineering buildings, highways, airports, tunnels, bridges, and dams.
Management and Construction Techniques	— Organizing and controlling the job.	— Techniques used to construct buildings, highways, airports, tunnels, bridges, and dams.
Marketing and Finance	— Performance bonds. — Payment bonds.	— Financing various types of construction projects. — Marketing various types of construction projects.
Social and Environmental Impacts		— Impact of various types of construction on the quality of life.
Equipment, Tools, and Safety	— Protecting the worker. — Protecting the public. — Protecting the environment.	
Trends in Technology		— Types of construction projects.

Chapter 10 The Decision to Build	Chapter 11 Designing and Engineering the Project	Chapter 12 Construction Processes
— Existing structures. — New structures.	— Designing functional structures. — Designing attractive structures. — Structural engineering. — Mechanical and electrical engineering.	— Role of design and engineering in the construction process.
— Selecting the site. — Acquiring a site.	— Architectural drawings. — Structural drawings. — Mechanical drawings.	— Preparing the site. — Building the foundation. — Installing utilities. — Finish work.
— Letter of commitment. — Mortgage notes. — Interest rates. — Bonds. — Appropriations.	— Systems cost. — Presentation models.	
— Impact of zoning laws on site selection.	— How design affects attitude.	
	— Impact of design and engineering on safety. — Using computers to design and engineer safe structures.	— Earthmoving equipment. — Finishing tools. — Installation tools. — Framing tools and equpiment.
— Trends in building new structures. — Trends in modifying existing structures.	— Trends in design.	— Trends in construction process.

	Chapter 13 The Completed Project	Chapter 14 Student Enterprises
Design and Engineering	— Checking the quality of design.	— Making plans and specifications. — Estimating materials. — Planning and scheduling work.
Management and Construction Techniques	— Punch list. — Certificate of occupancy.	— Forming a construction company. — Building a structure. — Selecting management. — Selecting labor.
Marketing and Finance		— Marketing construction projects. — Financing construction projects. — Projecting financial need. — Calculating profit and loss.
Social and Environmental Impacts	— Impact of inspections on quality.	— Working with others.
Equipment, Tools, and Safety	— Maintenance. — Repair.	— Developing a safety program. — Operating tools and equipment in a safe manner.
Trends in Technology	— Trends in preventive maintenance.	— Research in the construction process.

Chapter 15 Preparing for Construction Careers	Chapter 16 Careers in Construction	Notes
	— Careers in engineering and design.	
— Gain work experience. — Apprenticeships.	— Careers in management. — Labor. — Contractor.	
	— Careers in sales. — Careers in advertising. — Careers in accounting.	
— Job interviews. — Making career choices. — Educational requirements.	— Career interest.	
	— Careers in safety.	
	— TSA and VICA programs.	

Overview

CONSTRUCTION TECHNOLOGY: TODAY AND TOMORROW consists of a four-component program for teaching and learning. It includes:

- **Student Text** — a textbook for learning about construction techniques and technologies used in today's world.
- **Teacher's Annotated Edition** — consists of the full Student Text, with teaching suggestions and annotations included on the text pages, plus a bound-in Teacher's Manual.
- **Teacher's Resource Guide** — contains such items as teaching suggestions, visual aids, lesson plans, and section tests.
- **Student Workbook** — provides a wide selection of construction-related activities designed to attract students' interest and reinforce learning.

Each of the components listed above is described in detail on the following pages. Becoming familiar with each of the components will enable you to teach the course in a fashion that will allow your students to gain the greatest benefit from the course.

Section I. Introduction. The chapters in this section provide a general introduction to the main topics in construction technology. They examine the relationship of construction technology to society. Aspects of construction safety also are examined.

Section II. Materials, Tools, Processes. This section discusses the materials, tools and equipment, and processes used in construction technology. Recent and anticipated changes in construction technology are explored in this section.

Section III. The Construction Company. This section discusses the organization of construction enterprises and the general business of construction, especially as it relates to administration and financing.

Section IV. The Construction Project. This section discusses the various types of construction projects, including project design and engineering. It also covers construction processes. This section includes a chapter that presents a student enterprise designed to develop basic building skills.

Section V. Careers. This section discusses the various careers available in construction technology. It also provides information on preparing for these careers.

▌▌▌▌ The Student Text

The CONSTRUCTION TECHNOLOGY: TODAY AND TOMORROW student text is the principal learning tool in the program. It is an information resource that will aid learning and hold students' interest. It includes special features to enhance this core unit in the learning program.

Sections

The chapters of the textbook are divided into five sections. Each of these sections deals with a major theme in construction technology.

Chapters

CONSTRUCTION TECHNOLOGY: TODAY AND TOMORROW contains sixteen chapters. Each chapter presents the topic information in a logical and easily understood manner. The chapter text is carefully organized. The distinctive heads and subheads indicate the main divisions of information in the text. The vocabulary of construction technology is defined on first use. New terms are set in boldface and explained. These terms are also listed in the "Terms to Know" list that opens the chapter. Terms set in boldface also are defined in the glossary.

Each chapter has the following parts:

- **Terms to Know.** This list of key terms appears at the beginning of each chapter. An understanding of these terms is central to a proper understanding of the information in the chapter.
- **Objectives.** Behavior-specific expected learning outcomes are listed at the beginning of each chapter. These can serve as guides for emphasis of text information. They also will suggest points of instruction that should be evaluated.
- **Did You Know?** These are brief informational features that explore information presented or suggested in the text.
- **For Discussion.** These follow each of the main informational units in the chapter, which are headed by number one heads, as shown immediately below.

Number One Heads Are Set in This Type Style.

The topics introduced in these brief sections are designed to prompt teacher-guided class discussion of points relating to text information.

- **Health and Safety.** These specially identified sections present information relating to health and safety. This information may be in the form of safety tips. The section might also provide information relating to the historical development of modern-day safe work practices.
- **Special-Focus Feature.** One of these illustrated features is presented in each chapter. It provides a general exploration of a topic related to the main theme of the chapter.

  Each chapter is followed by a Chapter Review section. This section consists of a chapter summary, chapter review questions, and activities.
- **Chapter Summary.** This summarizes the main informational points of the chapter. It provides, then, a capsule summary of important chapter information.
- **Chapter Review Questions.** Titled "Test Your Knowledge," these questions are

designed to prompt learning reinforcement of the main themes in the chapter.
- **Activities.** These end-of-chapter activities are designed to help the student develop basic skills in the areas of science, math, the social sciences, and language arts. The skills these activities are designed to develop are identified by symbols, which are shown here.

✳ Science	🌐 Social Studies
➗➕ Math	📖 Communications

Special Highlights

- **Four-Color Illustrations.** The many full-color photographs will attract students' interest, motivating them to learn about the new technologies explored in the text. The photographs and drawings provide a strong visual reinforcement for the themes and concepts discussed.
- **End-of-Section Activities.** Each section is supplemented by an activity section, which provides "hands-on" learning experiences. Each of these activities is designed to enhance the students' learning of the information presented in the text. The activities have been developed to meet the needs of students with varying skill levels.
- **Glossary.** The glossary presents a complete alphabetized list of the important terms in the text. Each of the terms is defined. This glossary includes definitions of the terms in the "Terms to Know" list at the beginning of each chapter.
- **Index.** A comprehensive index is a valuable tool, offering the reader immediate access to a text's information. In a technical book, the index is invaluable. It is a guide to the main themes and topics of the text.
- **Objectives.** The main learning goals for each chapter are designated by clearly written objectives, which open the chapter. These objectives present the themes of the chapter in broad outline. They identify the skills and abilities that can be developed from the careful study of the chapter.

The Teacher's Annotated Edition

CONSTRUCTION TECHNOLOGY: TODAY AND TOMORROW is also published in a Teacher's Annotated Edition. This is the book you are now reading. The Teacher's Annotated Edition differs from the student text in the following two ways:
1. The textbook pages include teaching suggestions in the bottom page margins. These annotations are keyed by number to passages in the text.
2. A comprehensive teacher's manual is bound in with the annotated text pages. This teacher's manual is printed in off-white paper.

The Annotations

In the Teacher's Annotated Edition, the annotations are printed in the bottom margins of the text page, making them immediately accessible. These annotations take various forms. They provide discussion questions, additional information, and activity suggestions. This variety allows you to select those teaching suggestions that best suit the needs of your students. Each annotation is keyed by number to a specific text passage on the page.

The Teacher's Manual

The Teacher's Manual bound into the Teacher's Annotated Edition makes class planning and teaching information immediately available. You are now reading the Teacher's Manual. For each chapter of the textbook, the Teacher's Manual includes:
- **Chapter Outline.** States the main topics discussed in the chapter.
- **Main Goal.** A brief statement of the principal instructional goal of the chapter.
- **Objectives.** A set of student-oriented objectives that the student should be able to achieve.

- **Key Facts.** Identify key points of information presented in the chapter.
- **Preparation.** Suggested teaching strategies designed to complement and enhance the instructional unit.
- **Resources.** Suggested supplementary materials that can be used to enhance the learning experience.
- **Teaching.** Offers supplementary activities that can be used in addition to those found in each chapter and the Student Workbook.
- **Evaluation.** Suggestions for reviewing important information with students.
- **Answers to Chapter Review Questions.** Provides the answers to the "Test Your Knowledge" questions found at the end of text chapters.

The Teacher's Manual also offers three course outlines. These present possible schedules for course programs of six, nine, and eighteen weeks.

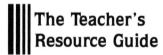

The Teacher's Resource Guide

The separate Teacher's Resource Guide provides a valuable supplement for the teacher. It includes the following resources:
- **Supplemental Information.** This includes information on mainstreaming special needs students, promoting consumer awareness, developing leadership, and entrepreneurship.
- **Chapter Lesson Plans.** There is one lesson plan for each of the sixteen chapters in the text. Each lesson plan contains the following:
— A visual master designed to reinforce learning of a key point in the chapter.
— Chapter objectives.
— Suggestions for introducing the lesson.
— Suggestions for teaching the lesson.
— Suggestions for follow-up assignments.
— Suggestions for evaluation.
- **Section Tests.** These section tests are designed to test students' knowledge of essential information in each of the chapters in the section.

- **Answer Key for Section Tests.** This answer key provides answers to the questions in the section tests.
- **Career Profiles.** These provide key information on specific careers within construction technology. The profiles discuss the necessary training and job responsibilities.

▐▐▐ The Student Workbook

The Student Workbook includes chapter reviews and activities designed to enhance students' retention of major themes presented in the text. Specifically, information in the Student Workbook includes:

- **Chapter Review Questions.** These questions are designed to evaluate students' retention of key information presented in the text. True-false, multiple-choice, matching, and essay-type questions are presented for each chapter.
- **Activities.** The activities are designed to challenge and develop skills at a variety of levels. These activities have been designed to draw on the information discussed in the text.

ESSENTIAL ELEMENTS FOR CONSTRUCTION SYSTEMS

The following list presents topics and concepts for a construction systems course in the trade and industrial education area. Also given are the page numbers of the CONSTRUCTION TECHNOLOGY: TODAY AND TOMORROW textbook that cover these topics and concepts.

Essential Elements	*Text Pages*
1. Safety	
1.1 information regarding safe operation of tools and equipment	51-65, 139, 177-180, 206, 276
1.2 appropriate state and federal safety laws	30, 54, 93, 124, 179, 245, 298
2. Social/cultural impacts of technology	
2.1 technological developments of the past and present	12-19, 24-25, 54, 79-105, 111, 112, 114, 122, 131, 136, 137, 143-145, 163, 208, 212, 226, 235, 253, 263, 268, 286, 303, 351
2.2 procedures for assessing the impact of technological change on society and culture	12-19, 25-27, 143
2.3 information on predicting how technological development will impact future cultures and societies	17-19, 31, 43-44, 143
2.4 technology and the environment	16-17, 31, 37, 143-144, 214, 230
3. Technology and daily life	
3.1 evaluation of selected products according to given standards	135, 297-298
3.2 criteria for selecting, purchasing, and contracting services	174, 222-223
3.3 information that shows the relationships between communication, energy, and production technology	13-19, 38-41
3.4 computer-controlled systems and/or devices used in technology	142, 211
3.5 design process used in product development	28-29, 142, 239-242, 311-313
4. Tools, materials, and processes of technology	
4.1 information regarding the proper use of selected tools and equipment	110-131, 267-292
4.2 properties of a wide range of materials	135-138, 204-205, 267-292, 309-325
4.3 process of various technologies	110-131, 138-142, 267-292
4.4 conservation and recycling of products and materials	25, 137, 303
5. Problem solving	
5.1 creative problem solving using the scientific method	71-73
5.2 standards of measurement	110

ESSENTIAL ELEMENTS COMMON TO ALL INDUSTRIAL TECHNOLOGY EDUCATION COURSES

The following concepts and topics are common to all industrial technology education courses.

Essential Elements	*Text Pages*
(1) Leadership concepts and skills	
(A) demonstrate skills, characteristics, and responsibilities of leaders and effective group members	329, 374
(B) demonstrate a knowledge of parliamentary procedure principles	308
(C) plan and conduct leadership activities	308, 374
(D) prepare for effective citizenship and for participation in our democratic society	308, 374
(2) Concepts and skills related to successful employment and/or postsecondary training	
(A) identify employment opportunities and preparation requirements in chosen fields	340-357, 358-377
(B) identify effective methods to secure and terminate employment	340-357, 358-377
(C) demonstrate effective communication skills both oral and written and follow through on assigned tasks	133, 307-326
(D) demonstrate dependability and punctuality	307-326, 345
(E) demonstrate productive work habits and attitudes	307-326
(F) understand the importance of taking pride in the quality of work performed	307-326, 341-357
(G) recognize the dignity in work	307-326
(H) develop skills in planning and organizing work	133, 307-326
(I) apply required methods and sequences when performing tasks	110-131, 307-326
(J) apply principles of time management and work simplification when performing assigned tasks	307-326
(K) identify ethical practices and responsibilities	175-177
(L) understand the importance of the application of organized policies and procedures	180-187, 307-326

Essential Elements	*Text Pages*

(3) Concepts and skills associated with entrepreneurship

    (A) identify opportunities for business ownership — 155-163, 373-374

    (B) understand the risk and profit motive factor — 155-156, 373-374

    (C) understand the elements and advantages of the free enterprise system — 155, 373-374

    (D) explain the role of small businesses in the free enterprise system — 155-157, 373-374

(4) Concepts and skills associated with human relations and personality development

    (A) understand the importance of maintaining good health and proper appearance for effective job performance — 345

    (B) understand oneself and others — 341-344, 374

    (C) exercise self-control — 374

    (D) accept and use criticism — 309-325, 374

    (E) recognize basic human relationships as they relate to business success — 308, 374

    (F) demonstrate characteristics for successful working relationships — 307-326, 374

(5) Concepts and skills related to personal and business management

    (A) explain how management assists in reaching personal and family goals — 328

    (B) explain the management process — 155-166, 180-186

    (C) describe the role of management in controlling stress — 164

    (D) identify and understand personal checking accounts — 357

    (E) identify and understand personal loan application processes — 357

    (F) identify and understand different financial institutions — 354

    (G) identify the role and functions of business management — 164, 180-186, 307-309

    (H) understand the lines of authority — 155-166, 180-186, 307-309

    (I) identify effective supervisory techniques — 155-166, 180-186, 307-326

(6) Concepts and skills related to the application of safety practices

    (A) demonstrate safe operation of appropriate tools, machines, and equipment — 57-59, 307-326

    (B) maintain a safe and clean laboratory environment — 57-59, 307-326

    (C) investigate appropriate state and federal safety laws — 54, 177-180, 298

Essential Elements	*Text Pages*

(7) Concepts and skills related to social/cultural impacts of technology

    (A) investigate ideas and technological developments of the past and present — 12-19, 24-25, 40-43, 111, 112, 114, 122, 131, 208, 212

    (B) assess the characteristics of technological change on society and culture — 12-19, 27, 41-43

    (C) predict how selected technological developments will impact future cultures and societies — 17-19, 31, 43

    (D) explore the impact technology has on the environment — 16-17, 31, 41-43

(8) Concepts and skills related to the application of technology to daily life

    (A) evaluate selected products based on given standards or applications — 222-223, 297-298

    (B) develop criteria for selecting, purchasing, and contracting services — 161-163, 171-174

    (C) practice the servicing of selected products and equipment of technology — 133, 301-302

    (D) investigate the interrelationship of all technology areas — 12-19

    (E) use computer-controlled systems and/or devices related to each course — 142-143

    (F) apply the design process to product development — 28-29, 142-143, 222-223, 239-242, 311-313

(9) Concepts and skills related to the tools, materials and processes of technology

    (A) become proficient in the use of appropriate tools, machines, and equipment — 306-329

    (B) analyze the properties of a wide range of materials of technology through testing — 191-193, 330-331, 382-383

    (C) explore the processes of various technologies — 69-71, 110-131, 138-142, 267-292, 331-333

    (D) investigate and practice conservation and recycling of products and materials of technology — 25, 137, 303

(10) Concepts and skills related to the application of problem solving techniques

    (A) identify and creatively solve technological problems using the scientific method — 71-73

    (B) explore standards of measurement used in technology and apply measurement in the solution of problems — 68-69, 148-150, 190, 191-193, 330-331, 378-381, 382-383, 384-387

    (C) communicate oral, written, and computational technical information — 133, 171-174, 378-381, 384-387

Content Outline

The six-week, nine-week, and eighteen-week course outlines given below vary in length. This will affect the depth of coverage for each topic. Regardless of course length, the basic concepts of construction technology should be taught.

CONSTRUCTION TECHNOLOGY: TODAY AND TOMORROW Six-Week Course Outline
Section I.   Introduction . . . .(One Week)
    Key concepts from Chapter 1 through Chapter 3.
Section II.   Materials, Tools, and Processes . . . .(One Week)
    Key concepts from Chapter 4 through Chapter 6.
Section III. The Construction Company . . . .(One Week)
    Key concepts from Chapter 7 through Chapter 8.
Section IV. The Construction Project. . . . .(Two Weeks)
    Key concepts from Chapter 9 through Chapter 14.
Section V. Careers. . . . .(One Week)
    Key concepts from Chapter 15 through Chapter 16.

CONSTRUCTION TECHNOLOGY: TODAY AND TOMORROW Nine-Week Course Outline
Section I.   Introduction . . . .(One Week)
    Key concepts from Chapter 1 through Chapter 3.
Section II.   Materials, Tools, and Processes . . . .(Two Weeks)
    Key concepts from Chapter 4 through Chapter 6.
Section III. The Construction Company . . . .(Two Weeks)
    Key concepts from Chapter 7 through Chapter 8.
Section IV. The Construction Project . . . .(Three Weeks)
    Key concepts from Chapter 9 through Chapter 14.
Section V. Careers. . . . .(One Week)
    Key concepts from Chapter 15 through Chapter 16.

CONSTRUCTION TECHNOLOGY: TODAY AND TOMORROW Eighteen-Week Course Outline
Section I.   Introduction. . . . .(Three Weeks)
    Chapter   1: Introduction to Construction
    Chapter   2: Construction and Society
    Chapter   3: Construction Safety
Section II.   Materials, Tools, and Processes . . . .(Three Weeks)
    Chapter   4: Construction Materials
    Chapter   5: Construction Tools and Equipment
    Chapter   6: Construction Frontiers
Section III. The Construction Company . . . .(Two Weeks)
    Chapter   7: Organization of Construction Enterprises
    Chapter   8: The Business of Construction
Section IV. The Construction Project. . . . .(Eight Weeks)
    Chapter   9: Types of Construction Projects
    Chapter 10: The Decision to Build
    Chapter 11: Designing and Engineering the Project

Teaching Strategies

For the full potential of the CONSTRUCTION TECHNOLOGY: TODAY AND TOMORROW textbook to be realized, it must be complemented with a variety of teaching strategies. Educators must emphasize basic skills as well as hands-on skills if students are to become productive members of society. Students should be shown how to apply the skills they have learned in academic courses such as math, science, language arts, or social studies. This can be done through the activities presented at the end of each chapter and at the end of each section. To further aid the teacher, the text uses symbols to identify which basic skills (math, science, language arts, social studies) are being reinforced by the activity. Optional activities that can be used to enhance learning can be found in the Teacher's Resource Guide and Student Workbook.

Through use of the discussion questions in the Teacher's Annotated Edition, teachers can expand the level of learning. By effectively using these discussion questions, teachers can help develop higher-order thinking skills. By combining hands-on activities with the discussion questions, students can enhance basic problem-solving skills.

It is important to develop the potential of all students. This includes students with special needs. It is important to remember that special needs students will need to develop the same skills as other students. To accomplish this task, the teacher may need to adapt his or her teaching methods and classroom. For example, visually impaired students may need the opportunity to explore the classroom and lab area. This will allow them to become familiar with the facility surroundings. In classrooms, visually-impaired students should be seated in the front of the room. When conducting a lecture or demonstration, it is important to be specific. Identify each point or operation clearly.

You may also have hearing-impaired students in your courses. Like visually-impaired students, students with hearing impairments should be seated toward the front of the room. When lecturing, remember to speak clearly and distinctly in a normal tone of voice.

For teaching students with physical disabilities, your lab or classroom may need to be modified to eliminate physical barriers. Equipment and work areas should be arranged to accommodate wheelchair travel. Ramps should replace stairs.

For a more complete discussion of mainstreaming special needs students, see the Teacher's Resource Guide.

By providing students with basic academic and problem-solving skills, educators are preparing students for an active role in society.

CHAPTER 1 LESSON PLAN

INTRODUCTION TO CONSTRUCTION

Essential Elements for the Course: 1.2, 2.1, 2.2, 2.4, 3.5, 4.4
Common Essential Elements: (7 A, B, C, D), (8 F), (9 D)

▍▍▍Chapter Outline

I. Buildings and Much More
II. From Camels to Cranes
III. Highlights of the Construction Process
IV. The Price of Progress

▍▍▍Main Goal

The main goal of this chapter is to help students understand how construction technology has contributed to the development of today's society.

▍▍▍Objectives

As a result of studying this chapter, students will be able to:
1. Describe construction technology.
2. Identify the effects of construction on our world.
3. Explain the procedure for constructing a building.

▍▍▍Key Facts

- Construction technology is the use of tools, materials, and processes to build structures such as buildings, highways, and dams.
- The construction process refers to everything that happens from the decision to build the structure to the owner's acceptance of the completed structure.
- Financing is the term used to describe the money used to pay for a project.
- The general contractor is in charge of the construction work.
- Scheduling involves estimating the amount of time it will take to do each part of the job.
- The owner's acceptance of the completed project is called transfer of ownership. It includes a formal notice of completion that legally establishes that the job has been completed.
- Inspectors check to see that the job has been done properly and according to the contract.

▍▍▍Preparation

Preparation before introducing Chapter 1:
1. Gather the needed materials and supplies to conduct the chapter activities.
2. Duplicate any transparency masters, handouts, and lab sheets needed to introduce students to Chapter 1.
3. Before the lesson, identify examples of local construction projects that are being built to satisfy various community needs.
4. Contact an area architect, engineer, and/or general contractor to discuss what considerations are made when preparing plans for a construction project. Be sure to discuss site selection, financing, and selecting materials.
5. Assign students to read the chapter.

▍▍▍Resources

Books

Fales, J. F., Kuetemeyer, V. F., and Brusic, S. K. *Technology: Today and Tomorrow.* Mission Hills, CA: Glencoe/McGraw-Hill, 1988.

Harpur, P. (ed.). *The Timetable of History*. New York: Hearst, 1982.

Lux, D. G., Ray, W. E., Blankenbaker, E. K., and Umstattd, W. *World of Construction*. Mission Hills, CA: Glencoe/McGraw-Hill, 1982.

▐▐▐▐ Teaching

This chapter is basically introductory. Review the objectives for this chapter carefully. Then:

1. Divide the class into three or four groups. Each group should search through newspapers to identify a local construction project. Have the groups discuss the potential positive and negative effects of the construction project on the community.
2. Invite an architect or general contractor to visit the class and discuss his or her role in the construction process.

▐▐▐▐ Evaluation

After completing this chapter, assign the study questions at the end of the chapter. Check the students' mastery of the text information by comparing the students' answers against the answers given below.

To further assess the students' understanding of the material, assign Chapter 1 of the *Student Workbook*.

After students have studied all the chapters in the section, administer the section test in the *Teacher's Resource Guide*. Check their answers against the answers given in the Guide.

Answers to Chapter Review Questions

1. Homes, banks, stores, office buildings, schools, factories, recreational facilities. (Accept any five.)
2. Wells, irrigation systems, dams, and irrigation canals can be built to irrigate land for agricultural purposes.
3. Highways, airports, bridges, railroads, seaports, and pipelines are examples of structures that can be built to help meet our transportation needs.
4. By building sewage treatment plants to neutralize or remove harmful waste from water before it is returned to the environment.
5. The transcontinental railroad opened up vast new areas for settlement by providing a relatively easy method of transportation to the West. It also provided a means of communication with people in the rest of the United States.
6. Cranes, dump trucks, and bulldozers.
7. The owner and the contractor (construction company). Attorneys, realtors, and financing companies also may participate at some stage of the process.
8. The project plans give all the information necessary to build the structure as it was designed and engineered. They show the construction workers how to build the structure and what materials to use.
9. Making sure workers have access to the site, putting portable offices and rest rooms at the site, and installing temporary utilities such as water and electricity.
10. Construction sometimes has a harmful effect on the environment or on the people who live in the area. We must decide whether the good accomplished by the construction project outweighs its bad effects.

CHAPTER 2 LESSON PLAN

Construction and Society

Essential Elements for the Course: 2.3, 2.4, 3.3
Common Essential Elements: (7 A, B, C, D)

▌▌▌ Chapter Outline

I. The Built Environment
II. Construction and the Economy
III. Ecology and the Environment
IV. Cost of Construction

▌▌▌ Main Goal

The main goal of this chapter is to help students understand how construction has impacted both the society and the environment in which we live.

▌▌▌ Objectives

As a result of studying this chapter, students will be able to:
1. Define "the built environment."
2. Explain how construction contributes to the economy.
3. Identify two major concerns people have about construction.
4. Identify several factors that affect the cost of constructing a project.

▌▌▌ Key Facts

- Construction is the building of structures.
- Environment simply means "surroundings."
- Structures, along with other parts of the environment that people have shaped or altered, can be referred to as the built environment.
- Ecology is the study of the way plants and animals exist together. It also studies the relationships of plants and animals to their environment.
- A study that evaluates the effects of a project on the environment is called an environmental impact study.

▌▌▌ Preparation

Preparation before introducing Chapter 2:
1. Gather the needed materials and supplies to conduct the chapter activities.
2. Duplicate any transparency masters, handouts, and lab sheets needed to introduce students to Chapter 2.
3. Before the lesson, identify examples of local construction projects that provide personal and social benefits.
4. Invite local contractors, architects, and developers to discuss how alternative construction methods may be used to reduce construction costs.
5. Assign students to read the chapter.

▌▌▌ Resources

Books

Fales, J. F., Kuetemeyer, V. F., and Brusic, S. K. *Technology: Today and Tomorrow.* Mission Hills, CA: Glencoe/McGraw-Hill, 1988.
Harpur, P. (ed.). *The Timetable of History.* New York: Hearst, 1982.

Lux, D. G., Ray, W. E., Blankenbaker, E. K., and Umstattd, W. *World of Construction*. Mission Hills, CA: Glencoe/McGraw-Hill, 1982.

▌▌▌▌ Teaching

This chapter is basically introductory. Review the objectives for this chapter carefully. Then:

1. Using the newspaper to locate construction projects, have students discuss whether the project was designed to provide personal or social benefits.
2. Using the real estate section of the newspaper, have the students compare the cost of home construction today with the cost of home construction ten years ago. Ask students to discuss ways to reduce rising construction costs.
3. Using a local construction project, ask students to discuss the social, economical, and environmental effects the project may have on the community.

▌▌▌▌ Evaluation

After completing this chapter, assign the study questions at the end of the chapter. Check the students' mastery of the information by comparing the students' answers against the answers given below.

To further assess the students' understanding of the material, assign Chapter 2 of the *Student Workbook*.

After students have studied all the chapters in the section, administer the section test in the *Teacher's Resource Guide*. Check their answers against the answers given in the Guide.

Answers to Chapter Review Questions

1. A person's total surroundings.
2. Food, shelter, and clothing.
3. Construction contributes to our social lives by providing meeting places where people can be sociable.
4. By attracting newcomers to the community, where they spend their money, and by providing jobs for many people.
5. Building a dam can control flooding and provide electricity, irrigation, and a reservoir that can serve as a recreational area.
6. Building a dam can decrease soil fertility, increase the salt level of the soil, raise the water table, displace people, cost a great deal of money, endanger wildlife, and flood historic sites and agricultural land. (Accept any three.)
7. Endangered Species Act.
8. To assess the impact of a proposed construction project on the environment.
9. Land, materials, and labor costs.
10. More people now live in apartments and condominiums because private homes are too expensive.

CHAPTER 3 LESSON PLAN

Construction Safety

Essential Elements for the Course: 1.1, 1.2, 2.1
Common Essential Elements: (6 A, B, C), (9 C), (10 A, B)

▐▐ Chapter Outline

I. Accident Prevention
II. Developing a Safety Prevention Program

▐▐ Main Goal

The main goal of this chapter is to help students understand that safety is essential to the success of any construction project.

▐▐ Objectives

As a result of studying this chapter, students will be able to:
1. Identify two major safety concerns in the construction industry.
2. Describe the safety measures taken by construction companies to protect workers on the job.
3. Understand the importance of safety rules and regulations in your school laboratory.
4. Describe first-aid techniques used in case of an accident.

▐▐ Key Facts

- An accident is an unexpected happening that results in injury, loss, or damage.
- A safety factor is an extra measure of strength added to the design of a structure.
- Safety rules are regulations aimed at preventing accidents and injuries in the work place.
- The Occupational Safety and Health Administration (OSHA) sets standards that regulate safety at construction sites.
- Labor unions are worker-controlled organizations that are formed to present the demands of the workers to the management of the company.
- First aid is the immediate care given to a person who has been injured. The purpose of first aid is to temporarily relieve the pain caused by the injury or to protect the wound until further medical attention can be provided.

▐▐ Preparation

Preparation before introducing Chapter 3.
1. Gather the needed materials and supplies to conduct the chapter activities.
2. Duplicate any transparency masters, handouts, and lab sheets needed to introduce students to Chapter 3.
3. Before the lesson, talk to local contractors, architects, and developers about the safety practices they use when planning and constructing structures.
4. Contact the nearest OSHA agency. Obtain a copy of the safety regulations used for construction projects.

▐▐ Resources

Books

Fales, J. F., Kuetemeyer, V. F., and Brusic, S. K. *Technology: Today and Tomorrow.* Mission Hills, CA: Glencoe/McGraw-Hill, 1988.

Harpur, P. (ed.). *The Timetable of History.* New York: Hearst, 1982.

Lux, D. G., Ray, W. E., Blankenbaker, E. K., and Umstattd, W. *World of Construction.* Mission Hills, CA: Glencoe/McGraw-Hill, 1982.

▐▐▐ Teaching

Since safety is essential to any construction project, it is important that students understand the importance of good safety practices. Review the objectives for this chapter carefully. Then:

1. Divide the class into groups of three. Have each group create a video commercial illustrating the proper use of a lab tool or machine.
2. Have students identify safety features found in their school and shop area.
3. Visit a nearby construction site. Ask students to identify worker safety practices and workplace safety features.
4. Have students discuss the importance of safety from the point of view of both the worker and owner.

▐▐▐ Evaluation

After completing this chapter, assign the study questions at the end of the chapter. Check the students' mastery of the information by comparing the students' answers against the answers given below.

To further assess the students' understanding of the material, assign Chapter 3 of the *Student Workbook.*

After students have studied all the chapters in the section, administer the section test in the *Teacher's Resource Guide.* Check their answers against the answers given in the Guide.

Answers to Chapter Review Questions

1. Five safety features that can help protect the public are safety barriers, security fences, caution signs, protected walkways, and security guards.
2. The two major safety concerns of the construction industry are (1) to build safe structures, and (2) to provide construction workers with a safe place to work and knowledge of safety rules.
3. A worker with good safety shows concern for his or her own safety as well as the safety of others.
4. Insurance companies are concerned about safety because if a worker is injured on the job, they may have to pay his or her medical expenses.
5. If you do not know how to operate a tool or machine, you should ask your instructor to help you.
6. When lifting heavy objects you should ask for help. You should lift using the muscles in your legs, not those in your back.
7. You should not carry tools in your pocket because many tools have sharp edges and points that might cut you, especially if you were to slip or fall.
8. Three-prong plugs should have all prongs intact to avoid the possibility of giving a severe electrical shock.
9. Only an extinguisher approved for use on Class C fires should be used to put out an electrical fire.
10. The purpose of first aid is to temporarily relieve the pain caused by an injury or protect the wound until further medical attention can be provided.

CHAPTER 4 LESSON PLAN

Construction Materials

Essential Elements for the Course: 1.2, 2.1
Common Essential Elements: (7 A)

||| Chapter Outline

I. Concrete
II. Lumber and Wood Composites
III. Masonry
IV. Metals
V. Other Materials
VI. Fasteners

||| Main Goal

The main goal of this chapter is to help students gain a knowledge of the basic materials used in a variety of construction activities.

||| Objectives

As a result of studying this chapter, students will be able to:
1. List and identify the ingredients of concrete.
2. Identify the types of wood and wood composites used in construction.
3. Describe two kinds of masonry that are used in construction.
4. Identify the uses of different kinds of metals in construction.
5. Identify and describe materials used for insulation, interior surfaces, roofing, and flooring in construction.
6. Identify several types of adhesives and mechanical fasteners and explain their uses.

||| Key Facts

- Concrete is a mixture of sand, rocks, and a binder.
- Portland cement is the binder for concrete. Portland cement is a mixture of clay and limestone that has been roasted in a special oven called a kiln.
- Aggregate is the sand and rock used in concrete. The main purpose of aggregate is to take up space. About seventy-five percent of a batch of concrete is aggregate.
- Admixtures are anything added to a batch of concrete other than cement, water, and aggregate.
- Concrete has a great amount of compression strength, which means it can carry a lot of weight per square inch (psi).
- Softwood does not refer to wood that is soft; it refers to wood that comes from coniferous (evergreen) trees.
- Hardwood is wood that comes from deciduous trees. These trees shed their leaves each season.
- Dimension lumber is lumber that measures between 2 and 5 inches thick.
- Board lumber is lumber that measures less than 1½ inches thick and 4 or more inches wide.
- Nominal size is the size of the lumber when it is cut from the log.
- Wood composites are those products that are made from a mixture of wood and other materials.
- Plywood is made of several thin plies, or veneers, of wood that have been glued together.
- Particleboard is made of wood chips that have been pressed and glued together.
- Waferboard is made of large wood chips that are pressed and glued together and then cured with heat.

- Hardboard is made up of very small, thread-like fibers of wood that are pressed together.
- Fiberboard is made from vegetable fibers such as those from corn or sugarcane stalks.
- Paneling is the term used to describe hardboard or plywood panels that have been prefinished.
- Laminated beams are long, thin strips of wood that have been glued together.
- Laminated joints are made of three parts: two flanges and a web. The flanges are at right angles to the web, forming a cross-section that looks like the capital letter I.
- Masonry is the process of using mortar to join bricks, blocks, and other units of construction.
- Mortar is a combination of masonry cement, sand, and water.
- Masonry cement is basically a commercially prepared mixture of portland cement and hydrated lime.
- Steel that is used to support any part of a structure is called structural steel.
- Structural steel can be processed into a number of different shapes and sizes. These standard shapes and sizes are called standard stock.
- Reinforcing bars are steel bars that run through the inside of the concrete.
- Metals that do not contain iron are called non-ferrous metals.
- Insulation helps keep heat from penetrating the building in the summer and cold from penetrating in winter.
- A special vapor barrier is needed to prevent water from condensing.
- Asphalt is a petroleum product made from crude oil.
- Various kinds of flooring or floor covering are used in buildings.
- Adhesives are materials that hold, or bond, other materials together.
- Mastics are thick, pastelike adhesives.
- Contact cement is an adhesive that is applied to the surface of materials and then allowed to dry before the materials are combined.

Preparation

Preparation before introducing Chapter 4:
1. Gather the needed materials and supplies to conduct the chapter activities.
2. Duplicate any transparency masters, handouts, and lab sheets needed to introduce students to Chapter 4.
3. During the lesson, discuss with the students the materials used in the construction industry.
4. Familiarize yourself with the construction projects in your area. Try to identify the various materials used to construct the project.
5. Since this chapter discusses several types of materials, it would be a good opportunity for students to conduct a materials test. Therefore, you should obtain or purchase several pieces of materials-testing equipment. It's a good idea to check with your science department.
6. Assign students to read the chapter.

Resources

Books

Fales, J. F., Kuetemeyer, V. F., and Brusic, S. K. *Technology: Today and Tomorrow.* Mission Hills, CA: Glencoe/McGraw-Hill, 1988.

Lux, D. G., Ray, W. E., Blankenbaker, E. K., and Umstattd, W. *World of Construction.* Mission Hills, CA: Glencoe/McGraw-Hill, 1982.

Teaching

Review the objectives for this chapter carefully. Then:
1. Divide the class into three groups. Assign each group a different type of construction (e.g., residential housing, high-rise structures,

highways, bridges). Have each group create a list of the materials needed to construct project.

2. Divide the class into groups of three. Assign each group a materials testing problem. Problems could include:
   - Testing the strength of plain concrete relative to the strength of reinforced concrete.
   - Testing the strength of hard and soft woods relative to the strength of composite woods like plywood, particleboard, waferboard, fiberboard, prefinished panels, laminated beams, and laminated joints.

3. Have the students place different types of interior and exterior finishing materials in bowls of water. Have the students compare the materials over a period of time.

4. Have the students make a laminated board by gluing together thin pieces of wood.

5. Divide the class into groups of three. Have each group take scrap pieces of sheet metal and bend them into different beamshapes (e.g., I-shape, L-shape, channel, flat). Using a testing fixture, test each shape for deflection and compare the results.

▐▐▐▐ Evaluation

After completing this chapter, assign the study questions at the end of the chapter. Check the students' mastery of the information by comparing the students' answers with the answers given below.

To further assess the students' understanding of the material, assign Chapter 4 of the *Student Workbook*.

After students have studied all the chapters in the section, administer the section test in the *Teacher's Resource Guide*. Check their answers against the answers given in the Guide.

Answers to Chapter Review Questions

1. The main ingredients of portland cement concrete are portland cement, water, and aggregate.
2. The main purpose of aggregate in concrete is to take up space.
3. An admixture is anything that is added to concrete other than cement, water, and aggregate. Examples are color, accelerator, and retarder.
4. Softwood comes from coniferous, or evergreen, trees; hardwood comes from deciduous trees.
5. Most of the lumber used in construction is made of softwood.
6. Nominal size is the size of the lumber when it is cut from the tree; actual size is the finished size after the lumber has been dried and smoothed.
7. The types of wood composites are plywood, particleboard, waferboard, fiberboard, prefinished panels, laminated beams, and laminated joists. (Accept any two.)
8. Two common types of masonry are brick and concrete block.
9. The purpose of mortar is to hold the units of masonry together.
10. Two types of steel reinforcers for concrete are reinforcing bars and mesh.
11. Three common types of insulation material are fiberglass, cellulose, and plastic.
12. Four kinds of flooring that are commonly used in buildings are carpet, floor tile, wood flooring, and terrazzo.

CHAPTER 5 LESSON PLAN

Construction Tools and Equipment

Essential Elements for the Course: 1.2, 2.1, 4.1, 4.3, 5.2, 5.3, 6.16
Common Essential Elements: (2 C, H, I), (7 A), (8 C), (9 C), (10 C)

▌▌▌ Chapter Outline

I. Hand Tools
II. Power Tools
III. Equipment
IV. Heavy Equipment

▌▌▌ Main Goal

The main goal of this chapter is to expose students to the various tools and equipment used in the construction industry.

▌▌▌ Objectives

As a result of studying this chapter, students will be able to:
1. List the four categories of construction tools and equipment, and give two examples of each.
2. Recognize and know the uses of various hand tools and power tools.
3. Recognize and know the uses of various kinds of construction equipment.
4. Describe three pieces of heavy equipment.

▌▌▌ Key Facts

- Hand tools are tools that use power supplied by a person.
- Folding rules and tape measures are used to measure construction materials.
- Digital rules are used to measure relatively long distances.
- Framing squares are used to measure 90-degree angles at the corners of framework and joints.
- A level is a long, straight tool that contains one or more vials of liquid. It is used to make sure that something is exactly horizontal (level) or vertical (plumb).
- A chalk line or chalk box is used to mark a straight line.
- The face, or pounding surface, of the claw hammer is used to drive nails. The opposite face is a V-shaped notch called a claw, which is used to remove nails from boards.
- Sledgehammers are heavy hammers that are used to drive stakes into the ground and to break up concrete and stone.
- One of the most common types of pry bar has a chisel at one end and a chisel with a claw for pulling nails at the other end.
- The standard screwdriver has a flat tip and is designed to fit a standard slotted screw.
- The phillips screwdriver has a tip shaped like an X.
- A spiral ratchet screwdriver is one that relies on a pushing force rather than a twisting force.
- A ripsaw has chisel-like teeth designed for ripping or cutting with the grain of the wood.
- A crosscut saw is used to cut across the grain of the wood.
- A backsaw is a special kind of handsaw that has a very thin blade. The backsaw is used to make very straight cuts, such as those on trim and molding.
- A hacksaw is used to cut metal.
- Wood chisels are used to trim wood.
- Cold chisels are used to cut metal objects.
- A nail set is used to drive finishing nails below the surface of wooden trim and molding.

- Pipe wrenches are used to turn objects that are round, such as pipes.
- Brick trowels are used to place and trim mortar between bricks or concrete blocks.
- A bull float is used to smooth the surface of wet concrete.
- A radial arm saw consists of a motor-driven saw blade that is hung on an arm over a table. This type of saw is used mostly for crosscutting various pieces of wood.
- A table saw consists of a blade mounted on an electric motor beneath a tablelike surface.
- A miter gage is an attachment used to cut an angle using a table saw.
- A portable circular saw is used to cut materials that are difficult to cut with stationary tools.
- A power miter saw is a circular saw mounted over a small table. The saw pivots to enable the worker to cut various angles in wood.
- A saber saw has a knife-shaped blade that reciprocates (moves up and down) to cut curves.
- Power drills are used for drilling holes in wood, metal, and concrete.
- The chuck is the part of a drill that holds the twist drill bit, or bit.
- Pneumatic hammers, or jackhammers, are used to break up concrete or asphalt paving.
- A rotary hammer operates with both rotating and reciprocating action. It is used to drill holes in concrete.
- Equipment is a term that refers to large, complex tools and machines.
- A transit measures horizontal and vertical angles.
- Surveyors use a surveyor's level to find an unknown elevation from a known one.
- Water pumps are used to remove water so that work can be done.
- A concrete pump moves concrete from the concrete mixer to the concrete forms efficiently.
- Conveyors are used to move materials other than fluids from one location to another.
- Ironworkers use arc welding machines to weld materials such as steel beams at a construction site.
- A laser-powered welder uses a concentrated laser beam that can heat metal to temperatures over 10,000°F.

- Heavy equipment includes machines designed to do jobs that might be impossible to do by hand.
- A crawler crane is mounted on metal treads so that it can move over rough terrain.
- A truck crane is mounted on a truck frame so that it can be driven to the site.
- A tower crane has a built-in jack that raises the crane from floor to floor as the building is constructed.
- An excavator is a machine that is used for digging. It scoops up earth from one place and deposits it in another.
- A backhoe is a type of excavator that is used for general digging.
- A trencher is a special kind of excavator that is used to dig trenches, or long, narrow ditches, for pipelines and cables.
- A tractor equipped with a front-mounted pushing blade is known as a bulldozer.
- Machines with large scoops used for shoveling are called front-end loaders.
- A scraper is a machine that is used for loading, hauling, and dumping soil over medium or long distances.
- A grader is an earthworking machine that is used to grade, or level, the ground.
- A compactor, or roller, is used to compact the soil of a roadway just before the road is paved.
- Pavers are used to place, spread, and finish concrete or asphalt materials.

▌▌▌▌ Preparation

Preparation before introducing Chapter 5:
1. Gather the needed materials and supplies to conduct the chapter activities.
2. Duplicate any transparency masters, handouts, and lab sheets needed to introduce students to Chapter 5.
3. Collect a variety of examples of the tools and equipment described in this chapter.
4. Assign students to read the chapter.

‖‖ Resources

Books

Fales, J. F., Kuetemeyer, V. F., and Brusic, S. K. *Technology: Today and Tomorrow.* Mission Hills, CA: Glencoe/McGraw-Hill, 1988.

Lux, D. G., Ray, W. E., Blankenbaker, E. K., and Umstattd, W. *World of Construction.* Mission Hills, CA: Glencoe/McGraw-Hill, 1982.

‖‖ Teaching

Review the objectives for this chapter carefully. Then:

1. Divide the class into groups of three or four. Assign each group a hypothetical construction activity (e.g., remodeling a house, constructing a garage, building a highway, preparing a site for a new shopping mall). Then have students create a list of the tools and equipment needed to construct the project.
2. In a teacher-guided discussion, ask students to explain some of the social and environmental impacts surrounding the use of hand tools, power tools equipment, and heavy equipment.
3. Stress the importance of reading a rule accurately. Provide each student with a customary rule, a metric rule, and a length of stock. Then ask each student to measure the length and width of the stock using first a customary rule and then a metric rule. Refer students also to the metric activity on pages 384-387.

‖‖ Evaluation

After completing this chapter, assign the study questions at the end of the chapter. Check the students' mastery of the information by comparing the students' answers with the answers given below.

To further assess the students' understanding of the material, assign Chapter 5 of the *Student Workbook.*

After students have studied all the chapters in the section, administer the section test in the *Teacher's Resource Guide.* Check their answers against the answers given in the Guide.

Answers to Chapter Review Questions

1. Three problems that can occur when a tool is misused are (1) damage to the tool, (2) damage to the object that is being worked on, and (3) injury to the person using the tool.
2. The four main categories of construction tools and equipment are hand tools, power tools, equipment, and heavy equipment.
3. Three common hand tools are screwdrivers, hammers, and saws.
4. For cutting trim and molding accurately.
5. A radial arm saw.
6. Two stationary power tools are the radial arm saw and the table saw.
7. Two types of power tools that are used to fasten materials together are nailers and staplers. (Powder-actuated stud driver is also an acceptable answer.)
8. Equipment is a term that refers to large, complex tools and machines.
9. Water pumps are needed to pump ground water out of holes so that work can be done.
10. A laser-powered welder is used to weld heat-resistant metals because this type of welder can reach temperatures in excess of 10,000 °F. (5,540 °C.)
11. Types of heavy equipment that are used in construction are cranes, excavators, bulldozers, front-end loaders, and highway construction equipment. (Accept any four.)
12. Four types of equipment that are used specifically for highway and parking lot construction are scrapers, graders, compactors, and pavers.

CHAPTER 6 LESSON PLAN

Construction Frontiers

Essential Elements for the Course: 1.1, 2.1, 2.2, 2.3, 2.4, 3.1, 3.4, 3.5, 4.2, 4.3, 4.4, 6.3, 6.13, 6.14, 6.15, 6.16, 6.18
Common Essential Elements: (8 E, F), (9 C, D), (10 B)

‖‖ Chapter Outline

I. New Materials
II. New Methods
III. Computers
IV. The Future

‖‖ Main Goal

The main goal of this chapter is to introduce students to the new tools and methods used in construction.

‖‖ Objectives

As a result of studying this chapter, students will be able to:
1. Describe several new construction materials.
2. Describe how computers are being used in construction.

‖‖ Key Facts

- Materials are the substances from which products are made.
- An adhesive is any substance that can be used to adhere, or bond, one object to another.
- Geotextile material is like a large piece of plastic cloth.

- Oriented-strand board is made from small, crooked trees that otherwise would be unprofitable to harvest.
- Com-ply®, or composite-ply, is made of several plies of veneer strips laminated to a core particleboard.
- Micro-lam® is made of pieces of veneer that have been laminated in a parallel direction.
- Components of structures and even whole structures are now being built in factories and shipped to the building site. Such buildings are called prefabricated units.
- Another method of construction that falls somewhere between prefabrication and traditional construction is called modular construction.
- A module is simply a standard unit that has been chosen by a manufacturer, such as 4 inches.
- Computer-aided design (CAD) speeds up the designing and engineering work of a project.

‖‖ Preparation

Preparation before introducing Chapter 6:
1. Gather the needed materials and supplies to conduct the chapter activities.
2. Duplicate any transparency masters, handouts, and lab sheets needed to introduce students to Chapter 6.
3. Collect examples of construction projects generated with a CAD system.
4. Visit a local lumber yard or cabinetmaking shop that uses a CAD system to generate drawings. Some systems will even generate a 3-D drawing, a framing drawing, and a complete bill of materials.
5. Preview various computer-aided drafting and cost-estimating software packages. (Refer to the reference section below.)

6. Contact the Homer Owner Research Foundation and obtain a copy of the Smart House video.
7. Assign students to read the chapter.

|||| Resources

Books

Fales, J. F., Kuetemeyer, V. F., and Brusic, S. K. *Technology: Today and Tomorrow.* Mission Hills, CA: Glencoe/McGraw-Hill, 1988.

Lux, D. G., Ray, W. E., Blankenbaker, E. K., and Umstattd, W. *World of Construction.* Mission Hills, CA: Glencoe/McGraw-Hill, 1982.

Software

CADDRAW
Kitchen Sink Software
903 Knebworth Ct.
Westerville, OH 43081

QUICK DRAFT
Interactive Microware, Inc.
P. O. Box 139
State College, PA 16804

AUTOSKETCH
AUTOCAD
Autodesk, Inc.
2320 Marinship Way
Sausalito, CA 94965

CONSTRUCTION ESTIMATOR
Mesa Research, Inc.
RT. 1, Box 1456A
Waco, TX 76710

Addresses

National Association of Home Builders
15th & M Street, N.W.
Washington, DC 20005

|||| Teaching

Review the objectives for this chapter carefully. Then:

1. Using a popular computer-aided drafting software package, have students design a drawing that will solve a simple construction problem (e.g., room addition, vacation home, garage with work area, space station living quarters). Ask students to discuss the advantages and disadvantages of computer-aided design.
2. Using a popular construction estimating software program, have students calculate the cost of a simple construction project. (This activity could be combined with Activity 1.)
3. In a teacher-guided discussion, ask students to explain some of the social and environmental impacts surrounding the use of new construction materials and techniques.
4. Visit a truss, mobile home, or modular home company. Have the students identify non-traditional building materials and techniques.
5. Show the Home Builders ResearchFoundations video entitled "Smart Houses." Have the students discuss the advantages, disadvantages, and potential impacts of such technology.
6. Refer students to the section on adhesives in Chapter 4. Ask them to list the adhesives mentioned there. Then ask them to find out about as many other adhesives as possible and make a list of materials that can be fastened by each.

|||| Evaluation

After completing this chapter, assign the study questions at the end of the chapter. Check the students' mastery of the information by comparing the students' answers with the answers given below.

To further assess the students' understanding of the material, assign Chapter 6 of the *Student Workbook.*

After students have studied all the chapters in the section, administer the section test in the *Teacher's Resource Guide.* Check their answers against the answers given in the Guide.

Answers to Chapter
Review Questions

1. Adhesives are faster to use than nails.
2. Liquid storage tanks, roofing, protective coatings, waterproofing materials, engineering fabrics, and fasteners. (Accept any four.)
3. Oriented-strand board is a wood material made from small, crooked hemlock, poplar, and pine trees.
4. It is 30 percent stronger. It uses 35 percent more of each tree. It virtually eliminates warping, twisting, and shrinking.
5. To keep soil in place and help prevent erosion.
6. To find and maintain elevations, to weld heat-resistant metals, and to drill holes in very hard surfaces.
7. Prefabricated units are self-contained units or buildings that are built in a factory, then shipped to the building site.
8. Modular construction.
9. It speeds up the work, and it provides great accuracy.
10. Computers can schedule the tasks for a project, keep track of the schedule, keep track of materials and labor costs, and do record-keeping tasks such as payroll, inventory, and billing.

CHAPTER 7 LESSON PLAN

Organization of Construction Enterprises

Essential Elements for the Course: 2.1, 6.1, 6.9, 6.10
Common Essential Elements: (3 A, B, C, D), (5 B, C, G, H, I), (8 B)

▌▌▌ Chapter Outline

I. Types of Ownership
II. Types of Construction Companies
III. Company Organization

▌▌▌ Main Goal

The main goal of this chapter is to help students understand how construction companies are formed and organized.

▌▌▌ Objectives

As a result of studying this chapter, students will be able to:
1. Define and explain the types of business ownership.
2. Explain the difference between a general contractor and a construction management company.
3. Describe the relationship between the general contractor and subcontractors.
4. Explain the organization of a typical construction company.

▌▌▌ Key Facts

- A company that is owned by one person is known as a proprietorship.
- Two or more people can form a business as a partnership.
- A corporation is a company that is owned by many different people.
- People buy ownership of a corporation by purchasing shares of ownership called stock.
- The individuals who own the stock are called stockholders.
- A board of directors is elected by stockholders to run the company.
- When two companies combine for the purpose of working on a certain project, it is called a joint venture.
- A general contractor is a company that undertakes an entire construction project.
- Specialty contractors specialize in one type of construction job.
- When a general contractor hires a specialty contractor, the specialty contractor is known as a subcontractor.
- Construction management companies are those that manage construction jobs without doing any of the physical construction.
- The home office is the company headquarters.
- The field engineer oversees the project and makes certain that the building is laid out properly.
- The project manager is the person in the home office who is directly responsible for a certain construction project.
- The field office is a temporary office that is established at the construction site.
- The construction superintendent is the person in charge of all construction proceedings.

▌▌▌ Preparation

Preparation before introducing Chapter 7:
1. Gather the needed materials and supplies to conduct the chapter activities.

2. Duplicate any transparency masters, handouts, and lab sheets needed to introduce students to Chapter 7.
3. Visit local construction companies and determine their type of ownership.
4. Contact your Secretary of State and obtain a sample article of incorporation.
5. Assign students to read the chapter.

Resources

Books

Fales, J. F., Kuetemeyer, V. F., and Brusic, S. K. *Technology: Today and Tomorrow.* Mission Hills, CA: Glencoe/McGraw-Hill, 1988.

Lux, D. G., Ray, W. E., Blankenbaker, E. K., and Umstattd, W. *World of Construction.* Mission Hills, CA: Glencoe/McGraw-Hill, 1982.

Software

CADDRAW
Kitchen Sink Software
903 Knebworth Ct.
Westerville, OH 43081

QUICK DRAFT
Interactive Microware, Inc.
P. O. Box 139
State College, PA 16804

AUTOSKETCH
AUTOCAD
Autodesk, Inc.
2320 Marinship Way
Sausalito, CA 94965

CONSTRUCTION ESTIMATOR
Mesa Research, Inc.
RT. 1, Box 1456A
Waco, TX 76710

Addresses

National Association of Home Builders
15th & M Street, N.W.
Washington, DC 20005

Teaching

Some of the activities in this chapter expand on those discussed in Chapter 6.

Review the objectives for this chapter carefully. Then:

1. Have the students organize a construction company to complete a construction project (e.g., scaled mock-up of a four-lane highway and a bridge, scaled mock-up of a vacation house, storage shed). The company should complete the following activities:
   - Nominate and elect company officials.
   - Design a company logo and stock.
   - Select a company superintendent, field engineer, general contractor, and subcontractor.
   - The company superintendent should oversee such activities as the design, cost estimation, and construction of the project.
2. Invite a local general contractor to class. Ask the contractor to describe the type of activity associated with his or her job.

Evaluation

After completing this chapter, assign the study questions at the end of the chapter. Check the students' mastery of the information by comparing the students' answers with the answers given below.

To further assess the students' understanding of the material, assign Chapter 7 of the *Student Workbook.*

After students have studied all the chapters in the section, administer the section test in the *Teacher's Resource Guide.* Check their answers against the answers given in the Guide.

Answers to Chapter Review Questions

1. A proprietorship has only one owner.
2. If a partnership fails, all the partners are equally responsible.

3. A corporation sells shares of ownership to many different people.
4. Stock is the shares of ownership sold by a corporation.
5. A joint venture is formed from two smaller companies for the purpose of doing a specific project.
6. A general contractor undertakes a whole project from start to finish; a subcontractor is a specialty contractor hired by a general contractor or management company to do a specific task related to a project.
7. A construction management company is responsible for seeing that a project is completed properly. The management company does not take part in the actual construction.
8. The two kinds of construction company offices are the home office and the field office.
9. The field engineer oversees the project and makes sure that the structure is laid out properly.
10. The construction supervisor is responsible for coordinating the work of the subcontractors and seeing that the work runs smoothly.

CHAPTER 8 LESSON PLAN

The Business of Construction

Essential Elements for the Course: 1.1, 1.2, 3.2, 5.3, 6.5, 6.9, 6.10, 6.11
Common Essential Elements: (2 K, L), (5 B, G, H, I), (6 C), (8 B), (9 B), (10 B, C)

IIII Chapter Outline

 I. The Bidding Process
 II. Contracts and Legal Responsibilities
 III. Organizing the Job
 IV. Controlling the Job

IIII Main Goal

The main goal of this chapter is to introduce students to the business functions surrounding a construction project.

IIII Objectives

As a result of studying this chapter, students will be able to:
1. Explain the difference between negotiating and bidding.
2. Explain the four main steps in the bidding process.
3. Describe four types of contracts.
4. Explain how bonds protect the owner of a construction project.
5. Describe two types of construction schedules.
6. Describe project control procedures.

IIII Key Facts

- The owner and the construction company negotiate, or discuss the terms of, the contract for the company to do the project.

- A bid or quote is the price for which a company will do the job.
- Overhead is the cost of doing business.
- The contract is a written agreement between the owner and the contractor.
- A lump-sum contract is a contract in which a lump sum (fixed price) is paid for the work to be done.
- In a cost-plus contract, the owner agrees to pay all the cost of construction, including materials and labor.
- An incentive contract is designed to reward or penalize the contractor, depending on when the job is complete. If the job is finished before the agreed-upon date, the contractor is awarded an amount of money that is specified in the contract. If the job is not done by the specified date, the contractor is penalized a certain amount of money.
- With a unit-price contract the contractor will charge by a unit of work.
- A bond is similar to an insurance policy. Bonds are meant to provide protection for the owner in the event the contractor does not follow the terms of the contract.
- A performance bond guarantees that the contractor will build the project according to the agreement.
- A payment bond is a guarantee that the contractor will pay his or her employees, subcontractors, and suppliers.
- The Occupational Safety and Health Administration (OSHA) is an agency of the federal government. It is responsible for making sure that workers have a safe place to work.
- A project manager is appointed to coordinate the money, workers, equipment, and materials for the job.
- A bar chart lists the months across the top of the chart and all the major jobs down the side of the chart. A bar is used to show the starting and completion dates for each job.

- The critical path method (CPM) chart is a diagram made of circles and lines. This kind of schedule is useful because it shows the critical parts of the job clearly.
- The contract superintendent controls all the activities at the site.
- Project control is the process of giving directions and making sure the job is done properly and on time.
- Project accounting is used by the contractor to keep accurate records of what has been done.
- Cost accounting is the procedure by which the company keeps track of the cost of the project.

‖‖ Preparation

Preparation before introducing Chapter 8:
1. Gather the needed materials and supplies to conduct the chapter activities.
2. Duplicate any transparency masters, handouts, and lab sheets needed to introduce students to Chapter 8.
3. Visit local construction companies and obtain samples of various types of bid and contract forms. Ask contractors to categorize contracts as lump sum, cost plus, incentive, and unit price.
4. Contact the nearest OSHA office to obtain sets of safety regulations used on various construction projects.
5. Obtain examples of a CPM and a bar chart.
6. Search through the newspaper and locate examples of contractors' bid advertisements.
7. Assign students to read the chapter.

‖‖ Resources

Books

Fales, J. F., Kuetemeyer, V. F., and Brusic, S. K. *Technology: Today and Tomorrow.* Mission Hills, CA: Glencoe/McGraw-Hill, 1988.

Lux, D. G., Ray, W. E., Blankenbaker, E. K., and Umstattd, W. *World of Construction.* Mission Hills, CA: Glencoe/McGraw-Hill, 1982.

‖‖ Teaching

Review the objectives for this chapter carefully. Then:
1. Introduce students to the processes used for preparing bids and estimating the cost of construction projects. Divide the class into four groups. Obtain a set of drawings for a local construction project. Have one group estimate the cost of materials. Have a second group estimate the labor cost. Have a third group estimate equipment cost. Have the fourth group estimate overhead cost. Since this is a hypothetical situation, you will need to generate a set of figures and list of prices for the students to use. Ask the students to discuss the consequences of inaccurately estimating and bidding construction projects.
2. Introduce students to the concept of scheduling construction projects. After the students have completed the activity above, have the class create a CPM and a bar chart for the project. Have the students discuss how poor planning can influence things like safety, cost, and profit.

‖‖ Evaluation

After completing this chapter, assign the study questions at the end of the chapter. Check the students' mastery of the information by comparing the students' answers with the answers given below.

To further assess the students' understanding of the material, assign Chapter 8 of the *Student Workbook.*

After students have studied all the chapters in the section, administer the section test in the *Teacher's Resource Guide.* Check their answers against the answers given in the Guide.

Answers to Chapter Review Questions

1. A company can get business by negotiating and by bidding.

2. (1) The type of work. (2) The location of the project. (3) Where to get plans and specifications. (4) The time and place of the bid opening.

3. The key person in the bid preparation process is the estimator.

4. Five kinds of costs that an estimator must consider when preparing a bid are the cost of materials, the cost of labor, the cost of equipment, the cost of subcontracted work, and the cost of overhead.

5. In a lump-sum contract, the total price is agreed upon before construction begins.

6. The incentive is money: if the contractor finishes the job early, he or she gets a bonus. If he or she finishes late, there is a penalty.

7. A payment bond protects the owner by making sure that the workers are paid, so that they cannot ultimately claim part ownership in the structure.

8. Two safety precautions that construction workers can take are wearing safety glasses, wearing gloves, and wearing hard hats. (Accept any two.)

9. Two common methods of scheduling are by bar chart and by the critical path method chart.

10. The construction superintendent controls all the work at this site.

CHAPTER 9 LESSON PLAN

Types of Construction Projects

Essential Elements for the Course: 1.1, 2.1, 2.4, 3.4, 4.2, 6.2, 6.6, 6.7
Common Essential Elements: (7 A)

||||Chapter Outline

   I. Buildings
  II. Highways
 III. Airports
 IV. Tunnels
  V. Bridges
 VI. Dams

||||Main Goal

The main goal of this chapter is to introduce students to various types of construction projects such as buildings, highways, airports, tunnels, bridges, and dams.

||||Objectives

As a result of studying this chapter, students will be able to:
1. Describe the three basic types of buildings.
2. Explain the general procedure for constructing a highway.
3. Describe the major construction tasks involved in building an airport.
4. Explain two general procedures that can be used to construct a tunnel.
5. Describe some special construction techniques needed to build a dam.
6. Identify and describe five ways in which bridges can be constructed.

||||Key Facts

- Residential buildings are those in which people reside, or live.
- Commercial buildings are those designed to accommodate businesses.
- Industrial buildings house the complex machinery that is used to manufacture goods.
- Highway construction is the general term used for the construction of any road or street.
- The simplest type of bridge, the slab bridge, consists of a concrete slab supported by abutments.
- An arch bridge is one in which an arch is used to carry the weight of the bridge.
- Truss bridges are supported by steel or wooden trusses, or beams that are put together to form triangular shapes.
- A cantilever bridge is used for fairly long spans.
- Suspension bridges are suspended from cables made of thousands of steel wires wound together.
- A dam is a structure that is placed across a river to block the flow of water.
- A spillway is a safety valve that allows excess water to bypass the dam.
- A cofferdam, or watertight wall, must be built to keep water out of the workers' way.

||||Preparation

Preparation before introducing Chapter 9:
1. Gather the needed materials and supplies to conduct the chapter activities.
2. Duplicate any transparency masters, handouts, and lab sheets needed to introduce students to Chapter 9.
3. Search the surrounding area to find new or existing examples of construction

projects like buildings, highways, airports, tunnels, bridges, and dams.

4. Assign students to read the chapter.

||||Resources

Books

Fales, J. F., Kuetemeyer, V. F., and Brusic, S. K. *Technology: Today and Tomorrow.* Mission Hills, CA: Glencoe/McGraw-Hill, 1988.

Lux, D. G., Ray, W. E., Blankenbaker, E. K., and Umstattd, W. *World of Construction.* Mission Hills, CA: Glencoe/McGraw-Hill, 1982.

||||Teaching

Review the objectives for this chapter carefully. Then:

1. Introduce students to the process involved in designing and planning an airport. Divide the class into groups of three or four students. Provide each group with two 18" x 24" pieces of ¼" graph paper. Using traditional drafting techniques, have each group lay out and design an airport for a medium-sized city. Be sure each design includes the following:
   - runways
   - taxiways
   - aprons
   - parking lots and roadways
   - passenger and freight terminals
   - hangars
   - control towers
   - fire stations
   - maintenance buildings

   After each group has completed their design, have them present their design to the rest of the class. Then guide the students in a discussion of the social and environmental impact an airport can have on a community.

2. Introduce students to the concept of bridge design. This can be done by having the students design, build, and test a bridge that will span a nine-inch gorge for $800,000 or less. Divide the class into groups of two or three.

Have each group research basic bridge designs. Using either traditional drafting equipment or computer-aided design equipment, have the students make a scaled drawing of their bridge design. The bridge must stay within the following specifications:
   - 12" long
   - 3" tall
   - 3" wide
   - 1" under carriage (optional)
   - No obstruction inside the structure.
   - A platform across the center of the structure. (This is to be used to hang weight from.)

Next, provide each group with a materials and price list. The materials used on this construction project will be toothpicks and glue. Your materials and parts list may include:
   - toothpicks $8,000
   - glue $5,000/2 ounce
   - pieces of paper used when designing the project $5,000/sheet
   - equipment rental $3,000/day
   - use of test equipment $1,000

Have each group of students construct a bridge. When all the bridges have been completed, have each group test their design for strength and efficiency. Place two tables the same height nine-inches apart. Have each group weigh their bridge. Then place the bridge across the tables. Add small amounts of weights to each bridge. When the bridge fails, have the students calculate the bridge's efficiency factor. The efficiency factor is equal to the weight of the bridge divided by the amount of weight the bridge held.

||||Evaluation

After completing this chapter, assign the study questions at the end of the chapter. Check the students' mastery of the information by comparing the students' answers with the answers given below.

To further assess the students' understanding of the material, assign Chapter 9 of the *Student Workbook.*

After students have studied all the chapters in the section, administer the section test in the *Teacher's Resource Guide.* Check their answers against the answers given in the Guide.

Answers to Chapter Review Questions

1. Residential, industrial, and commercial.
2. Reinforced floors for heavy equipment; special furnaces; chemical-resistant warehouses; chemical baths (any two).
3. Bituminous concrete and portland cement concrete.
4. Runways, taxiways, aprons, and parking lots.
5. Specially trained airport planners and engineers.
6. Explosives are used to blast the rock, which can then be removed.
7. Reinforced concrete slab bridges.
8. Suspension bridges.
9. A safety valve that allows excess water to bypass a dam.
10. A temporary, watertight wall that allows workers to construct the underwater portions of a dam.

CHAPTER 10 LESSON PLAN

The Decision to Build

Essentials Elements for the Course: 2.1, 2.4, 3.2, 6.1, 6.11, 6.12
Common Essential Elements: (8 A, F)

Chapter Outline

I. Modifying an Existing Structure
II. Building a New Structure
III. Financing
IV. Building Sites

Main Goal

The main goal of this chapter is to help students understand the decision-making processes used by the construction industry. This chapter discusses decisions relating to building and renovating, financing construction projects, and selecting a building site.

Objectives

As a result of studying this chapter, students will be able to:
1. Identify two construction-related alternatives to building a new structure.
2. Describe the difference between private and public building projects.
3. Describe the process of selecting and acquiring a building site.
4. List three sources of funds for construction projects.

Key Facts

- Alterations are changes in the structural form of a building or other structure.
- Renovation is the process of restoring the original charm or style of the building, while at the same time adding modern conveniences such as air-conditioning.
- When a construction project belongs to an individual or a company, it is known as a private project.
- Public projects are projects paid for with tax money. They belong to the whole community.
- A feasibility study is done to gather information about the proposed project.
- Zoning laws tell what kinds of structures can be built in each zone.
- A contract is a written agreement that states the terms of the sale.
- Through the power of eminent domain the government has the right to buy property for public purposes even though the owner does not want to sell.
- A letter of commitment states the terms and conditions that are required for the payment of the loan.
- A mortgage note is actually two documents. The note is a document in which the lender agrees to finance the project under certain conditions and at a specified rate. The mortgage pledges the property as security for the loan.
- Interest is the price the borrower pays for using the lending institution's money.
- A bond is a type of note by which various amounts of money are borrowed from many different people or institutions at once.

Preparation

Preparation before introducing Chapter 10:
1. Gather the needed materials and supplies to conduct the chapter activities.
2. Duplicate any transparency masters, handouts, and lab sheets needed to introduce students to Chapter 10.

3. Check with your local city planner and obtain several copies of city zoning maps.
4. Preview popular spreadsheet programs to find one that can be set up to calculate mortgages, given the interest rate and length of the loan.
5. Locate and obtain a film or video showing the construction of the St. Louis Arch.
6. Assign students to read the chapter.

‖‖‖ Resources

Books

Fales, J. F., Kuetemeyer, V. F., and Brusic, S. K. *Technology: Today and Tomorrow.* Mission Hills, CA: Glencoe/McGraw-Hill, 1988.

Lux, D. G., Ray, W. E., Blankenbaker, E. K., and Umstattd, W. *World of Construction.* Mission Hills, CA: Glencoe/McGraw-Hill, 1982.

‖‖‖ Teaching

Review the objectives for this chapter carefully. Then:

1. Introduce students to the concept of modifying an existing structure. Divide the class into groups of three or four students. Provide each group with a set of plans for an existing structure. Have each group modify the structure to satisfy a clients' needs (e.g., a room addition, a deck, an attached garage). After each group has completed their design, have them present their design to the rest of the class.
2. Introduce students to the concept of city zoning. Divide the class into three groups. Provide each group with a map of the city. Assign each group a construction project (e.g., shopping mall, housing subdivision, automobile assembly plant). Have each group determine an appropriate building site. After each group has selected their site, have them share and defend their selection to the rest of the class.
3. Provide the students with a copy of a zoning map. Have students identify the city's residential, commercial, and industrial areas.
4. In a teacher-guided discussion, ask the students to describe both the positive and nega-

tive social and environmental effects associated with placing a dam across a river.
5. Using a popular computer spreadsheet software program, have students calculate mortgages and interest for various loans. Have students calculate a $100,000 loan over 15, 20, and 30 years at 6%, 10% and 14% interest rates. Ask students to discuss how length of loan and interest rate affects total cost and monthly payment.

‖‖‖ Evaluation

After completing this chapter, assign the study questions at the end of the chapter. Check the students' mastery of the information by comparing the students' answers with the answers given below.

To further assess the students' understanding of the material, assign Chapter 10 of the *Student Workbook.*

After students have studied all the chapters in the section, administer the section test in the *Teacher's Resource Guide.* Check their answers against the answers given in the Guide.

Answers to Chapter Review Questions

1. Alterations and renovation.
2. Public and private ownership.
3. To gather information about a proposed project and to find out if the project is practical.
4. Zoning laws.
5. Location, cost, and physical characteristics.
6. A contract.
7. The right of the government to buy property for public use even though the owner does not want to sell.
8. The money to build private construction projects is usually borrowed from a lending institution in the form of a mortgage.
9. Public projects can be financed by tax money or by money raised by selling bonds.
10. A type of note in which money can be borrowed from several different sources at one time.

CHAPTER 11 LESSON PLAN

Designing and Engineering the Project

Essential Elements for the Course: 1.2, 2.1, 3.5, 6.4
Common Essential Elements: (8 F)

||| Chapter Outline

I. Designing
II. Engineering
III. The Final Design
IV. Architectural and Engineering Services

||| Main Goal

The main goal of this chapter is to introduce students to the processes used in designing and engineering structures.

||| Objectives

As a result of studying this chapter, students will be able to:
1. Explain the difference between designing and engineering.
2. Name two important aspects of design.
3. Define live loads and dead loads and give an example of each.
4. Describe the three general categories of engineering.
5. Describe the various drawings used in the final design.
6. Explain who provides architectural and engineering services.

||| Key Facts

- Designing is the process of deciding what a structure will look like and how it will function.
- Engineering is the process of figuring out how the structure will be built and what structural materials will be used.
- Preliminary designs or first sketches show what the structure might look like.
- Structural engineering is the process of selecting appropriate materials from which to build a structure.
- The dead load of a structure is the combined weight of all its materials.
- A live load is a variable, or changeable, load.
- A safety factor is extra strength that is built into a structure to provide a wide margin of safety.
- The mechanical and electrical setups of a structure are commonly referred to as its infrastructure.
- Engineering efficiency is important in construction.
- The drawings show the plans for a structure in graphic form.
- The specifications tell the contractor exactly what materials to use and how to use them.
- Architectural drawings are those that show the layout of the building.
- The floor plan shows the layout of all the rooms on one floor of a building.
- The site plan shows what the site should look like when the job is finished.
- Elevations are drawings that show the outside of a structure.
- A section drawing is one that shows a section, or slice, of the structure.
- A detail drawing is one that shows a particular part of the structure.
- A structural drawing gives information about the location and sizes of the structural materials.
- Mechanical plans are prepared for the plumbing and piping systems.

- The electrical plans show the location of all the light fixtures, switches, and other electrical devices.
- Most specifications for large construction projects follow the format presented by the Construction Specification Institute (CSI).
- Specification writers are people who write project specifications for most large construction companies. Specification writers must have a good understanding of construction practices and an up-to-date knowledge of materials.
- Scale models are sometimes made to help visualize how the final design will look. These models have proportions that the finished building will have.
- A model that is made to show people how the finished design will look is called a presentation model.
- Sometimes a study model of a design is made so that the design can be tested.
- A consultant is an expert in a specific area.

||||Preparation

Preparation before introducing Chapter 11:
1. Gather the needed materials and supplies to conduct the chapter activities.
2. Duplicate any transparency masters, handouts, and lab sheets needed to introduce students to Chapter 11.
3. Check with a local architect to obtain several examples of construction plans. Try to find examples for projects like residential homes, office complexes, roads, bridges, and superstructures.
4. Preview popular computer-aided design programs. Be sure the programs can be used to lay out simple floor plans.
5. Assign students to read the chapter.

||||Resources

Books

Fales, J. F., Kuetemeyer, V. F., and Brusic, S. K. *Technology: Today and Tomorrow.* Mission Hills, CA: Glencoe/McGraw-Hill, 1988.

Lux, D. G., Ray, W. E., Blankenbaker, E. K., and Umstattd, W. *World of Construction.* Mission Hills, CA: Glencoe/McGraw-Hill, 1982.

Software

CADDRAW
Kitchen Sink Software
903 Knebworth Ct.
Westerville, OH 43081

QUICK DRAFT
Interactive Microware, Inc.
P. O. Box 139
State College, PA 16804

AUTOSKETCH
AUTOCAD
Autodesk, Inc.
2320 Marinship Way
Sausalito, CA 94965

||||Teaching

Review the objectives for this chapter carefully. Then:
1. Divide the class into groups of three or four. Supply each group with a set of floor plans of a construction project. Have students identify live loads and dead loads in the structure. Also, have students discuss the plan's layout and floor plan. Finally, be sure the students notice the various symbols used throughout the plans.
2. Introduce students to the concept of designing a construction project. Using either traditional or computer-aided drafting techniques, have students create a simple floor plan for a single-story ranch-style home. Provide the students with the following specifications:
   - The design must cost less than $100,000.
   - The design must be for a house of 2,000 square feet or less.
   - The design must include two or three bedrooms, one or two bathrooms, a kitchen, a family room, and a garage. An optional room might be a living room, dining room, or utility room.

Once the students have completed their floor plan, have them create an elevation drawing for the front and right side of the house. In a teacher-guided discussion, ask students to discuss how computers have impacted and influenced the design and engineering aspects of the construction industry.

3. Divide the class into groups of two students. Provide each group with a set of plans for an existing structure. Have each group modify the structure to satisfy a client's needs (e.g., a room addition, a deck, an attached garage). After each group has completed their design, have them present their design to the rest of the class.

|||| Evaluation

After completing this chapter, assign the study questions at the end of the chapter. Check the students' mastery of the information by comparing the students' answers with the answers given below.

To further assess the students' understanding of the material, assign Chapter 11 of the *Student Workbook*.

After students have studied all the chapters in the section, administer the section test in the *Teacher's Resource Guide*. Check their answers against the answers given in the Guide.

Answers to Chapter Review Questions

1. Designing is the process of deciding what a structure will look like and how it will function. Engineering is the process of figuring out how a structure will be built and what structural materials will be used.
2. Function and appearance.
3. The live load is a variable, or changeable, load. The people in a building are part of its live load. A dead load is the combined weight of the building's materials. The lumber in a building is part of its dead load.
4. To allow extra strength and a margin of safety.
5. Floor plan, site plan, elevations, section drawing, detail drawing.
6. Specifications describe materials and explain the procedures used to perform each task. Specifications describe details that cannot be easily shown on a drawing.
7. Presentation models and study models.
8. Using a simulation program. The computer can simulate what will happen to the structure under certain conditions.
9. Projects such as houses, churches, office buildings, and shopping centers.
10. Heavy construction projects such as bridges, roads, and utility systems.
11. The consultant may have special knowledge of some part of the project.

CHAPTER 12 LESSON PLAN

Construction Processes

Essential Elements for the Course: 1.1, 2.1, 4.1, 4.2, 4.3, 6.2, 6.7
Common Essential Elements: (9 C)

▌▌▌ Chapter Outline

I. Preparing the Site
II. Building the Foundation
III. Building the Superstructure
IV. Installing Utilities
V. Finish Work

▌▌▌ Main Goal

The main goal of this chapter is to help students understand the processes used in the construction industry. These processes include preparing the site, building the foundation, constructing superstructures, installing utilities, and performing finishing work.

▌▌▌ Objectives

As a result of studying this chapter, students will be able to:
1. Explain the process of preparing a construction site.
2. Describe three major types of structural work.
3. Explain the difference between a frame structure and a bearing-wall structure.
4. Describe three basic types of utility systems.
5. Describe five major types of finish work.

▌▌▌ Key Facts

- The land on which a project will be constructed is called the site.

- Laying out the site is the process of identifying the location of the proposed structure on the property.
- The boundaries of the building are usually marked by batter boards. A batter board is a board held horizontally by stakes driven into the ground.
- Excavating, or digging, can begin as soon as the site has been laid out.
- The first step in soil stabilization is to determine the load-bearing ability of the soil. This is the amount of weight that soil can safely support without shifting.
- The banks or walls of soil are covered with sheets of steel called sheathing. The sheathing is usually held in place by long strips of metal that are driven into the earth. This method of holding sheathing in place is called shoring. Shoring can also be used without sheathing to stabilize soil and reduce the chance of cave-ins.
- The foundation is the part of the structure that is beneath the first floor. The rest of the building, beginning with the first floor, is called the superstructure.
- The footing is the part of the structure that distributes the structure's weight.
- The wall that is built directly on the footing is called the foundation wall. It transmits the weight of the superstructure to the footing.
- Forms are the molds that contain the concrete until it hardens.
- A slump test is done to check the workability of the concrete.
- Screeding is the process of moving a straight board back and forth across the top of the form. This removes any excess concrete and levels the top of the concrete.
- Floating is the process of moving coarse aggregate down into the concrete, leaving only fine aggregate and sand on top.

- The final smoothing of concrete is called troweling.
- A roof truss is a preassembled frame of wood or steel that is designed to support a roof.
- A bearing-wall structure is one in which heavy walls support the weight of the building.
- A frame structure is one in which a frame supports the weight of the building.
- Sheathing is a layer of material that is placed between the framing and the finished exterior to provide additional insulation.
- Utility installation is a two-stage process. The first stage, roughing in, is the installation of the basic pipes and wiring that must be placed within the walls, floor, and roof. The finishing stage of utility installation readies the utilities for use.
- The service drop is the wiring that connects a building to the electric company's overhead or underground wires.
- The service panel is a box that contains circuit breakers for each individual, or branch, circuit.
- Conduit is a pipe through which individual wires can be pulled.
- Nonmetallic sheathed cable is made of several wires wrapped together inside a plastic coating of insulation.
- Armored cable is made of several wires inside a flexible metal casing.
- Special trim called molding is used to cover joints where floors, walls, and ceilings meet.

4. Preview popular computer-aided design programs. Be sure the programs can be used to do interior designs and landscaping.
5. Assign students to read the chapter.

 Resources

Books

Fales, J. F., Kuetemeyer, V. F., and Brusic, S. K. *Technology: Today and Tomorrow.* Mission Hills, CA: Glencoe/McGraw-Hill, 1988.

Lux, D. G., Ray, W. E., Blankenbaker, E. K., and Umstattd, W. *World of Construction.* Mission Hills, CA: Glencoe/McGraw-Hill, 1982.

Software

CADDRAW
Kitchen Sink Software
903 Knebworth Ct.
Westerville, OH 43081

QUICK DRAFT
Interactive Microware, Inc.
P. O. Box 139
State College, PA 16804

AUTOSKETCH
AUTOCAD
Autodesk, Inc.
2320 Marinship Way
Sausalito, CA 94965

Preparation

Preparation before introducing Chapter 12:
1. Gather the needed materials and supplies to conduct the chapter activities.
2. Duplicate any transparency masters, handouts, and lab sheets needed to introduce students to Chapter 12.
3. Check with a local architect to obtain several examples of construction models. Try to find examples for projects such as residential homes, office complexes, roads, bridges, and superstructures.

Teaching

Review the objectives for this chapter carefully. In doing so you will find that many of the concepts discussed in Chapter 11 can be expanded in Chapter 12. Therefore, some of the activities discussed below are continued from Chapter 11.
1. Introduce students to the concept of interior design. Using the drawings generated in Chapter 11 and traditional or computer-aided drafting techniques, have students create an interior design for at least one room of their

floor plan. Be sure students consider flexibility, view lines of sight, and traffic patterns when creating their design.

2. Introduce the students to frame construction. Using the floor plan from Chapter 11, and materials like balsa wood or cardboard, glue, and construction paper, have the students build a scale model of their design. When conducting this activity, it is important to include the following steps:

   A. Have the students cut out their floor plan and glue it to a piece of cardboard.
   B. Using traditional framing techniques and ¼" cardboard or balsa wood strips, have the students frame the exterior walls.
   C. Once the exterior walls have been completed, have the students glue the walls on to the floor plan.
   D. When the students have finished the exterior walls, have them frame and glue the interior walls.
   E. Once the students have finished all of the walls, have them frame and glue the roof trusses.
   F. Finally, using different types of materials like construction paper and sandpaper, have the students apply interior and exterior coverings to the structure.

   Other activities that can be used to reinforce the same concepts include building a full or one-half scale model of a corner section and/or constructing an 8' x 10' storage shed.

3. Introduce students to the techniques used to construct a foundation wall. Divide the class into groups of two or three. Provide each group with a box 8" deep by 2' x 2' filled halfway with dirt and strips of wood to represent two-by-sixes and two-by-fours on a ¾" scale. Have the students construct forms for a wall 8' high and 12' long on a ¾":1' scale. Thin pieces of wire can be used for reinforcing rod. Finally, have the students mix either concrete or plaster and pour it into the forms.

4. Divide the class into groups of two or three. Using standard concrete blocks and wet sand, have students construct and plumb a block wall measuring 3' high and 10' long. Have

the students discuss the potential consequences of a poorly constructed foundation.

5. Introduce the concept of installing utility systems into structures. Using a corner section or lab trainer, have students wire a simple electrical circuit. The circuit could include wiring a receptacle and a light using both a single pole and a three-way switch.

6. Introduce students to the concept of landscaping. Using the drawings generated in Chapter 11 and traditional or computer-aided drafting techniques, have students create a landscape design for their house plan. Have students discuss how landscaping can affect such things as the appearance and selling price of a house.

▐▐▐▐ Evaluation

After completing this chapter, assign the study questions at the end of the chapter. Check the students' mastery of the information by comparing the students' answers with the answers given below.

To further assess the students' understanding of the material, assign Chapter 12 of the *Student Workbook*.

After students have studied all the chapters in the section, administer the section test in the *Teacher's Resource Guide*. Check their answers against the answers given in the Guide.

Answers to Chapter Review Questions

1. The three steps involved in preparing a site are surveying the site, clearing the site, and laying out the site.
2. The markers that identify building boundaries even after excavation has begun are called batter boards.
3. A long, narrow excavation that is meant to hold pipelines is called a trench.
4. Three methods of soil stabilization are pounding or rolling, sheathing and shoring, and adding chemicals to the soil.

5. The two basic parts of a structure are the foundation and the superstructure.

6. Screening, floating, and troweling are used to smooth the surface of concrete.

7. In a bearing-wall structure, heavy walls support the weight of the building.

8. The three main structural parts of a building are the floor, walls, and roof structure.

9. A roof truss is a preassembled frame of wood or steel that is designed to support a roof.

10. Two types of roofing that can be used on flat roofs are built-up roofing and membrane roofing.

11. The three main types of utility systems are plumbing systems, electrical systems, and HVAC systems.

12. The three basic types of electrical wiring are conduit, nonmetallic sheathed cable, and armored cable.

13. The system that controls the temperature inside a building is called an HVAC, or heating, ventilation, and air conditioning system.

14. Three common types of floor covering are floor tiles, sheet goods, and carpet.

15. To finish the area outside of a structure, the structural details must be completed. Roads and parking lots must be paved. Landscaping must be completed, and general cleanup must be done.

CHAPTER 13 LESSON PLAN

The Completed Project

Essential Elements for the Course: 1.2, 2.1, 3.1, 4.4, 6.11
Common Essential Elements: (6 C), (8 A, C), (9 D)

||||Chapter Outline

I. Final Inspection
II. Transferring Ownership
III. Service and Repair

||||Main Goal

The main goal of this chapter is to introduce students to the processes used to conduct a final inspection, the steps used for transferring ownership, and the methods used to service and repair completed construction projects.

||||Objectives

As a result of studying this chapter, students will be able to:
1. Describe the final inspection process.
2. Explain what a punch list is, who makes it, and what is done with it.
3. List the steps to transfer ownership of a construction project.
4. Explain how releases protect the owner.
5. Explain the difference between maintenance and repair and give one example of each.

||||Key Facts

- The final inspection is made after the construction project has been completed.

- As the inspection is being made, the inspectors make a list of things they see that need to be corrected. This list is called a punch list.
- For a building to be approved for use, a certificate of occupancy must be issued by the building inspection department. This certificate shows that the building has passed the building inspector's check of the structure.
- A notice of completion is a legal document that lets everyone know that the job is finished.
- A claim is a legal demand for money.
- A release of claims is a legal document in which a contractor gives up the right to file any claim against the owner.
- A lien is similar to a claim, except that the owner's property becomes security for the amount due the worker.
- A release of liens is a formal, written statement that everyone has been properly paid by the contractor.
- A warranty is a guarantee or promise that a job has been done well or that the materials have no defects.
- As the owner receives releases, warranties, and other items, he or she makes the final payment. This is the last step in transferring ownership.
- Maintenance is a method of taking care of an object or structure so that it continues to function the way it was intended.
- A repair is the process of restoring an object or structure to its original appearance or working order.

||||Preparation

Preparation before introducing Chapter 13:
1. Gather the needed materials and supplies to conduct the chapter activities.

2. Duplicate any transparency masters, handouts, and lab sheets needed to introduce students to Chapter 13.
3. Check with your local building inspector to obtain several examples of a punch list. Try to find examples for projects such as residential homes, office complexes, roads, bridges, and superstructures.
4. Check with your local building inspector to obtain examples of certificates of occupancy, notices of completion, releases, and warranties for various types of construction projects.
5. Assign students to read the chapter.

‖‖ Resources

Books

Fales, J. F., Kuetemeyer, V. F., and Brusic, S. K. *Technology: Today and Tomorrow.* Mission Hills, CA: Glencoe/McGraw-Hill, 1988.

Lux, D. G., Ray, W. E., Blankenbaker, E. K., and Umstattd, W. *World of Construction.* Mission Hills, CA: Glencoe/McGraw-Hill, 1982.

‖‖ Teaching

Review the objectives for this chapter carefully. Then:
1. Have students create a punch list for their house or school. Have students identify needed repairs and potential corrections.
2. Have students identify sources of maintenance, both routine and preventive, for their school or homes.
3. Invite a local building inspector to visit the class and discuss the nature of his or her job with the class.
4. Have the students discuss the potential consequences if safety inspections were not required at construction sites.

‖‖ Evaluation

After completing this chapter, assign the study questions at the end of the chapter. Check the students' mastery of the information by comparing the students' answers with the answers given below.

To further assess the students' understanding of the material, assign Chapter 13 of the *Student Workbook.*

After students have studied all the chapters in the section, administer the section test in the *Teacher's Resource Guide.* Check their answers against the answers given in the Guide.

Answers to Chapter Review Questions

1. The final inspection of a construction project is made after a construction project has been completed.
2. The final inspection is made by a team of inspectors including representatives of the owner, the architect or engineer, and the contractor.
3. A punch list is a list of corrections that need to be made to a project. The punch list is compiled by the team of inspectors that make the final inspection.
4. The contractor is responsible for seeing that all the needed corrections are made.
5. The certificate of occupancy is issued by the local building inspection department.
6. Two types of releases that an owner should get from a contractor are a release of claims and a release of liens.
7. A warranty is a promise or guarantee that a job has been done well or that the materials have no defects.
8. Two kinds of warranties are contractor's warranties and supplier's warranties.
9. The last step in transferring ownership from the contractor to the owner is the final payment from the owner to the contractor.
10. Maintenance is a method of taking care of an object or structure so that it continues to function properly. Repair is the process of restoring an object or structure to its original appearance or working order.

CHAPTER 14 LESSON PLAN

Student Enterprise

Essential Elements for the Course: 3.5, 4.2, 6.4, 6.5, 6.6, 6.9, 6.10, 6.16
Common Essential Elements: (1 A, B, C, D), (2 C, D, E, F, G, H, I, J, L), (4 D, E, F), (5 A, G, H, I), (6 A, B), (8 F), (9 A, B, C), (10 B)

Chapter Outline

I. Forming a Construction Company
II. Building the Construction Project
III. Determining Profit or Loss

Main Goal

The main goal of this chapter is to provide the students with a hands-on experience in construction by forming a student enterprise and building a simple construction project.

Objectives

As a result of studying this chapter, students will be able to:
1. Participate in the formation of a class company.
2. Participate in estimating and planning a construction project.
3. Participate in building a structure as a member of a class construction company.

Key Facts

- Speculation means that you build the project and then find someone to buy it.
- To build a project on contract means that you have a buyer before you start.

- Unit cost is the cost of the material per selling unit.

Preparation

Preparation before introducing Chapter 14:
1. Gather the needed materials and supplies to conduct the chapter activities.
2. Duplicate any transparency masters, handouts, and lab sheets needed to introduce students to Chapter 14.
3. Use the drawing provided in Chapter 14 to build a balsa wood model of the storage shed construction project.
4. Visit local companies to obtain sample stock certificates, job descriptions, job applications, and organizational charts.
5. Assign students to read the chapter.

Resources

Books

Fales, J. F., Kuetemeyer, V. F., and Brusic, S. K. *Technology: Today and Tomorrow.* Mission Hills, CA: Glencoe/McGraw-Hill, 1988.
Lux, D. G., Ray, W. E., Blankenbaker, E. K., and Umstattd, W. *World of Construction.* Mission Hills, CA: Glencoe/McGraw-Hill, 1982.

Teaching

Since Chapter 14 is an activity-based chapter, the following activities may be used to enhance the students' learning experience. Review the objectives for this chapter carefully. Then:
1. The position of project manager can be used to oversee activities like the creation of a bill

of materials, preparation of a construction schedule, development of a safety program and building the structure.

2. The position of finance manager can be used to oversee activities like creation of stock, obtaining bids for materials, placing purchases for needed materials, keeping track of expenses, and calculating profit and loss.

3. The position of marketing director can be used to oversee activities like creating a video-taped commercial, posters, or a newsletter advertising the product.

4. The position of personnel director can be used to oversee activities like creating job descriptions, developing a job application, and conducting interviews.

||| Evaluation

After completing this chapter, assign the study questions at the end of the chapter. Check the students' mastery of the information by comparing the students' answers with the answers given below.

To further assess the students' understanding of the material, assign Chapter 14 of the *Student Workbook*.

After students have studied all the chapters in the section, administer the section test in the *Teacher's Resource Guide.* Check their answers against the answers given in the guide.

Answers to Chapter Review Questions

1. The personnel director.
2. To build a project and then find someone to buy it.
3. The cost of the material per selling unit.
4. Joining student clubs and participating in their activities.
5. It helps schedule work.

CHAPTER 15 LESSON PLAN

Preparing for Construction Careers

**Essential Elements for the Course: 2.1
Common Essential Elements: (2 A, B, D, F), (4 A, B), (5 D, E, F)**

||| Chapter Outline

I. Determining Your Career Interests
II. Exploring Career Possibilities
III. Getting the Right Education

||| Main Goal

The main goal of this chapter is to help students understand some of the methods used to make possible career decisions.

||| Objectives

As a result of studying this chapter, students will be able to:
1. Know where to find information relating to construction careers.
2. Identify careers related to construction.
3. Know the different sources of training for construction-related careers.

||| Key Facts

- A job is a paid position at a specific place or setting.
- A career is a sequence of related jobs that a person holds throughout his or her working life.
- Your interests are all those things you most like to do.
- An aptitude is a natural talent for learning a skill.

- An ability is something you have already learned how to do or a skill you have mastered.
- Your values are your beliefs and ideas about things that you think are important.
- The *Occupational Outlook Handbook* contains information about two hundred careers. The careers, or occupations, are listed in the table of contents under large general classifications.
- The *Dictionary of Occupational Titles* (DOT) contains a description of over 20,000 jobs relating to many different careers, including those related to construction.
- General education is made up of all the basic courses, such as reading, writing, mathematics, science, and history, that are required in school.
- On-the-job training is the training that a person receives after he or she has been hired.
- An apprentice learns from a skilled worker while on the job. The apprentice also receives classroom instruction.
- A technical institute is a school that offers technical training for specific careers.
- A community college is a local two-year school that is usually supported in part by the state or local government.

||| Preparation

Preparation before introducing Chapter 15:
1. Gather the needed materials and supplies to conduct the chapter activities.
2. Duplicate any transparency masters, handouts, and lab sheets needed to introduce students to Chapter 15.
3. Check with your school library or guidance counselor to obtain materials on career information related to the construction industry.

Try to locate items like the *Dictionary of Occupational Titles* and *Occupational Outlook Handbook*.

4. Assign students to read the chapter.

|||| Resources

Books

Fales, J. F., Kuetemeyer, V. F., and Brusic, S. K. *Technology: Today and Tomorrow.* Mission Hills, CA: Glencoe/McGraw-Hill, 1988.

Farr, J. M., et. al. *The Work Book: Getting the Job You Want.* Mission Hills, CA: Glencoe/McGraw-Hill, 1984.

Kimbrell, Grady and Vineyard, Ben. *Succeeding in the World of Work.* Mission Hills, CA: Glencoe/McGraw-Hill, 1986.

Lux, D. G., Ray, W. E., Blankenbaker, E. K., and Umstattd, W. *World of Construction.* Mission Hills, CA: Glencoe/McGraw-Hill, 1982.

|||| Teaching

Review the objectives for this chapter carefully. Then:

1. Have students contact and interview somebody employed in a construction-related occupation. Ask students to collect information about the person's educational background, qualifications, and training.

2. Have students select a construction-related job. Ask them to conduct library research to determine the job's educational requirements, future trends, expected salary, and working conditions.

|||| Evaluation

After completing this chapter, assign the study questions at the end of the chapter. Check the students' mastery of the information by comparing the students' answers with the answers given below.

To further assess the students' understanding of the material, assign Chapter 15 of the *Student Workbook*.

After students have studied all the chapters in the section, administer the section test in the *Teacher's Resource Guide.* Check their answers against the answers given in the Guide.

Answers to Chapter Review Questions

1. A job is a paid position at a specific place. A career is a sequence of related jobs.

2. You should know your interests, abilities, aptitudes, and values before you choose a career.

3. You should consider your values when you make a career choice. If your values conflict with your career, you may be unhappy with your career choice.

4. An ability is something you already know how to do. An aptitude is a potential ability. It is a natural talent for learning a certain skill.

5. You can get career information by talking to relatives, friends, or neighbors; by doing research in a library; by participating in a school shop enterprise; and by taking a part-time job in a field in which you are interested.

6. Two publications of the U.S. Department of Labor are the *Occupational Outlook Handbook* and the *Dictionary of Occupational Titles.*

7. To locate an article about a career, you would use the *Readers' Guide to Periodical Literature.*

8. Taking a part-time job in a field that interests you exposes you to that field. Even if you only run errands, you can talk to other people who work there to get additional information about the field.

9. Four options are college, technical institute, community college, and industrial training.

10. A new worker who is being trained on the job is called a trainee.

CHAPTER 16 LESSON PLAN

Careers in Construction

Common Essential Elements: (1 A, C, D), (2 A, B), (3 A, B, C, D), (4 B, C, D, E, F), (9 B), (10 B, C)

Chapter Outline

I. Trades and Crafts
II. Construction-related Professions
III. Design and Engineering Professions
IV. Your Career Interests

Main Goal

The main goal of this chapter is to help students understand the various careers related to construction technology.

Objectives

As a result of studying this chapter, students will be able to:
1. Name some common construction-related trades and crafts.
2. Identify some construction-related professions.
3. Find more information about specific construction-related careers.

Key Facts

- Carpenters are tradespeople who work with wood and wood products.
- A bricklayer is a tradesperson who works with masonry.
- Electricians assemble, install, and maintain electrical wiring and fixtures.
- Plumbers install, maintain, and repair the plumbing systems.
- Pipefitters build and repair pressurized pipes to carry compressed air and steam in HVAC systems.
- The tradespeople that build steel-framed structures are called ironworkers.
- The people who run construction equipment are known as operating engineers.
- Laborers do supportive physical work at the construction site.
- Construction managers assign the work to the workers. They also check the work.
- The project manager is responsible for the construction project from start to finish.
- The manager directly in charge of one particular project is called the construction-superintendent.
- The estimator for a project carefully calculates what the job will cost.
- Surveyors measure and record the physical features of the construction site.
- Technicians are construction personnel who work in laboratories testing soil samples and materials.
- Office personnel is a general term for all the clerical and secretarial employees of a company, together with their managers and supervisors.
- Architects create new building designs.
- Engineers are responsible for the structural design of a project.

Preparation

Preparation before introducing Chapter 16:
1. Gather the needed materials and supplies to conduct the chapter activities.

2. Duplicate any transparency masters, handouts, and lab sheets needed to introduce students to Chapter 16.
3. Check with your school library or guidance counselor to obtain materials on career information related to the construction industry. Try to locate items like the *Dictionary of Occupational Titles* and *Occupational Outlook Handbook*.
4. Check with local construction-related industries and find out the methods they use to hire new employees.
5. Assign students to read the chapter.

||| Resources

Books

Farr, J. M., et al. *The Work Book: Getting the Job You Want*. Mission Hills, CA: Glencoe/McGraw-Hill, 1984.

Kimbrell, Grady and Vineyard, Ben. *Entering the World of Work*. Mission Hills, CA: Glencoe/McGraw-Hill, 1989.

Lux, D. G., Ray, W. E., Blankenbaker, E. K., and Umstattd, W. *World of Construction*. Mission Hills, CA: Glencoe/McGraw-Hill, 1982.

||| Teaching

Review the objectives for this chapter carefully. Then:

1. Have students search the classified ads of various large local newspapers to identify construction-related jobs. Ask students to discuss the types of information found in the ads. Have students discuss other sources for finding construction-related jobs.
2. Invite people from the construction industry to participate in a career day. Ask each participant to describe his or her work.

||| Evaluation

After completing this chapter, assign the study questions at the end of the chapter. Check the students' mastery of the information by comparing the students' answers with the answers given below.

To further assess the students' understanding of the material, assign Chapter 16 of the *Student Workbook*.

After students have studied all the chapters in the section, administer the section test in the *Teacher's Resource Guide*. Check their answers against the answers given in the Guide.

Answers to Chapter Review Questions

1. The three main categories of construction-related careers are trades and crafts, construction-related professions, and design and engineering professions.
2. Most tradespeople get their training on the job or through formal apprenticeships.
3. Four careers that are considered construction trades are carpenters, bricklayers, electricians, plumbers, pipefitters, ironworkers, and operating engineers. (Accept any four.)
4. Workers who assist tradespeople are called laborers.
5. A construction-related profession is a career in construction that requires formal schooling beyond high school.
6. Two differences between a project manager and a construction superintendent are (1) a project manager manages several different projects at once, while the construction supervisor directs one project at a time; (2) the project manager works at the home office, but the construction manager works at the field office of the project on which he or she is working.
7. The architect is responsible for the usefulness of space in a building.
8. The engineer is responsible for structural soundness.
9. Four types of engineers that might work on a large construction project are civil, structural, electrical, and mechanical engineers.
10. Two ways to find out more about a construction-related career are: looking it up in a career handbook, visiting a construction site, and taking a job as a laborer. (Accept any two.)

Construction Technology
Today and Tomorrow

Construction
Technology
Today and Tomorrow

James F. Fales, Ed.D., CMfgE
Professor and Chairman
Department of Industrial Technology
Ohio University
Athens, Ohio

GLENCOE/McGRAW-HILL
A Macmillan/McGraw-Hill Company
Mission Hills, California

Copyright © 1991 by Glencoe/McGraw-Hill Educational Division. All rights reserved. Printed in the United States of America. Except as permitted under the United States Copyright Act of 1976, no part of this publication may be reproduced or distributed in any form or by any means, or stored in a database or retrieval system, without prior permission of the publisher.

Send all inquiries to:
Glencoe/McGraw-Hill
15319 Chatsworth Street
P.O. Box 9509
Mission Hills, CA 91395-9509

ISBN 0-02-675754-0 (Student Text)
ISBN 0-02-675755-9 (Teacher's Resource Guide)
ISBN 0-02-675756-7 (Student Workbook)

1 2 3 4 5 6 7 8 9 10   95 94 93 92 91 90

ISBN 0-02-675758-3 (Teacher's Annotated Edition)

1 2 3 4 5 6 7 8 9 10   95 94 93 92 91 90

 ACKNOWLEDGMENTS

The publisher hereby gratefully acknowledges the cooperation and assistance received from many persons and companies during the development of *Construction Technology: Today and Tomorrow*. Special recognition is given to the following persons for their contributions:

Dave Pullias
Richardson Independent School District
Richardson, TX

Ken Smith
Technology Education Resource Teacher
Charles County Public Schools
La Plata, MD

James D. Stemple
Technology Education Teacher
Stafford Senior High School
Stafford, VA

Larry L. Stiggins
Technology Education Instructor
J.T. Hutchinson Junior High School
Lubbock, TX

Chapter number photo: Ping Amranand, Sylvania horse barn, Meadowfarm Stable, Orange, VA

Cover photo by Digital Art/Westlight

||| TABLE OF CONTENTS

INTRODUCTION

The construction industry today is an exciting and expanding field. When you think of construction, you may think of bulldozers and high-rise buildings. The world of construction involves much more, however. Construction involves not only the building of homes and office buildings. It is also concerned with the building of highways, tunnels, airports, and dams. It also involves more people than the construction workers you see on construction sites. Many others are working behind the scenes. These people are architects, engineers, and office workers, among others. Construction today is a large and growing industry. It builds on the technical accomplishments of the past. It also depends on more recent technological developments — inventions such as the laser and the computer.

Construction Technology: Today and Tomorrow provides a complete survey of the exciting construction industry. It allows you to explore all areas of this rapidly-growing field, including the most recent changes in technology. To give you some idea of the design of this text, let's discuss its organization. First, we'll discuss the photo-essay that opens the text. Then we'll discuss the table of contents and the various features in each of the text chapters.

THE ORGANIZATION OF THIS BOOK

Photo-Essay

Placed immediately before Section I, the photo-essay is the first part of this book. Titled "The Development of Construction Technology," this photo-essay provides a window on the exciting world of construction technology. With photos and text, it provides a general overview of the development of construction technology throughout history. In reading this photo-essay, look closely at the photos that accompany the text. They have been carefully selected to highlight the information in the text. Each photo carries a caption, or a description of what is shown in the photo. Read these captions carefully. They go beyond simply describing what is shown in the photo. They provide other valuable information that relates to the topics discussed in the text. When you have finished reading the photo-essay, you will have a better idea of the subjects that will be discussed in this book. You also will gain a greater knowledge of the historical developments that have led to the growth of construction technology.

Table of Contents

If you turn to the table of contents, you will see that this textbook has sixteen chapters. Each of these chapters discusses a separate topic in the field of construction technology. You also will notice that the chapters are grouped into sections. All of the chapters in a particular section relate to the basic theme of that section. Look, for example, at Section II ("Materials, Tools, and Processes"). You will see that each of the chapters in that section deals with the section topic.

Chapter Features

The features in each chapter are designed to help you learn the information presented there. Each chapter contains a variety of helpful and interesting features. These features will allow you to gain more information from this book. Each feature presents additional information relating to the topic being discussed. The types of features appearing in each chapter are discussed below. Watch for them as you read the chapters of this book.

- *Learning Objectives.* A short list of learning objectives appears at the beginning of each chapter. These learning objectives provide goals that you should set for yourself before you begin to read and study the information in the chapter. Then, as you read each chapter, you should occasionally refer back to the chapter objectives. By doing this, you will be able to make sure that you still have them in mind. These learning objectives are important. They relate to the key ideas in the chapter.
- *Terms to Know.* The Terms to Know also are listed at the beginning of each chapter. Each of these terms is set in **boldfaced type** within the chapter. Pay special attention to these terms. They signal important information. Each of the boldfaced terms in the chapter is also defined in the glossary at the back of the book.
- *Did You Know?* These short paragraphs offer information that builds on the information presented in the text. Usually, this new information relates construction technology to other subjects you may be studying. These subjects might be history, geography, or mathematics. All of these short features are designed to give you more information on construction technology.
- *Construction Facts.* Each chapter contains one long feature. This feature is usually toward the end of the chapter, just before the chapter review material. Each of these features highlights an important event in the history of construction technology. Each feature is illustrated with a photo or drawing chosen to provide more information on the subject.
- *For Discussion.* As you read the text, you may have some questions on the information. You might also want to share some of your ideas with the class. The short features titled "For Discussion?" will allow you to share your ideas with others. Each of these features presents a question relating to information in the text. These questions will provide a springboard for class discussion of an interesting topic.
- *Health and Safety.* Safe work habits are important in the construction industry. These features highlight health and safety practices and offer tips on working safely. They also highlight important events in the development of safe work practices.

End-of-Chapter Review Material

When you have finished reading each chapter, you will come to the end-of-chapter review material. This material consists of a chapter summary, chapter review questions, and activities. All of these are designed to help you and your teacher judge how well you have learned the information presented in the chapter. Remember the learning objectives at the beginning of the chapter? All of the material at the end of the chapter relates to these learning objectives. Let's look at each of the items in the end-of-chapter material.

- *Chapter Summary.* A summary is a statement of key points. The chapter summary is a statement, then, of the key points in the chapter. By reading the chapter summary, you can review the main points of information discussed in the chapter. You will want to read the chapter summary before you look at the review questions.
- *Test Your Knowledge.* The review questions at the end of each chapter are titled "Test Your Knowledge." They are designed to call your attention to the key points of information in the chapter. Your ability to answer these questions correctly will help you judge how well you have learned the information in the chapter.
- *Activities.* Each chapter closes with a set of short activities. Some of these activities are designed to develop skills in areas that relate to some of the other courses you may be taking. For most of these activities, you will not

need anything other than paper and a pencil. These activities follow the "Test Your Knowledge" questions.

Each of these end-of-chapter activities offers you an opportunity to develop a certain skill. The skills you can develop are in the areas of math, science, social studies, and communication. Each end-of-chapter activity is marked with one of the symbols shown below. These symbols identify the type of skill that can be developed by the activity.

 Math    **Social Studies**

 Science    **Communications**

Section and End-of-Section Activities

As mentioned above, the chapters of this book are grouped into sections. Each section deals with a specific theme in construction technology. A list of all the chapters in the section appears at the beginning of the section. These chapters are listed by number and title.

- *End-of-Section Activities.* A set of activities follows the last chapter in each section. These activities are longer than the activities that are included at the end of each chapter. These end-of-section activities also usually require materials other than paper and a pencil. They sometimes will provide you with an opportunity to build something. Also, they often present you with a chance to demonstrate teamwork. In some of these activities, you will be working in a two-person team or in a small group. Each of these activities is designed to make it easy for you to follow the directions. For every activity there is an objective, a list of the materials needed, and a numbered list of the steps of procedure.

Glossary and Index

- *Glossary.* Remember the boldfaced terms in the chapters? Each of these terms is listed

also in the glossary at the end of the book. A glossary is a list of terms explained. The glossary is alphabetized. If you need to know the meaning of a boldfaced term used in the text, look in the glossary. You will find its definition there.

- *Index.* The index is an important part of any book. Often, the value of a good index is not properly appreciated. The word *index* comes from the Latin word for "to indicate." An index entry, then, points you toward something. It helps you learn more about a term. If you would like to know where a certain subject is discussed in this book, look in the index. It will give you the numbers of the pages that provide information on that subject.

HEAD WEIGHTS

Turn forward a few pages to Chapter 1. You will notice that each major part of that chapter is introduced by a short title. These titles are set in different type sizes. The size of the type indicates the importance of the subject being discussed. These short titles are called "heads." There are heads in all of the chapters in this book.

The heads in a chapter can serve as stepping-stones in helping you gain information. They alert you to what will be covered in that part of the chapter. Before you read a chapter, scan the heads that introduce the various parts of the chapter. Scanning these heads will give you a general idea of the topics that will be discussed in the chapter.

Regardless of your career goals, you will find that this book is a helpful guide to one of the key technologies in the modern world — construction technology. By gaining a general knowledge of the materials and processes of this growing industry, you will have a better understanding of our modern and changing world.

THE DEVELOPMENT OF CONSTRUCTION TECHNOLOGY

TOOLS AND TECHNOLOGY

Technology is the use of technical methods to obtain practical results. Technology as it relates to construction is known as **construction technology**. The instruments of technology are tools. A tool is anything that makes a job easier. For example, a laser-guided bulldozer is a tool, just as is a common shovel. Because our age has developed complex tools, it has been called the Age of Technology.

The technology we use today builds on developments from throughout the entire experience of the human race. Our own time is the present stage of history, a word that comes from the Greek word for "to know." History, then, is the time about which we know. It stretches back from the present day to the end of that period known as prehistory. Prehistory is that time about which we know little. Much of human history and prehistory is concerned with the slow, but gradual, development of the technological skills needed for survival. Because shelter is a basic need, many of these skills related to construction.

Let's take a brief look at the history of construction technology. This will help give us a better appreciation of the construction developments of our own time.

SKILLS TO MEET BASIC NEEDS

Shelter, along with food and clothing, was one of the three main concerns of early humans.

A laser is a beam of intense light that can be accurately focused. The blade of this grader is guided by a laser. A sensing device on the blade follows the laser beam. The beam, then, guides the blade of the grader. It ensures that the blade cuts to a certain depth. The laser is a fairly new device. Its use in construction is just one example of the way in which the construction industry makes use of available technology.

The first shelters were natural—cave entrances and rock overhangs. These were not built or even greatly adapted for human use. They were merely found and used for what they were—protection from the weather.

As long as people camped in one place, the same shelter could be used day after day. However, as people moved in a ceaseless search for food, a new shelter would have been needed. If a natural shelter could not be found, a shelter would have to be built. From necessity, people developed basic construction skills.

These first shelters actually built by humans were made of available materials—tree branches and stones. These materials would have been used just as they were found. Early humans lacked the tools to greatly alter materials to suit their purposes. Though we might find them crude, these simple shelters would have stretched to the limit the technological skills of early humans.

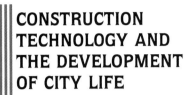

CONSTRUCTION TECHNOLOGY AND THE DEVELOPMENT OF CITY LIFE

At some point, people realized that it would be easier to carry a portable shelter rather than to build a new shelter at each campsite. To be portable, these shelters needed also to be light.

This dwelling of the Algonkian Amerindians was portable. It could be quickly taken down and transported to another place. It provided a reliable shelter.

Generally, they consisted of little more than a flexible covering, such as animal skins, stretched over an arrangement of poles. Still, as long as humans traveled from place to place, they were limited in their design of shelters. This limitation hampered their development of new construction skills.

The products of construction technology reflect the needs of society. In this view of a city block, you see several different types of buildings. Each type of building is used for a different purpose. Some are used as workplaces. Others are used as apartments. Others are used for recreation. The buildings shown here reflect the complexity of our modern social life. Today, we use certain buildings for certain purposes. In ancient times, most human activities were carried on in one place. The need for buildings for different purposes has proved a challenge to modern construction technology. Working with engineers, architects design buildings for a wide range of uses.

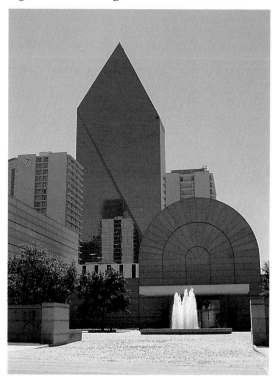

THE SPECIALIZATION OF SKILLS

When people learned to grow plants for food, they no longer needed to seek out a new food source each day. This development—the beginning of agriculture—led to the founding of human settlements. Settled in one place, people began to practice those construction skills that would ensure their survival in that place. They built fortifications and dug wells.

To earn their living, people began to concentrate on doing one thing well. For example, if they were farmers, they became better at growing crops. In short, people became more specialized in their job skills. Becoming more specialized, they also became dependent on others for the things they could not provide for themselves. To gain animals, food crops, and needed handmade items, they began to trade with others.

CONSTRUCTION TECHNOLOGY AND THE GROWTH OF TRADE

In this gradual development of trade there lay the seeds of a growing commerce. Commerce is the buying and selling of goods that require transportation from one place to another. The development of commerce was a major spur to the growth of construction technology. Commerce became important to the economy of these societies. The word economy relates to the production and sale of goods and services.

The economic survival of these early town-dwellers depended on a thriving commerce. To create and maintain this, they needed to develop the technical skills to build roads and bridges.

These were needed to establish trade routes, to link one town with the next. By making commerce easier, these transportation links helped ensure the survival of city life.

Some of these small towns prospered, becoming trading centers. In them, buildings of a more permanent nature began to be constructed. Again, the materials used would have been those at hand—stone and wood in Europe, clay in the Middle East. Now, though, the material was being shaped. Stone was being cut into building blocks. Tree trunks were being shaped into building beams. Clay was being formed into sun-dried bricks.

To meet these construction needs, there began to emerge a group of workers who gained most of their livelihood from the practice of a single construction skill. The skill may have been carpentry or stonemasonry. Such specialization allowed workers to set work standards. Using their skills, these workers learned to shape their environment, or surroundings, in new ways. They began to create a **built environment**. In time, changing slowly over a period of thousands of years, this built environment would develop into an environment recognizable to all of us. It would be the city.

Until fairly recently, humans spent a great deal of their energy fortifying the places in which they lived. Security was one of their principal considerations. Some of the largest early construction projects were fortifications. This Iron Age hill fort in Dorset, England is an example of such a fortification. The fort is known as Maiden Castle. The earth used to build Maiden Castle was moved by hand over a period of many years. The people who built the fort lived around it and inside it. In 70 A.D., the invading Romans conquered the people living here. The survivors were moved to a site 2 miles [3.2 km] away. There, a new town—visible in the distance—developed.

THE REBIRTH OF CONSTRUCTION TECHNOLOGY

As can be seen, a well-developed and vigorous city life was essential to the development of construction technology. In no period of human history was this shown more clearly than during the so-called Dark Ages. The Dark Ages is the name for the period from the fall of Rome in 476 to the rebirth of city life in about 1000. During this period of about 500 years, construction dropped off. Many of the roads and buildings of the Romans—who were master builders—were dismantled. Their stones were then used for other purposes, usually agricultural. City life diminished. People returned to working the land.

In about 1000, city life began to revive. Once again, there was a growth in the development of skilled trades, especially building trades. Commerce began to thrive. Better roads were needed, as were more bridges and more functional build-

The Romans were the first people to emphasize the importance of good roads. They were masters at roadbuilding. Used mainly to move troops rapidly throughout the empire, many of their roads were divided into slow and fast lanes. Also, their roads usually were built to follow a straight line. They went over natural obstacles, such as hills, rather than around them. Modern interstate highways employ both of these principles. They allow two lanes of traffic—fast and slow—in each direction. Whenever possible, interstates are laid out to run in a straight line—a straight line being the shortest distance between two points.

ings. Carpenters and stonemasons, as well as other skilled workers, organized themselves into groups called guilds. These set standards of workmanship. They also ensured that their members worked at an acceptable level of skill. The cathedrals of Europe—most of them built between 1100 and 1300—are the surviving momuments to the skills of these medieval carpenters and masons.

THE BUILT ENVIRONMENT

Just as the the prosperous growth of city life fostered the growth of construction technology, it also created problems for it to solve. As an example, let us look at London. In the late nineteenth century, that city became enormously overcrowded. This overcrowding caused serious transportation problems. City streets were crowded. The city had no efficient public transportation system. The roads into the city also were jammed with traffic. The transportation problem within the city was solved by the con-

The building of the medieval European cathedrals was an important point in the development of construction technology. Large teams of laborers and skilled workers were needed to complete these projects. Keeping track of materials and work schedules was a difficult task, requiring smooth organization. The task was not eased by the fact that construction was often carried on over a period of forty or fifty years. These cathedrals represent one of the most organized and sustained building efforts of the Middle Ages. This shows Notre Dame in Paris.

struction of the Tube. This subway was the world's first underground transportation system. Transportation into and out of London was greatly improved through the construction of a number of large railroad stations. Each of these construction projects involved the building of several different types of structures. Tunnels, bridges, overpasses, and roadways were all built as part of these projects.

In the United States, many of the outstanding construction projects of the nineteenth century also involved building transportation links. Two of the greatest marvels of construction were the transcontinental railroad and the Brooklyn Bridge (see page 263). Each of these massive construction projects drew on the latest construction technology of the day.

CONSTRUCTION TECHNOLOGY: TODAY AND TOMORROW

Some think of construction technology as relating only to buildings. However, it relates also to the building of highways and bridges as well as to the building of tunnels and airport runways. We travel to school or to work on roads and highways. These may pass through tunnels or across bridges. All of these — as well as the buildings in which we live, go to school, and work — are examples of the uses of construction technology. As you can see, the works of construction technology are essential in modern communication and transportation systems.

In our own time, we have used construction technology to build an efficient network of interstate highways, rail systems, and airports. This has freed us from the need to build our structures from the materials at hand. Look around you and you will find that the materials used to construct the buildings in which you live and go to school were probably brought from another place. As materials have become more readily available, builders have been able to concentrate more on their use. This has led to the use of construction materials that save time. Of course, these materials can also cut costs and provide greater strength and safety. New high-strength steels have enabled us to build structures that would have been impossible before. Plastics have found an increasing use in construction. New instruments, such as lasers, also are being used in construction.

In our own century, one of the most spectacular construction projects has been the Verrazano-Narrows Bridge. With a length of 4,260 feet (1,298 m), it spans New York Harbor to connect Staten Island with Brooklyn. Its suspension cables weigh nearly 10,000 tons each. Perhaps the most famous of the New York bridges is the Brooklyn Bridge. For more information on the Brooklyn Bridge, refer to page 263.

Modern transportation systems allow builders a wide choice of construction materials. On the American frontier, the log cabin was the principal dwelling in the midwest. The sod house was built in the Plains states of Nebraska and North and South Dakota. Each of these dwellings, like the dwellings of humans long ago, was built using available resources. Today, an expanded construction technology and an effective transportation system allow builders to choose from a wide range of building materials. Modern skyscrapers are built from a variety of materials.

These new developments in construction technology are encouraging. They have given us the confidence and ability to undertake massive construction schemes. One of these is the Chunnel, the undersea link between England and France (see page 235).

Projects such as the Chunnel require careful organization. Each stage of construction must be carefully coordinated with the others. Computers will be essential in managing such large construction projects. Such great projects will once again test the limits of our construction skills. In testing these skills, we are again working against the same limits imposed on the first people who sought to build a simple shelter from the materials at hand. Once again, we will be testing our skills against the circumstances. If we meet the challenge, we will have expanded the frontiers of construction technology. We will have met new goals. As before, these goals will encourage us to work still harder to focus the uses of construction technology to meet our needs.

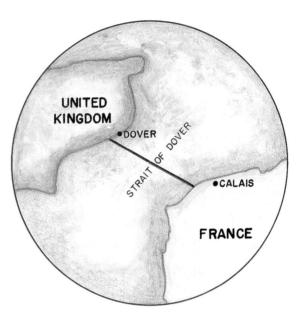

The dream of the Chunnel has fascinated Europeans for over 150 years. Previous attempts to build such a tunnel beneath the English Channel have failed. Now, the technology and financing are available. Construction has now begun on what some see as the construction project of the century. For more information on this exciting project, refer to page 235. The map on the right shows the route of the undersea Chunnel between the United Kingdom and France.

A computer is hardware. The programs that are used on a computer are known as software. A number of computer programs are especially designed to assist builders in managing construction projects. For example, computers can be used in ordering materials and scheduling construction activities. They also can be used to prepare financial projects and assess the profit and loss on a construction project. In the management of a large construction project, the computer can be a valuable tool. This shows construction drawings created on a computer.

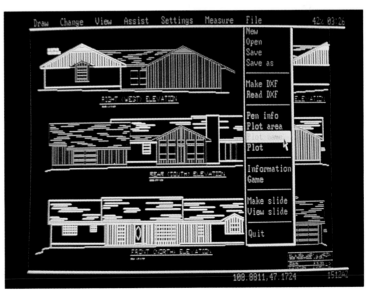

SECTION

I

INTRODUCTION

CHAPTER **1** INTRODUCTION TO CONSTRUCTION

Terms to Know

construction process
construction
  technology
financing

general contractor
scheduling
transfer of
  ownership

Objectives

When you have completed reading this **1**
chapter, you should be able to do the
following:
- Describe construction technology.
- Identify the effects of construction in our
  world.
- Explain the basic procedure for constructing a building.
- Explain why a construction project should
  be considered carefully before it is begun.

1. Resources:
- Chapter 1 Lesson Plan in the Teacher's Manual
  in this Teacher's Annotated Edition and in the
  Teacher's Resource Guide.
- Chapter 1 Study Guide in the Student Workbook.
- Chapter 1 Visual Master in the Teacher's Resource
  Guide.

The construction industry as we know it is the result of thousands of years of development. Today we have heavy equipment and sophisticated tools that help us construct tall buildings and other large structures within a short period of time. Fig. 1-1.

The tools and equipment, as well as the processes construction workers use to build structures, are the result of construction technology. **Construction technology** can be described as our use of tools, materials, and processes to build structures such as buildings, highways, and dams. To say this another way, construction technology refers to all the knowledge we have gained about how to build structures to meet our needs.

BUILDINGS AND MUCH MORE

When we think of construction, we generally think first of buildings. However, construction includes every type of structure that people build. Construction plays such a universal role in our lives because almost every type of need can be at least partially satisfied by some type of construction.

Community Development

Construction plays an important part in shaping the communities in which we live. Most communities have homes, office buildings, churches, factories, banks, stores, schools, and recreational facilities. Fig. 1-2. In the development of these structures, construction technology is helping us satisfy our needs for shelter, education, employment, and recreation, as well as many other needs. The construction of power plants and sewer and water systems meets our utility needs. The construction of broadcasting towers for radio and television stations makes communication within the community and with the rest of the world more convenient.

Agricultural Needs

Construction also provides many agricultural aids. We build wells and irrigation systems to

Fig. 1-1. The construction of a modern skyscraper draws on the full range of available tools in construction technology.

1. Discuss how the amount of labor needed to build structures has been reduced as more sophisticated tools and equipment have been developed.

Fig. 1-2. Construction contributes to community development by providing homes and facilities for community services.

2. Ask each student to list five recent construction projects in their community. Ask the student to list the need or needs met by each project.

irrigate otherwise nonproductive land. Fig. 1-3. For larger applications, we build dams to create reservoirs. Then we can construct irrigation canals from a river or reservoir to supply water to farms in the area. This method is also used to provide water supplies for whole communities.

Transportation Needs

Our transportation needs are also met by construction. Highways, bridges, and airports are built to help people travel from place to place. However, construction does more than just help people travel from one place to another. For example, the construction of railroads and seaports allows us to move large amounts of freight by land or by water.

The construction of pipelines enables us to move resources such as water, natural gas, and oil over long distances economically. The most outstanding example of a pipeline is the Trans-Alaska, or Alyeska, pipeline. Fig. 1-4. This 800-mile (1290-km) pipeline allows producers to transport oil from oil fields in Prudhoe Bay

Fig. 1-4. The Alyeska pipeline was constructed to transport oil some 800 miles (1290 km) across the frigid Alaskan terrain.

in northern Alaska to the Port of Valdez in southern Alaska. Before the pipeline was built, oil companies could not tap the vast amounts of oil in Prudhoe Bay simply because they had no way to transport the oil to other parts of the country.

Fig. 1-3. Irrigation canals can be constructed to supply water to land that otherwise could not be used for farming.

Did You Know?

An aqueduct is a structure for carrying water from one place to another. Though the water usually flowed in open channels in an aqueduct, pipe was sometimes used. In a sense, then, an aqueduct was similar to a pipeline. Ancient Rome was served by several aqueducts. It has been estimated that, in the first century A.D., these aqueducts supplied Rome with about 38,000,000 gallons of water — or about 38 gallons per person. Three of the ancient Roman aqueducts have been repaired for use today.

1. Ask your students if any have flown over the Great Plains. If they have, ask if they have noticed the large green circles where land has been irrigated. Discuss the environmental impact of this irrigation on the environment.

2. Show photos of ancient Roman aqueducts. Point out the use of the arch as a supporting structure. Point out that sometimes a series of arches — one above another — was used.

Fig. 1-5. The construction of sewage treatment plants allows us to remove or neutralize harmful wastes from liquid sewage before the water is returned to lakes and streams.

Sanitation Needs

Even our sanitation needs can be met by construction. The building of sewage treatment plants helps protect our environment by neutralizing or removing harmful wastes from the water we use. The water is then returned to its source. From its source, the water can be reused to irrigate land or to supply water to nearby communities. Fig. 1-5.

Did You Know ?

Ancient Rome had a sewage system. Rainwater was drained into the Tiber river by drains built into the surface of the earth. However, by the sixth century B.C., the water was carried to the Tiber through enclosed drains. As well as carrying off rainwater, these sewers also carried off the water that had been used in the public baths.

1. Discuss present day sewage treatment. Explain how soluble chemicals and nutrients can destroy the quality of the water in our rivers and lakes.

National Development

The benefits of construction are not limited to individual communities. Construction can also affect the development of a country. For example, the building of the transcontinental railroad, which was finished in 1869, encouraged pioneers to settle the far reaches of the western United States. Fig. 1-6. The railroad made transportation reasonably safe and convenient. After the railroad was completed, people and supplies could be carried from Omaha, Nebraska, to Sacramento, California, in five to six days. Before the construction of the railroad, this same trip took as long as three to four months by wagon. The railroad also improved long-distance communication between people in the East and the West. A letter transported by train could be carried much more safely and quickly than one transported by wagon.

The construction of highway and road systems also has made transportation more convenient. Our highways and roads make it possible to travel by automobile to any of the thousands of towns and cities in our country.

2. Discuss the impact of the interstate highway system on the railroads in recent years.
3. How has the increased use of trucks and automobiles affected the use of energy in the United States?

Fig. 1-6. The construction of the transcontinental railroad opened up vast areas of the western United States for settlement.

1   In addition, these highways and roads comprise a valuable network of pathways that are indispensable in transporting food, materials, and manufactured products by truck. As a result, communities can be established almost anywhere that roads can be built. People can now
2   live farther from their jobs and still be within commuting distance. Fig. 1-7.

Fig. 1-7. The construction of highways and roads has allowed for the growth of cities and towns by making transportation more convenient.

1. Discuss the effects that construction has had on the availability of farmland.
2. As a city expands, driving time from the edge of the city to the central business district often increases. Mention that, in some cities, buildings near the central business district have been converted to apartments.

For Discussion

1. In what ways has the interstate highway system changed the way you live? Are you now able to buy food that might have been unavailable before? Are there any other changes?
2. How would the life of a pioneer in the West have been improved through a nearby source of transportation?

||| FROM CAMELS ||| TO CRANES

The construction technology of today is based on the discoveries made by many people over a period of thousands of years. The first construction tools were handmade, hand-held tools made of rocks or animal bones. Later, people found ways to refine the tools so that they could work better and faster. They also domesticated animals—such as camels, horses, and even water buffalo and elephants—to use as "beasts of burden." For a long time, animals such as these provided the greatest force available for moving heavy building materials around construction sites.

Today cranes, dump trucks, bulldozers, and many other types of equipment help construction workers move and lift large amounts of heavy materials. Fig. 1-8. The conversion from beasts of burden such as camels to sophisticated machines such as cranes did not occur overnight, however. The development of new machines and processes to help us do work is actually the result of many significant advances that took place over a period of many years.

Fig. 1-8. Cranes are now used to lift and move heavy materials.

For Discussion

The text mentions that certain domesticated animals were used to move building materials at construction sites. What limits would the use of such animals place on construction activities and building design?

1. Mention that the horsepower rating given to bulldozers and other construction equipment reflects our previous dependence on animals to move construction materials.

2. Have students research and report on the ways in which construction practices were changed by developments such as the steam engine, the internal combustion engine, and the electric motor.

HIGHLIGHTS OF THE CONSTRUCTION PROCESS

The term **construction process** refers to everything that happens from the decision to build a structure to the owner's acceptance of the completed structure. The construction process involves the owner of the structure and the construction company that builds the structure. Sometimes various other parties—such as attorneys, realtors, and financing companies—also participate at some stage of the process. In this section you will become familiar with the basic steps in planning and building a structure.

Fig. 1-9. This gas station is located near an interstate highway interchange. Why is this a good place to construct a gas station?

Planning a Project

Every construction project begins with several decisions. The first decision is whether or not to build a structure. Once this decision has been made, other decisions are needed. Where should the structure be built? When? How much will it cost? Who will build it? All of these decisions and many more must be made.

Selecting a Site

Choosing the right site or location for a structure is important. For example, fast food restaurants should be built on sites that are easy for people to get to. Fig. 1-9. Factories should be built near good transportation routes. The best location for a school is in the community it will serve.

After a site has been selected, the procedure of acquiring the site begins. Usually a realtor handles the negotiations. When the buyer and seller agree, a contract is signed.

Financing

Financing is the term used to describe the process of obtaining the money used to pay for a project. Construction projects cost a lot of money. A public project, such as a school build-

ing, is funded through taxes and bonds. A private project, such as a house, generally is financed by one or two people. Usually, people have to borrow the money to pay for private construction projects.

Did You Know?

Every construction project must be paid for. In the nineteenth century, many American railroads received land from the federal government. This land was along the path of the railroad. Because the railroads then sold most of this land to settlers, they obtained money with which to help finance the building of the railroad. In all, this grant of federal land totaled 131,000,000 acres.

1. Stress that the construction process begins before any actual construction takes place. Remind the students that construction takes place to fill a need—which must first be identified.

2. Mention that studies are sometimes conducted to determine if a perceived need is real. A study can also be used to determine if a construction project can be economically profitable.

Preparing the Plans

At this time many decisions are made about how the structure should look and how it will function. These decisions are made by architects or engineers and are approved by the owner. The final decisions are written into a set of project plans that identify all the details of the project. Fig. 1-10. The project plans give all the information necessary to build the structure as it was designed and engineered. The plans show the construction workers how to build the structure and what materials to use.

Building the Project

When the final plans are ready, the owner must determine who will do the construction work. The owner hires a construction company, or **general contractor**. The general contractor is in charge of the construction work. When the owner and the contractor agree on the cost of the construction, they sign a contract and construction can begin.

Organizing the Work

After the contract is signed, the job of organizing begins. The organization of a construction project is accomplished in part by scheduling.

Scheduling involves estimating the amount of time it will take to do each part of the job. The contractor prepares a schedule for the work that identifies who will do what job and in what order. Fig. 1-11.

Next, the job site must be organized. This includes making sure that workers have access to the site. Portable offices and restrooms, as well as temporary utilities such as water and electricity, are needed.

Completing the Project

As the job progresses, managers must make sure that the construction tasks are being done properly and on time. The contractor keeps charts and records of the progress. The object is to get the job done on time and to stay within the established budget.

Fig. 1-11. This construction manager uses a bar chart to help schedule construction tasks in the right order.

Fig. 1-10. The project plans contain all the information necessary to build a structure.

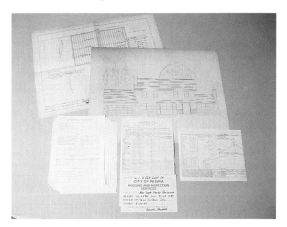

1. Show the class a set of plans and specifications for a building. (If your district has a vocational building construction program, you may be able to get a set from the instructor.)

2. Discuss why the scheduling of work on a construction project is so important.
3. Explain that limited space on many construction sites requires that materials be carefully organized.

Completing the project includes finishing the structure itself as well as completing all of the exterior work, such as paving and landscaping. It also includes cleaning up the construction site after the building is finished.

When all of this work has been done, the project is ready for the final inspection. Inspectors check to see that the job has been done properly and according to the contract. Fig. 1-12.

During the inspection, the inspectors make up a list of things to be corrected. The contractor has to make the necessary corrections by a certain date. Once the corrections are completed, another inspection is made.

When everyone is satisfied that the contract requirements have been met, the owner accepts the completed project. This is called the **transfer of ownership**. It includes a formal notice of completion, which legally establishes that the job is done. At this time the owner makes the final payment to the contractor. Now the owner takes on the responsibility for the maintenance and repair of the structure and grounds.

Fig. 1-12. These people are performing the final inspection for this building. They will note anything that has not been done correctly.

For Discussion

Discuss the qualities a person should look for in a general contractor.

HEALTH & SAFETY

Safety on a construction site is important. You may have noticed that fences are sometimes placed around large construction sites. As construction technology has developed, the number of regulations covering the safety of construction workers has increased. Workers today are provided with more protection on the job than were construction workers one hundred years ago. Much of this increased protection has resulted from state and federal laws. Also, consumer groups are watchful for unsafe job practices.

1. Explain that most commercial projects cannot produce income until they are finished. Therefore time means money to the owner. Sometimes the owner may offer a bonus for getting the job done early.

2. Have students list things that they would check during the final inspection of a house. Keep this list. After Chapter 14, ask them to prepare another list. Compare the two lists.

THE PRICE OF PROGRESS

Much progress has been made in the construction industry since our ancestors used stone or bone tools to construct their dwellings. In general, most people agree that the progress we have made in construction technology has been useful and good. However, construction is not without some drawbacks. For example, every time we clear a tract of land for a new construction project, we alter, or change, a part of our natural environment. Figs. 1-13 and 1-14.

In many cases the construction project destroys the natural habitat of a variety of plants and animals. As a result of the widespread building to accommodate human growth, many plants and animals have become extinct. Therefore, the possible effects of a proposed construction project should be weighed carefully before the decision is made to begin building. By making responsible decisions, we can build structures that will do as little harm as possible to the environment and still provide for our needs.

Fig. 1-13. Even though most construction projects are beneficial to people, we must consider whether their benefits outweigh any possible negative effects on our environment.

1. Ask the students to write a short report on a plant or animal that has been endangered due to construction.

2. Obtain an environmental impact statement that has been prepared for a proposed construction site. Discuss some parts of the study with the class.

Fig. 1-14. The water behind this dam covers land that was once part of several small family farms.

For Discussion

Are you aware of any construction projects in your neighborhood that have been built on land that was covered with trees or bushes? Did the builders make any attempt to keep some of the trees or bushes? Did they plant any new trees or bushes? In your opinion, were any trees or bushes removed unnecessarily?

Construction Facts

A GOOD ARCH TAKES TIME

A monumental symbol of the twin spirits of freedom and exploration, the Gateway Arch in St. Louis is the tallest freestanding arch in the world. The stainless steel arch stands 630 feet (190 m) high—as tall as a 63-story building.

In the late 1940s, the people of St. Louis saw the need for a memorial to commemorate the Louisiana Purchase of 1803 and the westward expansion that resulted. A national competition was held in 1947 to select a design for the monument. A deceptively simple arch, the entry of architect Eero Saarinen, was the winner of the competition.

Saarinen's original design presented severe engineering problems. For example, his original design called for a nonstructural stainless steel covering over structural steel members. With this design, the arch could not withstand the forces to which it would be subjected. Even a light wind would twist the arch and break it off at its base.

It was not until 1961 that construction began on a perfected arch. However, many new problems were yet to be encountered. For example, special crawler derricks had to be used to carry the upper sections of the arch into place. Also, at the 530-foot level, a stabilizing strut had to be placed between the two legs of the arch.

In 1965, seventeen years after its conception, the arch was completed. Large jacks were used to push the legs of the arch apart so that the final section, the keystone section, could be inserted.

The finished arch has withstood the test of time. For more than 20 years it has towered over St. Louis as a huge symbol of the role of that city as the "Gateway to the West." This beautiful and masterfully engineered structure is considered by many to be an architectural triumph.

1. Ask one or more students to volunteer to prepare a short report on the Gateway Arch in St. Louis. Ask the student or students to report to the class.

2. Ask a student or group of students to make a model of the Gateway Arch for display purposes.

R E V I E W

Chapter Summary

The construction industry today reflects developments in technology occurring over thousands of years. Today's construction technology helps to meet our agricultural, transportation, and sanitation needs. Construction, especially as it relates to transportation, has also been important in national development. Construction processes must be carefully planned. A site must be selected. Financing must be obtained. Plans must be prepared and the work must be carefully organized by the contractor in charge of the project. In all building projects, it is essential that as little harm as possible be done to the environment.

Test Your Knowledge   1

1. Name at least five types of structures that can be built to aid in the development of a community.
2. What types of structures can be built to provide agriculture aid in areas where irrigation is necessary?
3. Name four types of structures that can be built to help meet our transportation needs.
4. How can our sanitation needs be met by construction?
5. Explain how the construction of the transcontinental railroad affected the development of the western United States.
6. Name three types of equipment that construction workers use today to help lift and move heavy materials.
7. Who are the two principal participants in any construction project? Who else may be involved?
8. What is the function of the project plans for a construction project?
9. Name three tasks that are included in organizing a job site.
10. Why must we consider carefully all of the effects of construction before we begin to build?

1. The answers to the Test Your Knowledge questions are in the Teacher's Manual at the front of this Teacher's Annotated Edition.

REVIEW

Activities

1. Choose a construction project that was recently completed in your community. Make a presentation to your class to explain the effect of that construction project on your community.

2. Do research on a major construction project such as the Erie Canal, the Alyeska pipeline, or Hoover Dam. Write a one-page report on the effects of the construction project on the environment and on society.

3. Use old newspapers and magazines to create a construction-related collage on a piece of cardboard. Design your collage so that it illustrates one of the following themes:
   • Community development
   • National development
   • Progress in construction
   • Process of construction
   • Environmental impact of construction

CHAPTER **2** CONSTRUCTION AND SOCIETY

Terms to Know

built environment
construction
ecology

environment
environmental
    impact study

Objectives

When you have completed reading this
chapter, you should be able to do the
following:
- Define *built environment*.
- Explain how construction contributes to
  the economy.
- Identify two major concerns people have
  about construction.
- Identify several factors that affect the cost
  of a construction project.

1. Resources:
- Chapter 2 Lesson Plan in the Teacher's Manual
  in this Teacher's Annotated Edition and in the
  Teacher's Resource Guide.
- Chapter 2 Study Guide in the Student Workbook.
- Chapter 2 Visual Master in the Teacher's Resource
  Guide.

Construction, or the building of structures, plays an important part in our lives. Through construction we are able to meet our basic need for shelter. Homes, apartment buildings, and hotels are common examples of buildings that we construct to provide us with shelter. Through construction we also build office buildings, factories, and other buildings that, in addition to providing shelter, provide us with places to work. Construction is also the process by which we build roads, highways, bridges, and tunnels that we use in transporting people and products from place to place. As you can see, construction plays an important role in our society. Construction is a primary activity by which we shape our environment to better suit our needs.

HEALTH & SAFETY

Did you know that a building can be "sick"? Some new and remodeled office buildings contain materials that give off harmful fumes. In some cases, this problem is worsened because the building is closed. Because the windows do not open, the toxic fumes build up within the building. It is estimated that as many as 10 percent of the workforce are sensitive to such fumes. In some cases, the solution is clear. The material giving off the harmful fumes (carpet, for example) can be replaced. In other cases, the solution is not as simple.

THE BUILT ENVIRONMENT

Environment simply means "surroundings." Most often when we think of the word *environment*, we think of trees, lakes, and mountains. However, structures such as buildings, bridges, and highways are part of the environment, too. These structures, along with other parts of the environment that people have shaped or altered can be referred to as the **built environment**. Fig. 2-1. Our built environment is ever changing to meet current needs. Old buildings are often renovated (renewed). Other buildings are torn down and new buildings take their places.

Fig. 2-1. The fountain, sidewalks, and other structures in this park were built by people. These structures are part of our built environment.

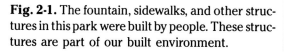

1. All construction projects do not have the same level of importance to society. Ask students to identify a project that is very important, one that is of average importance, and one that is of little importance. Ask students to give their reasons.

2. Explain to the class how the built environment in one location can affect the environment hundreds of miles away. Acid rain might be used as an example.

Personal Benefits

We all have the common needs for food, clothing, and shelter. The need for shelter is satisfied directly by construction. For example, we live in houses and apartments that shelter us from the weather. Fig. 2-2. Some of these houses and apartments are fancier and more expensive than others. Each has been constructed with the basic elements of a foundation, walls, and a roof.

The construction industry indirectly satisfies other needs, such as needs for food and clothing. For example, stores, factories, and warehouses are constructed to provide manufacturing space and places to store and sell clothing. Food processing plants are constructed that make it possible to process large quantities of food in short periods of time. This helps us keep up with the ever-increasing demand for food. Once the food is processed, it is stored and sold in buildings that have been constructed for that purpose. Fig. 2-3.

Fig. 2-3. Grocery stores are specialized buildings designed and constructed to store, display, and sell food.

Fig. 2-2. These apartment buildings were constructed to shelter several hundred families.

Food and clothing do not depend on construction directly. They would still be available if stores and factories could not be built. However, the existence of these buildings makes food and clothing more accessible and provides us with better-quality products.

Social Benefits

In addition to meeting personal needs, construction affects our social lives. People are social beings. We like to interact with one another. Living in a community makes such interactions possible. Playgrounds, public swimming pools, and other recreational facilities are just a few products of construction that help satisfy our need to socialize. Fig. 2-4.

Construction also helps us share our experiences and culture. The construction of large facilities allows people to gather at cultural functions such as concerts, ballets, and plays.

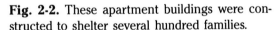

1. Make the class aware of how the growth of suburbia led to the development of shopping malls as the distance to central business districts became longer.

2. Ask students to list some of the ways that the school building is used to meet the social needs of their community.

Fig. 2-4. Recreational facilities such as this ski lodge are constructed to help us meet our social needs and wants.

Fig. 2-5. A museum offers a place for us to learn about the past.

Museums, libraries, and art galleries help people learn more about their society. Fig. 2-5. Community centers and auditoriums provide places for people to gather to decide important issues or to share interests.

Communication

Because of fast-changing technology, communication systems are changing and improving rapidly. We can communicate over long distances conveniently and with great speed. Our communication systems are so sophisticated that we can communicate with people across the world without leaving our homes. Television broadens our world by bringing news and informative programs about the world directly into our living rooms. Fig. 2-6.

Our communication systems require the construction of transmission towers, relay stations, and radio and television studios. Many people are involved in designing and constructing the

Fig. 2-6. Construction plays an important role in many types of communication. This television broadcasting studio required the construction of many unusual structures.

different components of communication systems. Architects, engineers, contractors, and other workers contribute to the construction of these systems.

1. Have a student or group of students study and report on the facilities necessary for the operation of a television station.

2. Point out that a great deal of today's communication is relayed by satellites in space. Then ask the students to conduct research regarding the vehicle assembly building at the Kennedy Space Center.

Transportation

Transportation systems seem to have made the world smaller and each person's horizons wider. Because of our excellent transportation systems, we can live and travel practically anywhere. Railways, highways, bridges, and airports are construction projects that make travel fast and convenient.

When you think of transportation systems, you probably think first about the vehicles that carry us from place to place. However, in many cases the pathways are as important as the vehicles in providing safe and efficient transportation. For example, trains could not operate without a system of tracks. Automobiles would travel more slowly and be less convenient to use if we did not have an effective system of roads and highways. This system of roads and highways represents major construction efforts. In the United States there are over 4 million miles (6.4 million km) of roads and 300 thousand miles (480 thousand km) of railroad tracks. Fig. 2-7.

Fig. 2-7. The construction of an effective road and highway system has made travel by automobile more efficient.

Did You Know ?

The wheels of modern trains are, of course, guided by rails. In the Bronze Age, people in the eastern Mediterranean constructed ruts in roads. These ruts were 3 to 6 inches (76 to 152 mm) deep, about 8 inches (203 mm) wide, and about 50 inches (1.27 m) apart. The function of the ruts was the same as the function of the rails in a railroad—to guide the wheels. The ruts were used to guide the wheels of carts and wagons. Of course, this made the transportation of goods easier.

1. Have a student or group of students research and report on the difference between the construction of a railroad roadbed and the roadway of a super highway.

For Discussion

1. In what ways has the design of buildings been influenced by the fact that human beings are social creatures?
2. Why are rivers in the United States no longer greatly used for passenger travel?

2. Contact the state highway department and the county road commission to find out the average cost of building one mile of primary interstate highway and one mile of two-lane secondary road.

41

CONSTRUCTION AND THE ECONOMY

The construction industry affects our nation's economy by employing millions of people. Within the construction industry are many different types of jobs. The obvious jobs of carpenter, plumber, and electrician are not the only jobs offered by the construction industry. Construction workers also include architects, engineers, accountants, and managers. Each job provides workers with income that allows them to buy the things they need and want. This process of earning and spending money contributes to the health of our economy.

Construction and community growth are closely related. As a community grows, the number of available jobs also grows. Constructing a new factory or business attracts workers to a community. Fig. 2-8. When new workers and their families move to a community, they purchase houses and use the community's goods and services. They generate business that improves the economy. As a community grows, more highways and utilities are needed. Thus there is a need for more construction.

Fig. 2-8. When this new factory is completed, additional jobs will be available for people living in nearby communities.

Fig. 2-9. The damming of water by the Aswan High Dam in Egypt has had some harmful effects on Egyptian agriculture.

ECOLOGY AND THE ENVIRONMENT

Ecology is the study of the way plants and animals exist together. It also studies the relationship of plants and animals to their environment. The changes we make that affect our natural environment can be critical. If we make a poor decision, we may damage our environment beyond repair. For example, in the 1960s, the Egyptians built the Aswan High Dam on the Nile River. Fig. 2-9. The Aswan dam is 364 feet

1. Make the students aware that the construction industry frequently leads the economy into a period of recession and also out of a recession.

2. Discuss how the paving of large areas of land for parking lots may affect the local ground water level. Draw attention to the use of ground water recharge basins as a solution to this problem.

(111 m) high. According to those who favored the dam, it would control seasonal flooding of farmland and residential areas. It would provide electricity for half the population of Egypt. It would also create approximately 1 million acres (404,680 ha) of new farmland through irrigation. When the dam was built, these benefits did occur. However, many unforeseen environmental effects also occurred.

Before the dam was built, the seasonal floods brought new nutrients to the farmland every year. Now that the floods have been controlled, the land is beginning to lose its fertility. The salt level in the land has risen by 10 to 15 percent, making it unsuitable for growing some kinds of crops. Another effect of the dam is coastal erosion, which has required the construction of costly dikes to keep the land from washing away.

The Aswan High Dam has also affected Egyptian culture. The dam has caused the water table to rise, threatening to cover monuments such as the Temple of Karnak. Fig. 2-10. Many of the Nubian people whose ancestors lived along the banks of the Nile, have been displaced. To support themselves, these people will have to learn to farm the irrigated land.

Fig. 2-10. The Temple of Karnak is one example of ancient Egyptian architecture that is threatened by the rising water table in Egypt.

Did You Know?

The soil in the Nile delta is some of the richest soil on earth. For centuries it has provided Egyptian farmers with land on which they could grow crops. The Aswan High Dam, completed in 1971, slowed the flow of the Nile through the delta. This allowed the waters of the Mediterranean Sea, which is saltwater, to flow farther up the Nile. As a result, the delta land covered by this seawater absorbed some of its salt. This salt in the soil lessens the usefulness of the land for farming.

The Aswan High Dam is only one example of how an uninformed decision can have unpredicted or harmful effects on our environment. In the United States, research committees study the effects of proposed major construction to try to identify in advance the harm it may cause. We also have a law, the Endangered Species Act, that helps protect animals and plants in danger of extinction because of human activities.

Political pressures, however, often bring about exemptions from and exceptions to the rules.

1. Ask students to read about one of the large dam projects in their own country. Ask them to write a report on its advantages and disadvantages. Ask them to conclude whether the project was environmentally sound.

2. Draw a parallel between the Aswan High Dam and some of the dams built in the United States. Some of these dams covered pre-Columbian archeological sites as well as evidence of more recent native American culture.

In Tennessee, for example, the construction of the Tellico Dam caused a great deal of controversy. Research committees found the dam to be economically unfeasible. Furthermore, 5,600 acres of agricultural land would be lost if the dam were built, as well as 280 archeological sites listed in the National Register of Historic Places. Also, scientists discovered that a species of minnow, the snail darter, would be threatened with extinction. The dam would remove the snail darter's only existing natural breeding ground. Fig. 2-11.

The dam would supply $2.7 million in electricity annually. The reservoir created would provide a recreational area. Because of these factors, political pressures to build the dam were strong. The protests of the environmentalists were overruled, and the dam's builders were exempted from complying with the Endangered Species Act. The agricultural land and the historic sites were lost. Fortunately, scientists were able to transplant 2,000 snail darters to another river in Tennessee, where they seem to be doing fine. If the transplant had not been successful, a whole species of life would have been destroyed.

As we plan new structures to meet our needs, we must give thought to both the built and the natural environment. The effects of a proposed construction project on the natural environment need to be evaluated. We must consider the preservation and conservation of open space, water resources, air quality, and animal and plant life.

A study that evaluates the effects of a project on the environment is called an **environmental impact study**. The environmental impact study is meant to bring to light the effect of a construction project on the environment. The federal government requires environmental impact studies on almost all construction projects that are built with federal money. Fig. 2-12.

Fig. 2-11. The snail darter is an example of a fish threatened by extinction due to our construction activities.

Fig. 2-12. The area shown here has been contaminated by industrial contaminants. These ecologists are measuring its effects. To prevent damage to the environment, an environmental impact study is required for any new construction project that uses federal money.

1. In some areas sewage that has not been treated to remove all soluble minerals is being used to irrigate. Some estimate that in fifty years such land will contain so much heavy metal (lead, etc.) that it will be unfit for raising crops. Discuss this.

2. Point out that a decision is often based upon the least costly choice. Politicians are not elected by future generations. Thus, we as today's voters must insist that our government do long-range environmental planning.

In many cases construction can improve the natural condition of the environment. For example, if mud slides often *erode* (wear away) a hilly area, retaining walls can be built to hold back the soil. Other construction projects, such as a water treatment plant, can improve our natural resources so that a community can use them. Fig. 2-13. Such a construction project, if well planned, can complement the natural environment. Each situation has to be evaluated on its own merit.

For Discussion

Are there examples of construction projects in your neighborhood that have improved the environment?

COSTS OF CONSTRUCTION

Most construction projects are very expensive. The high cost of construction is having a profound impact on our society. To understand the impact it is necessary to understand what makes up construction costs.

One large construction expense is the land on which a structure is built. The cost of the site for the average house is about 20 percent of the house's total cost. Also, construction projects must be built with sturdy, durable materials. The costs of structural materials—lumber, steel, and concrete—constitute a major building expense. Fig. 2-14.

Many other factors also contribute to the overall cost of a construction project. Construction workers must earn a living wage. *Overhead*, or the cost of running the company, and the company's profit must also be included in the cost.

Fig. 2-13. The construction of a water treatment plant provides a place where water can be made safe for human consumption.

1. Explain to students that while the finished project has an impact on the environment, the ways in which construction is done may cause problems. For example, extensive earthwork near a trout stream could cause serious soil erosion and sedimentation of the stream. This is why many states require all construction projects to use geotextiles to minimize erosion.

Fig. 2-14. Traditional building materials such as wood are becoming more expensive. Their costs contribute to the overall cost of construction, which is rising steadily.

Because of the high cost of construction, many people who probably would have purchased houses ten years ago now live in apartments or condominiums. In many cases, condominium and apartment dwellers share common walls with neighbors on both sides, upstairs, and downstairs. These conditions require that the people be considerate so as not to disturb one another's privacy. Even a loud alarm clock can sometimes be heard in the room next door. Insulation in the walls does not always eliminate all of the noise.

Although apartments and condominiums provide less privacy, they often include recreation facilities. For example, many apartments and condominiums have their own swimming pools and tennis courts. Fig. 2-15. Also, apartment and condominium dwellers rarely are responsible for yard work and for maintenance and repair of the building.

As construction costs continue to rise, more and more people will be affected by these and similar changes. Also, pressure will increase to keep costs low. New, less expensive materials undoubtedly will be developed to take the place of more expensive ones. These new materials may even change the appearance of the buildings we construct in the future.

For Discussion

In your neighborhood, there may be buildings of many different styles. The buildings may be constructed using a variety of materials. Discuss some of the reasons for the use of various styles. Discuss also the reasons why some building materials may have been chosen over others.

1. Discuss and list on the board the factors — besides raw land costs — that are included in the final price of a lot in a subdivision.

2. Explain to students how material costs rise and fall due to supply and demand. Also illustrate how energy costs impact on the cost of manufacturing and distributing construction materials.

1   **Fig. 2-15.** The individual units in this condominium building are built around a pool. Those who live in the condominium have access to the pool.

1. Mention that multiple dwelling units existed in ancient times. For example, small apartment buildings were found in ancient Rome.

Construction Facts

Years ago, every town had a town square or village green. This served as a central meeting place for townspeople and a place for special events. The town square served a real need in the community. Now we have shopping malls. Look around you next time you are in a shopping mall. We shop there, certainly, but we also meet and socialize there, just as townspeople in the past socialized in the town square.

The shopping mall as we know it today came into being in 1956 in Edina, Minnesota. Southdale Mall, designed by Victor Gruen, was the first fully enclosed shopping mall.

Gruen was an Austrian architect working in America. He believed that people spent too much time isolated, driving here and there. He thought that a community needed a place for people to be together face to face. Also, he saw a way to use land more efficiently by grouping stores together instead of placing them throughout the city. Gruen's idea for enclosing the mall solved the weather problems for shoppers, too.

The success of the Southdale Mall proved that Gruen's idea worked. In fact, his idea worked so well that Southdale Mall became the model for new malls all across the nation. Gruen knew that the mall could meet a social need by providing a center for human activity that was exciting, comfortable, and fun. There are now hundreds of shopping malls across the country. The mall shown here is in Texas.

1. Point out that most successful shopping malls have one or more anchor stores. An anchor store is one that is connected to the mall. However, it is built so that it can be isolated from the mall for firefighting purposes. These anchor stores act as magnets to draw people to the mall, where they may then shop at some of the smaller stores.

CHAPTER **2**

REVIEW

Chapter Summary

Construction plays an important part in our lives. Through construction, we alter our environment by creating the built environment. Construction creates personal benefits and social benefits by improving communication and transportation. It affects the economy by employing millions of people. Construction projects also affect the environment. Before constructing a project, possible harm to the environment should be carefully studied. Construction can be expensive. The cost of construction must include the price of the land and materials, as well as the cost of labor. The increasingly high cost of construction may lead to the development of less expensive building materials.

Test Your Knowledge ¹

1. What is an environment?
2. Name three personal benefits that construction makes possible either directly or indirectly.
3. How does construction contribute to our social lives?
4. Name two ways in which construction affects the economy of a community.
5. Name three beneficial results that building a dam might have.
6. Name three harmful results that building a dam might have.
7. What law in the United States is aimed at preserving plants and animals threatened by extinction?
8. What is the purpose of an environmental impact study?
9. Name three major types of costs that are involved in a construction project.
10. Name one major effect that the high cost of construction has had on our society.

1. The answers to the Test Your Knowledge questions are in the Teacher's Manual at the front of this Teacher's Annotated Edition.

REVIEW

Activities

 1. Choose a construction project that has had a profound effect on the environment. The project may be a dam, a nuclear power plant, a canal, or a similar project. Find newspaper and magazine articles that discuss the effects of the project on the environment. Share your findings with your class.

 2. Do research to find out more about environmental impact studies. For example, find out what a study tells about a proposed project and how a study affects the final decision to build or not to build a structure. Write a one-page report about your discoveries.

 3. Find a place in or around your community where the natural environment could be improved by construction. Describe the improvement you think could be made and how it would affect the natural environment.

 4. In 1980 a rare subspecies of butterfly, the Palos Verdes Blue butterfly, was placed on the federal government's list of endangered species. This rare butterfly lived only in a small area of land, overgrown with locoweed, south of Los Angeles on the Palos Verdes peninsula. In 1983 the city of Rancho Palos Verdes destroyed the butterfly's habitat to build an athletic playing field. The tiny creature is now thought to be extinct. Write a one-page report on the Palos Verdes Blue butterfly. Discuss whether or not the playing field should have been built.

CHAPTER

3 CONSTRUCTION SAFETY

Terms to Know

accident
first aid
labor unions
Occupational Health
and Safety
Administration
(OSHA)

safety factor
safety rules

Objectives

**When you have completed reading this ▮
chapter, you should be able to do the
following:**

- Identify two major safety concerns in the
  construction industry.
- Describe the safety measures taken
  by construction companies to protect
  workers on the job.
- Understand the importance of safety rules
  and regulations in your school laboratory.
- Describe first aid techniques to use in
  case of an accident.

1. Resources:
- Chapter 3 Lesson Plan in the Teacher's Manual
  in this Teacher's Annotated Edition and in the
  Teacher's Resource Guide.
- Chapter 3 Study Guide in the Student Workbook.
- Chapter 3 Visual Master in the Teacher's Resource
  Guide.

Safety is a major concern in the construction industry. While the potential for accidents exists in any business, the nature of construction increases the possibility of accidents. Therefore, no study of construction would be complete without a review of safety.

The two safety issues that most concern construction workers are safe working environments and building structures that are safe for people to inhabit or use. The primary concern of safety programs in the construction industry is to prevent injury to people and damage to property. In this chapter you will learn how the construction industry endeavors to meet the needs for safety in these areas. You will also learn how you can practice safe construction techniques in your school laboratory.

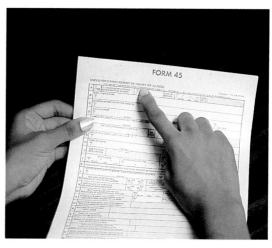

Fig. 3-1. Most construction companies require that an accident report be filled out for any accident, no matter how minor. The accident report helps supervisors correct problems and maintain a safe environment for employees.

ACCIDENT PREVENTION

An **accident** is an unexpected happening that results in injury, loss, or damage. Some accidents are minor, such as getting a splinter in your finger. Other accidents are serious, causing severe property damage, personal injury, or even death. All accidents, both minor and severe, can and should be prevented by taking appropriate safety precautions.

Every accident has a cause, or reason why it happened. Fig. 3-1. An accident may be caused by the carelessness or forgetfulness of a worker. For example, a worker who is hammering nails into a board and is not paying attention to what he or she is doing might hit a finger with the hammer. Accidents may also be caused by faulty equipment. For example, a broken electrical cord on a power tool might cause someone to get an electrical shock. Fig. 3-2. These are only a few examples of how an accident may be caused.

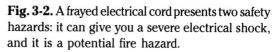

Fig. 3-2. A frayed electrical cord presents two safety hazards: it can give you a severe electrical shock, and it is a potential fire hazard.

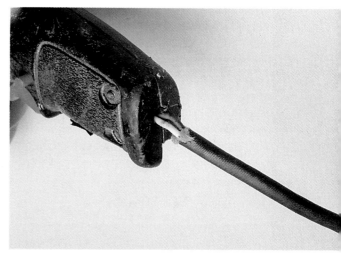

1. Only major construction accidents are reported by the news media. Encourage students to contribute such articles. Post such articles on the bulletin board. Talk about those safety rules that may have been broken. Discuss how such an accident might have been avoided.

2. Explain that one of the most important parts of an accident report is the section that identifies the cause of the accident and suggests a remedy to avoid similar future accidents.

Whenever an accident happens, regardless of its cause, it has an effect on someone. A worker may be hurt, or there may be equipment or property damage. Of course, time is lost also, which puts the work behind schedule. As a result, all accidents cost money. The cost of construction rises because of accidents, so that the structure costs more in the long run. Also, insurance rates are higher, which contributes to the overall cost of a project.

For Discussion

Safety rules may be general and refer to work practices as a whole. Safety rules may also be specific and refer to a certain work practice (such as working with electrical wiring). List three general safety rules.

CONSTRUCTION SAFETY

The primary concerns of safety in construction are to prevent injury to people and to prevent damage to property. There are two major ways to assure safety in the construction industry. One is to design safe structures. The other is to make sure that the workers have a safe place to work and know how to work safely. The workers then have the responsibility to follow company safety regulations to prevent accidental injury or damage to property.

Designing Safe Structures

All structures must be designed so that they are safe to inhabit and use. Fig. 3-3. For exam-

1. Explain that, when a serious accident occurs, the work of many people may be interrupted. The level of production may not be normal for some time after the accident. This affects the profitability of the job.

Fig. 3-3. This building was carefully planned by engineers so that it will be able to bear the weight of the construction materials as well as that of the people and things it will contain.

ple, buildings must be strong enough to support their own weight as well as the weight of all the people and things inside. Bridges must be wide enough and have strong enough foundations to support the heaviest vehicles they will carry. Roads, water towers, buildings, and every other kind of construction project must also be designed for safety.

Did You Know?

The ancient Romans thought that architecture was the art of building. They thought that architecture was concerned mainly with three ideas. The first of these was the stability, or safety, of the building. The second was the appropriate use of space in the building. The third was the attractiveness of the building.

To make sure that structures are strong enough for their intended uses and will not fail, engineers and architects use a safety factor. A **safety factor** is an extra measure of strength added to the design of a structure. For example, if an elevator must be able to carry ten people, the engineer may actually design the elevator to hold fifteen people. This safety factor helps prevent the elevator from failing due to overload.

Promoting Worker Safety

Most construction companies create and enforce a set of company safety rules. **Safety rules** are regulations aimed at preventing accidents and injuries in the workplace. The company's safety rules are taught to new workers before they begin working at a construction site, or *job site*. Special training sessions also may be held for workers already on the job. These sessions inform the workers about proper safety practices.

The safety rules developed by construction companies are usually just common sense. Most construction companies require workers to wear hard hats. These hats protect the workers' heads from falling objects. Fig. 3-4. Ear protection may be required in some construction areas to protect against harmful noise such as that from a concrete saw or jackhammer. Safety shoes protect workers' feet from the danger of heavy

Fig. 3-4. Most construction sites are "hard hat areas." This means workers must wear hard hats to protect themselves from falling objects.

1. Building codes are used to ensure that buildings will be safe for their intended use. Some structures may have to meet the standards of several governmental units. For example, a hangar designed for use by a state university will have to be approved by the local building department, the appropriate state agency, and the Federal Aeronautics Administration.

objects being dropped on them. Safety belts and harnesses with life lines attached should be worn by workers who work at high levels.

Promoting worker safety also includes maintaining a safe job site. The use of equipment guards, caution signs, and safety storage cans are good ways to maintain a safe job site. Fig. 3-5. Maintaining clean work areas that are free of clutter also helps promote worker safety.

Another way in which a construction company can help create a safe working environment for employees is to maintain and repair company tools and equipment. This requires a routine inspection of all tools and equipment. Damaged and worn tools and equipment must be repaired or replaced because they present a health hazard to employees.

In addition to the construction companies, three other groups are involved in promoting worker safety. These groups are the United States government, insurance companies, and labor unions. These groups have different functions, but they share the common goal of preventing accidents on the job site.

Fig. 3-5. The guard on this circular saw covers the teeth on the blade to protect the worker's hands.

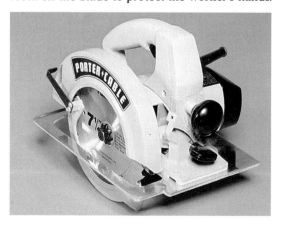

1. Explain to students why hard hats are designed to provide a gap between the top of the head and the hat. Explain that this gap provides a safety factor in case the falling object penetrates the top of the hat or the blow is very hard.

The Government

In 1970, the U.S. Congress created a regulatory agency known as the **Occupational Health and Safety Administration (OSHA)**. OSHA sets standards that regulate safety at construction sites. OSHA inspectors check on companies to make sure they are following these safety regulations. OSHA also inspects and approves safety products such as safety glasses and storage cans. If an OSHA inspector finds unsafe conditions at a job site, he or she informs the owner of the company. The inspector is authorized to shut down the construction job until the conditions are corrected.

Did You Know?

Lack of safety was a problem with early elevators. Prior to 1850, elevators were used mainly for lifting freight. These elevators were lifted by ropes, which sometimes broke. In 1853, Elisha Otis introduced an elevator that used a safety device to prevent it from falling. This safety device used a type of clamp that gripped the elevator guide rails. This clamp was activated when tension was lost on the hoisting rope. It was this basic development that opened the way to the development of the passenger elevator.

Insurance Companies

Insurance companies also are concerned about safety in construction. If a worker is injured on the job, an insurance company may have to pay his or her medical expenses. Insurance companies keep accurate records of accidents that happen at construction sites. The insurance

2. Have a student or group of students study and report on the various levels of safety violations recognized by OSHA. Ask them also to report on the action of the inspector at each level.

companies use these records to set *insurance rates*. These determine how much the company's insurance will cost. By working to prevent accidents, a construction company can keep its insurance rates low.

Labor Unions

Labor unions are worker-controlled organizations that are formed to present the demands of the workers to the management of construction and other types of companies. Workers form unions to increase their bargaining power. As members of a union, they are better able to negotiate for higher wages, shorter working hours, and improved working conditions.

Labor unions also negotiate for safer working conditions. For example, union workers in a job site may notice several safety hazards. The union may ask the construction company to eliminate these hazards. If the company managers take no action and the safety hazards are severe, the union workers may go on strike. To prevent workers from striking, the company may have to meet the workers' demands by increasing its safety measures.

Did You Know?

One of the first trade unions was formed in Tolpuddle, a small village in England. In 1833, six English farm laborers from that village formed a trade union. The purpose of their small trade union was to prevent their wages from being reduced. The laborers were arrested, and sentenced to banishment to a penal colony in Australia. The charge was "administering unlawful oaths." There was an enormous public outcry against this sentence. As a result, the men were set free in 1836. All but one of them returned to England.

1. Historically, labor unions have been responsible for the development of some safety standards. Guide students in a class discussion of this topic.

For Discussion

Can you name some of the features in the design of a school building that help make it a safe structure?

DEVELOPING A SAFETY PROGRAM

The best plan for accident prevention is to have a company safety program. The goal of a safety program is to achieve longer and longer periods of time without injury. One of the most important elements of a safety program is to develop good attitudes of safety among the workers. Then workers must be encouraged to follow general and specific safety rules concerning their personal safety while using tools and equipment. Fig. 3-6.

Fig. 3-6. This sign reminds the workers to work safely.

2. Emphasize that people should not trespass on construction sites. There are many hazards of which they are not aware. Emphasize that individuals should always ask permission before entering a construction site.

A company safety program also includes concern for the safety of the general public. Fig. 3-7. Sometimes security guards or security fences with locked gates can help ensure safety. Safety barriers, fences, and temporary protected walkways can be used to protect passersby from any danger at the construction site. The public should be allowed to view the project, but from a safe vantage point. This will ensure safety for spectators and good public relations for the company.

In the following paragraphs, you will learn more about the elements of a good safety program. You will find parallels between safety on a construction site and safety in your school laboratory. Read this information carefully before you begin any construction work in your laboratory.

Safety Attitudes

A good positive attitude toward a safety program or safety on the job is essential to the success of the program. If safety procedures and safeguards are not important to the worker, then the worker will disregard the rules and will not follow safe working procedures.

In most companies, the development of safe attitudes begins in employee training sessions. These sessions encourage safety attitudes as well as give instruction on safety practices. Much depends on a worker's attitude. You can give a worker safety instruction, but you cannot make the worker apply what he or she has learned. The worker must have the right attitude.

A worker who observes good personal safety practices is to be commended. Good personal safety practices are not enough, however. A worker with a good safety attitude must show concern for the safety of others. A safe worker is part of a safe team. Teamwork is an important element in safety. When team members are working safely together as a whole, then each member feels a responsibility to the team and wants to work safely for the good of the team. Fig. 3-8.

Fig. 3-7. This covered walkway protects pedestrians as they walk near the construction site.

1. Explain that an instructor, when covering safety rules in a training session, should explain why the practice being discussed is unsafe. He or she should also discuss the consequences of continuing an unsafe practice.

2. Emphasize that working safely involves developing safe working habits. Many times we perform an action without even thinking about it. If we can learn to do a job safely, it will be easy to continue doing it that way.

Fig. 3-8. Because construction workers work together as a team, each team member must think about everyone's safety.

HEALTH & SAFETY

In the nineteenth century, a worker who was injured on the job could do little about it. Generally, the employer was not responsible. However, in the late nineteenth century, there was an increased awareness of the need for safety in the workplace. At the same time, the employer began to take more responsibility for on-the-job injuries to employees. As a result of this, the employer sought to make the workplace safer for the employee. This resulted in a great decline in on-the-job injuries. As one example, accident rates for machine hazards are now only one-half of what they were forty years ago. This lowered accident rate is due mainly to the installation of protective devices on machines.

General Safety Rules

Most of the general rules for safety are just common sense rules. These rules are the same 1 for your school laboratory as they are for employees on a construction site. Violating these safety rules will endanger you and everyone else in the shop area. The following is a list of general safety rules you should know before beginning work in your construction laboratory. Following these rules may help you avoid serious injury.

1. Make sure an instructor is present in the shop area before you begin your work.
2. If you do not know how to operate a tool or machine, ask your instructor to help you. 2
3. Concentrate on your work at all times. Running in the shop area is not permitted. Before you begin any operation, carefully think 3 through every step that you will take. Identify any possible threats to your safety, and take immediate action to remove them. Do

1. Emphasize that eye protection should always be worn by anyone working in the lab.

2. Explain to students when and how they should use any special personal protective devices. See to it that they do so at all times.
3. Explain what you expect students to wear during lab activities. Be specific regarding appropriate dress.

not take chances. To do an operation safely often takes more time. However, it is better to spend time on safety than to suffer a serious injury. Remember, you can prevent most accidents by thinking *safety first*!

4. Keep your work area and all passageways clean and free of rubbish.

5. Keep your equipment in proper working order.

6. Stay alert when working with machinery.

7. When you are working with materials that may chip and fly into your eyes, wear safety glasses or goggles to protect your eyes. Fig. 3-9.

8. Wear hearing protectors or ear plugs in noisy work areas. These devices will help prevent your hearing from being damaged by excessive noise. Once damaged, your hearing cannot be restored.

9. Wear a respiratory mask when you are working in an area filled with dust or fumes. Fig. 3-10.

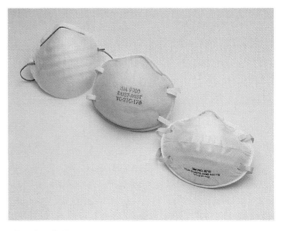

Fig. 3-10. Respiratory masks help protect workers from inhaling harmful particles.

10. Dress properly before you begin work. Remove jewelry such as necklaces, bracelets, watches, and rings. It is important to wear shoes at all times. Open-toed shoes such as sandals do not protect your feet from flying sparks or from sharp objects on the floor. Long hair should be tied back or placed securely under a cap. Hair can get caught in tools and machines and cause serious injuries.

11. Keep your mouth free of food and other objects. Chewing gum, toothpicks, and fasteners such as nails are hazardous to have in your mouth when working. An accidental slip or fall could cause you to choke on such items.

12. Use caution when lifting and moving objects. You can severely injure your back by lifting materials that are too heavy. Always ask for help when lifting heavy materials or carrying long objects. Lift using the muscles in your legs, not in your back.

13. Obey all safety signs in the shop area.

14. Be courteous to fellow students in the shop area. Arguing wastes time and energy, and may distract other workers in the shop area. Be willing to help others.

Fig. 3-9. Safety goggles provide eye protection. They help keep chips from flying into a worker's eyes.

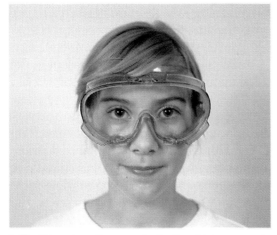

1. Explain why all power tools should be properly grounded.
2. Demonstrate how a ground fault interrupter will give the worker further protection.

15. Report all accidents to your instructor immediately. An accident report form should be filled out after an accident has occurred.
16. Know who the trained first-aid person is and where the first aid kit is.

Tool and Equipment Safety

Accidents involving tools and equipment generally occur because the operator has violated a safety rule. Many of these accidents can be avoided by observing the following safety rules:

1. Use tools and equipment only after you have received proper instruction in their use.
2. Use each tool and piece of equipment only to do the job for which it was intended. Do not attempt to modify tools or equipment.
3. Handle all tools and equipment with care. It is not safe or smart to throw tools down on work tables or to abuse equipment. Such actions can cause injuries or damage tools and equipment.
4. Carry tools in your hands, not in your pockets. Many tools have sharp edges and points that might cut you, especially if you were to slip or fall. It is also unsafe to carry too many tools at once.
5. Always check the electrical cords and plugs on portable power tools before using them. Cords should be in good condition with no frayed edges. Three-prong plugs should have all prongs intact. If the grounding prong is missing, the tool could give you a severe electrical shock. Also keep the cord well away from any cutting blades. Fig. 3-11.
6. Unplug portable power tools such as drills and sanders when they are not in use. Before plugging in a power tool, make sure all operating switches are off to keep from starting the tool accidentally.
7. When you operate portable power tools, be aware of your surroundings. Do not stand in water or work near live electrical wires.

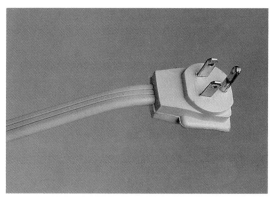

Fig. 3-11. This plug must be plugged into a grounded outlet to protect the worker from electrical shock.

8. Keep all guards in place, even when equipment is not in use.
9. Never touch moving parts on equipment. When you adjust equipment, make sure all switches are off and all moving parts have stopped.
10. Make sure a machine has completely stopped running before you leave the work area.
11. Report all damaged tools and equipment to your instructor to avoid accidents. If a tool or machine malfunctions, turn it off immediately.

Fire Safety

Fire prevention is an important part of any safety program. Since you may be working with potential fire hazards, it is important for you to learn some basic rules of fire safety. The safest procedure is to turn in a fire alarm regardless of the size of the fire and then promptly use a fire extinguisher to put the fire out. Emergency fire fighting equipment should be available in convenient locations. You should know where it is located.

1. Test the class on safety. Do not allow anyone to work in the lab who does not pass the general safety portion. Anyone who does not pass the tool and equipment portion should not be allowed to use the power tools.

2. As demonstrations are given on the use of various power tools, hand out a sheet of safety rules for each tool. Discuss these rules with the class.

The shop should be free of accumulated rubbish. Passageways should be clear of obstacles so that the exit is easily accessible if a fire should occur. All extinguishing equipment should be in its proper location, clearly marked, and in working order.

The following rules will help you prevent fires from starting. They will also give you a clear idea of what to do in case a fire breaks out:

1. Dirty rags soaked with oil, grease, or paint are a serious fire hazard. Place dirty rags in a proper safety can after use.
2. Flammable liquids such as paint and varnish should be stored in a well-ventilated place away from all furnaces and other heat sources. Fig. 3-12.
3. Make sure all electrical cords are in good condition. Frayed cords are a fire hazard.
4. Become aware of the location of fire extinguishers so that if a fire breaks out, you will not waste time searching for one.
5. Learn the proper way to use a fire extinguisher. Fig. 3-13.
6. Not all fire extinguishers can be used to put out all types of fires. For example, a water-type extinguisher should *never* be sprayed on an electrical fire. Figure 3-14 shows the four main classes of fire extinguishers—A, B, C, and multipurpose.
7. If a fire starts, quickly activate the nearest fire alarm to alert others of the danger. Then, if the fire is small and not spreading quickly, you may be able to control it with a fire extinguisher. If the fire is spreading quickly or cannot be extinguished, leave the building immediately.
8. If your clothing catches on fire, *do not run*! Drop quickly to the ground and roll from side to side to extinguish the flames.

These are basic fire safety rules that apply to all construction sites. Like other accidents, most accidental fires can be prevented by careful planning and foresight.

Always remember to *think safety first*!

Fig. 3-12. Store flammable materials such as paint and varnish in a dry, well-ventilated area away from heat.

1. Show the class the locations of fire extinguishers in the lab. Also point out the location of the nearest fire alarm. Discuss the procedures to be followed in case of a fire or fire alarm.

2. Explain the different kinds of fire extinguishers and the kinds of fires on which each one is effective. Refer the class to Fig. 3-14.

Fig. 3-13. The correct way to use a fire extinguisher.

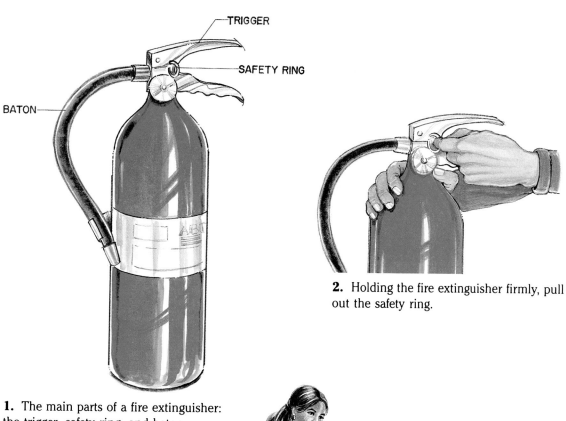

1. The main parts of a fire extinguisher: the trigger, safety ring, and baton.

2. Holding the fire extinguisher firmly, pull out the safety ring.

3. Pick up the extinguisher with one hand on the trigger. Use the other hand to aim the baton at the base of the fire. Squeeze the trigger to spray the extinguisher. Continue spraying until the fire is completely out.

1

1. Keep a record of any students who have missed key demonstrations on the safe use of any tools or equipment. Provide make-up demonstrations before allowing such students to use tools and equipment.

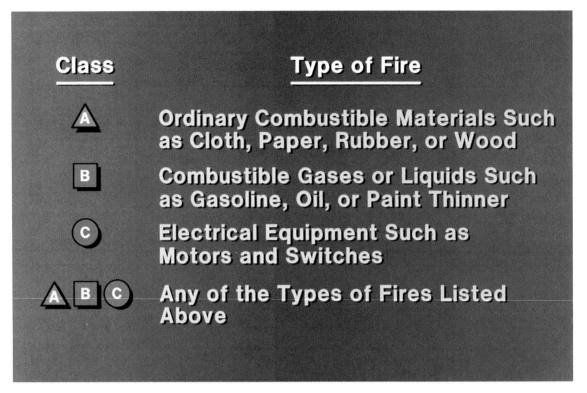

Class	Type of Fire
A	Ordinary Combustible Materials Such as Cloth, Paper, Rubber, or Wood
B	Combustible Gases or Liquids Such as Gasoline, Oil, or Paint Thinner
C	Electrical Equipment Such as Motors and Switches
A B C	Any of the Types of Fires Listed Above

Fig. 3-14. The four main types of fire extinguishers. All extinguishers are labeled to show the types of fires they can be used to put out.

Did You Know?

You may have heard of spontaneous combustion. This sometimes happens when oily rags are improperly stored. Basically, the combustible material in the rags joins with oxygen in the air. When this happens, small amounts of heat are created. As additional air joins with the combustible material, the temperature of the material rises. Finally, the rags burst into flame. Spontaneous combustion can be prevented by the exclusion of all air or by good ventilation.

1. Make the students aware that wood shavings and sawdust mixed with oil are also subject to spontaneous combustion.

First Aid

First aid is the immediate care given to a person who has been injured. The purpose of first aid is to temporarily relieve the pain caused by the injury or to protect the wound until further medical attention can be provided.

Being well trained in first aid procedures and having an adequately supplied first aid kit are essential ingredients in a safety program. Fig. 3-15. Everyone involved in construction should have a general knowledge of how to administer first aid. In addition, there should be at least one person present at all times who is well-trained in first aid.

A first aid kit that is fully equipped to handle emergency first aid needs should be located in a convenient place. Table 3-A provides a first aid table that explains the correct procedures to follow for several common industrial injuries.

Fig. 3-15. A well-stocked first aid cabinet is essential in any safety program.

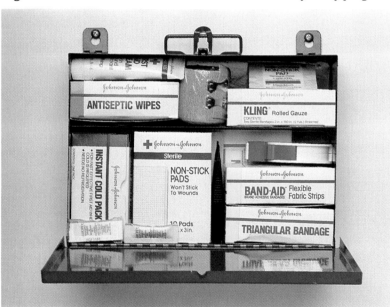

1. Familiarize the class with the basics of first aid. Refer the class to Table 3-A.

2. Develop a fire safety examination to be given to the class. Emphasize that anyone failing the exam must retake it until they pass it.

Injury	Actions To Be Taken
Bleeding	Minor cuts: Wash cut with soap under warm running water. To stop bleeding, press hard with sterile compress directly over wound, then bandage. Severe cuts: Try to stop bleeding by pressing hard with a sterile compress directly over the cut. If bleeding continues or cut is deep, take patient to a medical facility.
Burns	Mild: Hold 2-3 minutes under cold running water or in ice water. If pain persists, apply petroleum jelly or mild burn ointment and bandage. Severe: Apply dry protective bandage. Do not try to clean burn or break blisters. Keep patient calm, and transport to a medical facility as soon as possible.
Electric Shock	Turn off electrical power if possible. If patient is still touching source of shock, do not approach until power has been turned off. If necessary, pull patient away from source of shock using rope, wooden pole, or loop of dry cloth. If breathing stops, start rescue breathing. Take patient to a medical facility.
Eye Irritation (chemical)	Pour water into corner of eye, letting it run to other side, until chemical is thoroughly flushed out. Cover with bandage and take patient to a medical facility.
Eye Irritation (foreign object)	Follow same procedure as above to flush particle out of eye. If object cannot be flushed and is visible in eye, touch lightly with corner of moist handkerchief. If object cannot be removed or seen, take patient to a medical facility. Do not allow patient to rub affected eye.

Table 3-A. This table shows basic first aid procedures. You should be familiar with these procedures in case an accident occurs in your laboratory.

For Discussion

1. Discuss the characteristics a person must have if he or she is to develop a good safety attitude.
2. Teamwork is an important element in safety. To ensure good teamwork, what characteristics must the people on a team have?

1. Discuss why a small cut may not be as harmless as it might appear to be.

2. Relate teamwork on the construction site to teamwork in athletics. For example, the worker must know where his or her co-workers are if he or she is to keep from endangering them. No one wants an unsafe worker on their team.

Construction Facts

WHEN THE PRICE OF A JOB WAS YOUR LIFE

In New York City in the spring of 1911, a fire broke out one Saturday in the Triangle Shirtwaist Company. The fire swept through the eighth floor of the manufacturing plant. One thousand people were working there at the time. When they tried to escape, they discovered the doors were locked. The fire-fighting equipment inside the building was totally inadequate. When help finally arrived, 146 workers were dead. Hundreds more were injured.

The Triangle fire called attention to the unsafe working conditions in our nation's industries. Work was often brutal, many times done by children. The laming of one little girl by a treadle machine nearly caused a strike. Her employer refused to find other work for her. Men working in mines and for the railroads usually had the most dangerous positions. A brakeman, for instance, had to stand between two railroad cars coming together. Then he dropped the pin that joined them. A brakeman with all ten fingers was usually recognized as new on the job. As one person put it, companies valued mules more than human beings. Finally, public sympathy was aroused.

Real change did not happen, however, until companies began to realize that accidents hurt them, too. Accidents halted production, raised costs, and created conditions that made more accidents likely. During the late 19th and early 20th centuries, a safety movement supported by striking workers called for laws governing the workplace. Workmen's compensation laws stated that employers had to accept more responsibility for work injuries. Insurance and other health care programs came in later years.

Safety efforts paid off. Between 1926 and 1961, the rate of disabling injuries dropped from 32 percent to 6 percent. This drop in the accident rate was the result of reducing hazards and teaching workers accident prevention. Thanks to these and other safety measures, the industries of today are worlds apart from those of 100 years ago.

1. Invite a retired carpenter or other construction worker to present to the class a comparison of safety practices today with those of the time when he or she started working.

CHAPTER **3**

R E V I E W

Chapter Summary

Safety is a major concern in the construction industry. The primary concern of safety programs is to prevent injury to people and damage to property. To promote safety, the construction industry is careful to build structures that are safe to inhabit. They also promote worker safety programs. The United States government, insurance companies, and labor unions aid construction companies in promoting worker safety. A company safety program offers the best plan for accident prevention. In any safety program, good safety attitudes and general safety rules are important, as is fire prevention. Being well trained in first aid procedures and having an adequately supplied first aid kit is essential.

Test Your Knowledge

1. What five safety features can help protect the public near a construction site?
2. What are the two major safety concerns in the construction industry?
3. What distinguishes a worker with a good safety attitude?
4. Why are insurance companies concerned about safety on construction sites?
5. What should you do if you do not know how to operate a tool or machine?
6. Explain how heavy or bulky objects should be lifted and moved.
7. Why should you not carry tools in your pockets?
8. Why should you check to make sure three-prong electrical plugs are intact?
9. What type of fire extinguisher should be used to put out an electrical fire?
10. What is the purpose of first aid?

1. The answers to the Test Your Knowledge questions are in the Teacher's Manual at the front of this Teacher's Annotated Edition.

REVIEW

Activities

 1. Design a safety poster that illustrates the proper use of a particular tool or machine. On the poster make a list of precautions that should be followed to use the tool or machine.

 2. Make a list of accidents that could possibly occur in your shop. State why the accidents might happen and what could be done to prevent such accidents. Share your list with the class.

 3. Write a report about an accident that happened in the construction industry. In the report, explain how the accident occurred and what happened to the worker(s). You may want to visit a local construction company, talk to a construction worker, or read a newspaper or industrial safety magazine to gather the information for this report.

ACTIVITIES

Activity 1: Building a Studded Wall Model

Objective

After completing this activity, you should be able to demonstrate construction of a typical wall used in residential construction. This construction model will be to the scale of $1'' = 1'$.

Materials Needed
- $14\frac{1}{8}'' \times \frac{1}{4}'' \times 8''$ strips of balsa wood
- 2 dozen $\frac{3}{4}''$ wire brads
- 1 small container of glue

Steps of Procedure
1. Lay two $\frac{1}{8}'' \times \frac{1}{4}'' \times 8''$ strips of balsa wood face to face. Be sure the ends are even. Refer to Fig. A.
2. Starting from one end, draw a line on the edges of each piece $1\frac{5}{16}''$ apart. Including the line on each end, there should be seven of these lines. These lines will be the center marks for the wall studs. The piece of wood will be the top and bottom plates.
3. Nail and glue full studs ($\frac{1}{8}'' \times \frac{1}{4}'' \times 8''$) on all but the center marking. Fig. A.

4. Cut two strips of balsa wood to $6''$ lengths. Glue these to the inside of studs three and five. These pieces are called the trimmers. Fig. B.
5. Cut two $2\frac{1}{2}''$ pieces of balsa wood. Glue them face to face. This will be the window header. Fig. B.
6. Glue and nail the header to the top of the trimmer and between studs three and five.
7. Cut three $2''$ and three $1\frac{3}{4}''$ cripple studs from the $8''$ balsa wood. Fig. B.
8. Nail and glue the $1\frac{3}{4}''$ cripple studs to the top plate and header at the center stud mark location, and to the inside of studs three and five. Fig. B.
9. Nail and glue the $2''$ cripple studs to the bottom plate at the center stud marking location, and to the inside of studs three and five. Fig. B.
10. Cut a window sill $2\frac{1}{4}''$ in length.
11. Glue and nail the window sill to the tops of the cripple studs. Fig. A. You have now completed construction of the model wall.

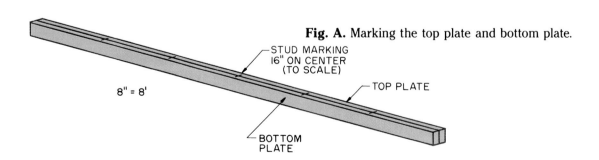

Fig. A. Marking the top plate and bottom plate.

STUD MARKING
16" ON CENTER
(TO SCALE)

TOP PLATE

8" = 8'

BOTTOM
PLATE

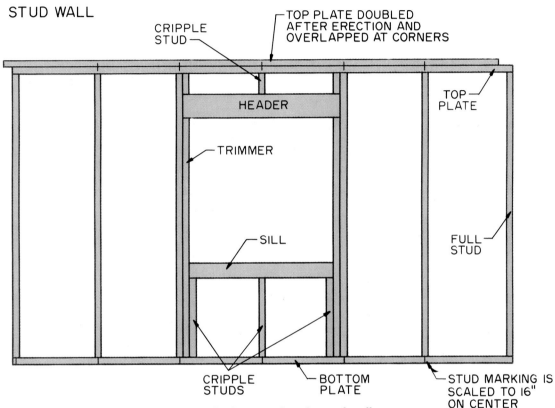

STUD WALL

CRIPPLE STUD

TOP PLATE DOUBLED AFTER ERECTION AND OVERLAPPED AT CORNERS

HEADER

TOP PLATE

TRIMMER

SILL

FULL STUD

CRIPPLE STUDS

BOTTOM PLATE

STUD MARKING IS SCALED TO 16" ON CENTER

Fig. B. Constructing the stud wall.

Activity 2: Learning about Paint Color and Heat Absorption

Objective

After completing this activity, you will be familiar with the basic techniques of the finishing process of painting. You will have developed basic painting skills in either brushing or spraying. You also will be familiar with the principles of passive solar construction. Passive solar construction is the use of construction techniques to reduce energy losses. While developing the skill to paint, you also will be able to identify those paint colors that have greater heat absorption characteristics.

ACTIVITIES

Materials Needed
- spray or brush-on paint (black, white, green, red, yellow, blue)
- 2 dozen 1"-wide paintbrushes
- 1 shoebox per student
- 1 6" × 16" piece of cardboard
- 1 roll clear-plastic food wrap
- hot glue gun and glue
- 12 thermometers
- scribe
- paint thinner
- 1 dozen scissors

Steps of Procedure
1. Each student should bring to class a shoebox with a lid. (A 6" × 16" piece of cardboard can be substituted for the lid.)
2. Your teacher will pass out the following materials to each student.
   - paint (in four colors)
   - 1 paintbrush
   - 15" of clear-plastic food wrap
3. Your teacher will make the following materials available for the use of all class members.
   - hot glue and glue gun

Fig. A. Dividing the box into evenly-sized compartments.

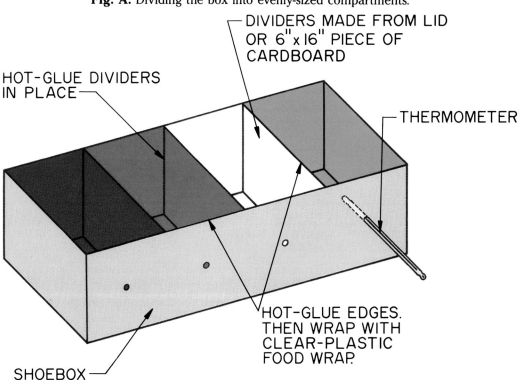

DIVIDERS MADE FROM LID OR 6"x16" PIECE OF CARDBOARD

HOT-GLUE DIVIDERS IN PLACE

THERMOMETER

HOT-GLUE EDGES. THEN WRAP WITH CLEAR-PLASTIC FOOD WRAP.

SHOEBOX

- thermometers
- scribes
- scissors
- paint thinner
- cleaning materials

4. Using the shoebox top or the $6'' \times 16''$ piece of cardboard, cut three pieces to match the height and width of the shoebox.
5. Hot-glue each of these pieces to the inside of the box to form four equal compartments. Fig. A.
6. Brush or spray each compartment a different color. Use all four colors.
7. After the paint has dried, turn the box on one side. Use a scribe to punch a hole in each compartment. Fig. A.

8. Coat the top edges of each compartment with hot glue. Coat the top of the divider and the side walls. Cover with plastic wrap. Press down the plastic wrap lightly so that it will be held by the glue.
9. Place each box right-side-up in sunlight or under a bright light. After 10 minutes, use a thermometer to check the temperature range in each compartment of the box. Insert the thermometer through the hole in each compartment.
10. What conclusions are you able to make from this experiment? Does paint color have an effect on the absorption of heat?

Activity 3: Describing Developing Technology

Objective

After completing this activity, you should be able to describe the basic development of a certain material, process, or tool in the area of construction technology.

Materials Needed
- plain paper (one sheet per student)
- 6 colored markers

Steps of Procedure
1. Divide a sheet of paper into four sections. Do this by first folding it in half from top to bottom. Then fold it in half from left to right. Unfold the paper. You have now divided the paper into four sections.

2. Brainstorm ideas for a construction-related topic. The topic may deal with any area of construction. For example, you might suggest ideas relating to the following topics:
   - materials
   - tools
   - safety
   - equipment
   - processes
   - structures
3. After choosing a particular topic, you should try to think of a "progression of development" that this item may have gone through. As an example of the general development of construction technology, you might refer to The Development of Construction Technol-

ACTIVITIES

Fig. A. The solution to one problem will sometimes create a new problem. Technology can be used to help solve problems.

DRAWING 1

People want to build a road between two villages. They find that the road will be blocked by a stream.

DRAWING 2

The people build a simple wooden bridge to span the stream.

DRAWING 3

The wooden bridge begins to crack beneath the weight of the wagon and its load.

DRAWING 4

To support the bridge, the people build a column of stones beneath the center of the bridge.

ogy, which begins on page 12. Each progression must show a problem that is being solved by using construction technology. Refer to Fig. A. Each progression should show:

- A problem (drawing 1).
- A solution through applied construction technology (drawing 2).

- A new problem related to and possibly caused by the solution (drawing 3).
- A solution for the new problem (drawing 4).

4. Sketch each development in one of the squares of your sheet of paper. You may use cartoon characters. You may even wish to include a little humor in your drawings. Write a caption for each drawing to explain what the drawing represents.

Activity 4: Making a Simple Electric Circuit

Objective

After completing this activity, you will have developed the basic skills needed to perform simple wiring activities. At the completion of this activity, you will be able to wire a plug, switch, light, and outlet into a circuit.

Materials Needed
- 1 wire cutter (side cutters)
- 1 wire stripper
- 1 screwdriver
- 6' of #12 − 2 Romex wire with ground
- 3 wire nuts
- 1 three-prong plug
- 1 receptacle and receptacle box
- 1 single-pull, single-throw switch and switch box
- 1 junction box with light canopy and bulb
- 1 mounting board (a 2' length of 2" × 4" will do)

- 6 ¼ " slotted screws
- 5 ½ " Romex box connectors

Steps of Procedure

There are three basic stages in this procedure: preparing the work station, running wires, and wiring the devices.

Preparing the Work Station

1. Cut the 6' section of #12 − 2 Romex wire with ground into three equal sections. Each section should be 2' in length.
2. Use the wire cutters to remove approximately 6" of the wire coating. Be sure not to cut any of the internal wires or their coatings. Perform this step at both ends of each wire.
3. Use the wire strippers to remove approximately ¾ " of the wire insulation from the ends of each wire.

4. Using two ¼ " screws, mount the receptacle box at one end of the 2×4. Now mount the switch box in the center. Mount the junction box at the remaining end of the 2×4.

Running Wires

1. Connect two Romex connectors to the receptacle box by placing one on each side. Tighten the lock-ring for each on the inside of the box.
2. Fasten a 2' length of wire through each of the Romex connectors so that approximately 6" of each wire remains inside the box.
3. Complete steps 1 and 2 once again for the switch box. Note that the feed line going into the switch box is the remaining end of the wire coming from the receptacle box.
4. Using the same method of fastening, connect the line coming out of the switch box to the junction box.

Wiring the Devices

1. Disassemble the plug. Insert the end of the wire through the plug cover. Tie an underwriter's knot 1 to 2 inches from the end of the wires. (Do not tie a knot in the ground wire.) This will keep the wire from being pulled from the end of the plug. See Fig. A.
2. Attach each wire to the appropriate terminal: black to brass, white to chrome, and ground to green.
3. Reassemble the plug. (Do not plug this in until all work has been completed and checked by your instructor.)
4. Next attach the receptacle. Fasten the black line coming into the receptacle box to a brass screw at the side of the receptacle. (Note

that for the receptacle and switching device there may be a strip gauge and hole to insert the wire.) Refer to Fig. B.

5. Now attach the remaining black line in the receptacle box to the remaining brass screw. This will allow a continuous flow of electricity to the switch box.
6. Attach the white wires to the chrome screws.
7. Attach the ground wire to the grounding terminal in the receptacle box and then to the green screw terminal of the receptacle. This will ground both the box and the receptacle.
8. To wire in the switch, fasten the black feed wire inside the switch box to one of the brass terminals at the side of the switch. Then fasten the remaining black wire to the brass terminal on the other side of the switch.
9. Connect the white neutral wires by twisting them together with the square nose of the side cutters and capping with a wire nut. Be sure no portion of exposed wire is visible under the cap.
10. Fasten the grounds to the box and the switch.
11. Fasten a 6" piece of black-and-white wire to your canopy light fixture. These are called wiring pigtails.
12. To complete the circuit, wire-nut the black wire from the junction box to the black pigtail from the light. Then connect the two remaining white wires and wire-nut together.
13. Ground the junction box.
14. Ask your instructor to check all work. Fig. B.
15. Fasten each device to each box.
16. Plug in the circuit. The outlet should be hot at all times. The switch will turn the light on and off.

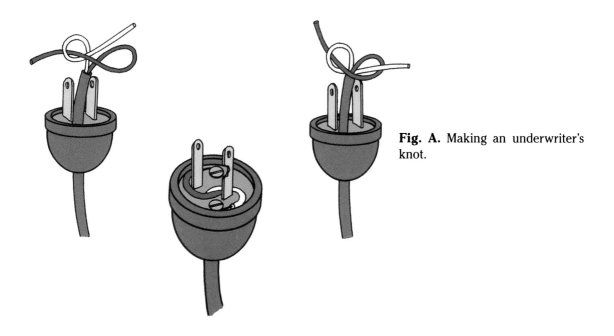

Fig. A. Making an underwriter's knot.

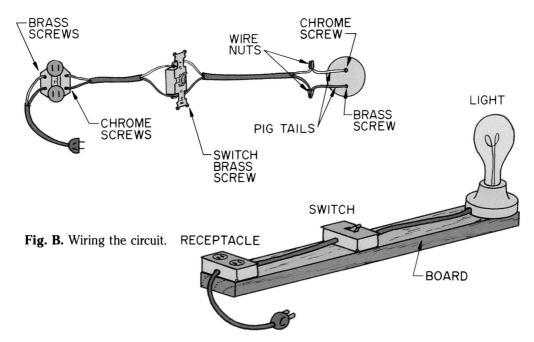

Fig. B. Wiring the circuit.

SECTION

II

MATERIALS, TOOLS, AND PROCESSES

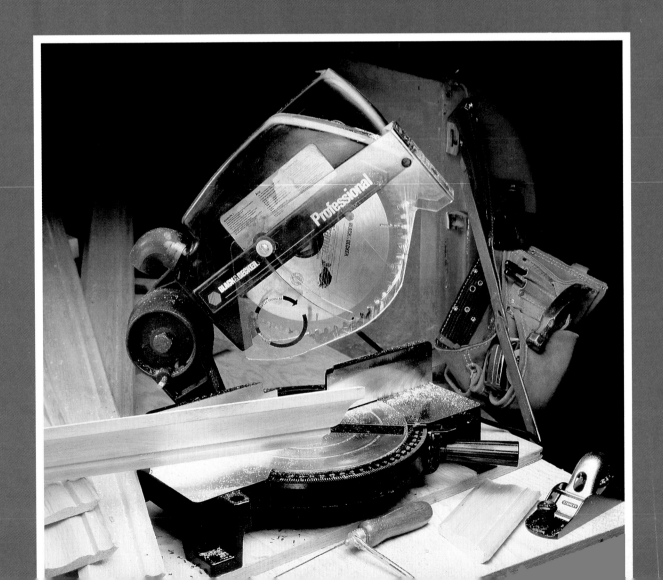

4 CONSTRUCTION MATERIALS

Terms to Know

adhesives
admixtures
aggregate
asphalt
board lumber
compressive strength
concrete
contact cement
dimension lumber

fiberboard
flooring
hardboard
hardwood
insulation
laminated beams
laminated joists
masonry

masonry cement
mesh
mortar
nominal size
nonferrous metals
paneling
particleboard
plywood

portland cement
reinforcing bars
softwood
standard stock
structural steel
vapor barrier
waferboard
wood composites

Objectives

When you have completed reading this **chapter, you should be able to do the following:**

- List and identify the ingredients of concrete.
- Identify the types of wood and wood composites used in construction.
- Describe two kinds of masonry that are used in construction.
- Identify the uses of different kinds of metals in construction.
- Identify and describe materials used for insulation, interior surfaces, roofing, and flooring in construction.
- Identify several types of adhesives and mechanical fasteners and explain their uses.

1. Resources:
- Chapter 4 Lesson Plan in the Teacher's Manual in this Teacher's Annotated Edition and in the Teacher's Resource Guide.
- Chapter 4 Study Guide in the Student Workbook.
- Chapter 4 Visual Master in the Teacher's Resource Guide.

The construction of a building requires hundreds of different materials. These materials must be chosen very carefully. The use of weak or inappropriate materials would result in an unsound and unsafe structure. It is therefore important that the people who work on a project know what materials are available. They must also know how to use each of the materials to the best advantage. For example, people who design and engineer a structure must make sure that the materials being used are appropriate for the project. The people who actually build the structure must use and install the materials correctly. This chapter will describe some common construction materials and will explain the uses of these materials. Fig. 4-1.

Fig. 4-1. This structure contains hundreds of different materials. The engineers and designers chose each type of material carefully to be sure it was the best choice for the project.

 CONCRETE

Basically, **concrete** is a mixture of sand, rocks, and a binder. Concrete is one of the most common construction materials. Today nearly every structure contains some concrete. Concrete is used in building houses, skyscrapers, airports, and highways. Fig. 4-2. Even sewer piper can be made of concrete.

There are two types of concrete. *Asphaltic concrete* is a black concrete that is made with asphalt and rocks. This kind of concrete is used for paving roads and parking lots. Most often, however, the term *concrete* refers to *portland cement concrete*. The main ingredients in portland cement concrete are:

- Portland cement.
- Water.
- Aggregate.
- Admixtures.

1. See how many different types of building materials the class can name. List them on the chalkboard as they are mentioned.

2. Students should be taught the proper terminology. For example, cement is the powder mixed with water to make the cement paste binder. Concrete is the mixture of cement, water, aggregates, and admixtures.

Fig. 4-2. Here the basic materials in concrete are being blended.

Portland cement is the binder for concrete. Portland cement is a mixture of clay and limestone that has been roasted in a special oven called a *kiln*. The dried mixture is crushed and ground into a fine powder, as shown in Fig. 4-3. This powder hardens when it is mixed with water. As the portland cement hardens, it makes the whole mixture *adhere*, or stick together.

Water is mixed with the cement to cause the chemical reaction needed to harden the concrete. This water-cement mixture is called *cement paste*. The strength of the concrete depends on the amount of water that is used. Too much water dilutes the cement paste. This makes a weak concrete mixture. Too little water does not allow the proper chemical reaction to occur in the cement, which also causes the mixture to be weak.

Did You Know?

Portland cement was not named for Portland, Oregon. Portland cement was invented in 1824 in England. It was produced from a mixture of limestone and clay. The resulting product was called portland cement because some thought that it looked like portland stone. This was a limestone that was used for building in England. By 1850, the technique for producing portland cement had been improved. By 1875, portland cement was being manufactured in the United States.

Fig. 4-3. Portland cement is sold by the bag. Each bag weighs 94 pounds (42 kg).

1. Assign students to perform an experiment with portland cement and water. Mix measured amounts of portland cement with different quantities of water. After two weeks, ask students to compare the appearance and strength of each cylinder. The conclusion is that if enough water is present to make a thick paste of the cement, the less water used, the stronger the mixture should be.

Aggregate is the sand and rocks used in concrete. The main purpose of the aggregate is to take up space. About 75 percent of a batch of concrete is aggregate. Fig. 4-4. However, each piece of aggregate must be coated with cement paste. If the aggregate is not covered completely, the concrete will not be strong.

Different sizes of aggregate are needed to make a good batch of concrete. *Fine aggregate*, usually sand, is actually any aggregate that is smaller than ¼ inch in diameter. *Coarse aggregate* is any aggregate that is larger than ¼ inch in diameter. Aggregate can be gravel, crushed rocks, or slag. *Slag* is a by-product of steel manufacturing. At one time, slag was thrown away. Now it is commonly used for aggregate.

Admixtures are anything added to a batch of concrete other than cement, water, and aggregate. Admixtures are used to give concrete certain characteristics. For example, if brown concrete is wanted, an admixture consisting of brown coloring is added while the concrete is being mixed. A *chemical accelerator* is an admixture that makes the concrete set up fast. A *retarder* is an admixture that makes the concrete cure more slowly.

Concrete has a great amount of **compressive strength**, which means it can carry a lot of weight per square inch (psi). For example, a concrete driveway may be made from 3,000 psi concrete. When it has cured, this concrete will support 3,000 pounds per square inch.

Concrete does not cure at once. As it dries, or sets, it becomes hard. Fig. 4-5. However, it is not as strong as it will be when it has cured. Curing time is about one month. As it cures, the concrete becomes stronger. By the end of a month, the concrete has developed most of its strength.

For Discussion

Discuss the ways in which building designs might be changed if concrete were no longer available.

Fig. 4-4. Aggregate mixed with portland cement.

Fig. 4-5. Concrete is poured into forms that hold it in place while it sets, or becomes hard. Forms give the concrete its final shape.

1. Point out that aggregates must be well graded (have the proper amount of each size of aggregate) to keep from having large voids that need to be filled with cement paste. They must also be dense, strong, and clean.

2. Have each student prepare a short report on one aspect of the history and manufacture of portland cement or the production and use of concrete.

LUMBER AND WOOD COMPOSITES

Wood was one of the first materials to be used in construction. Although other materials are now used to meet many construction needs, wood remains one of the most popular and useful construction materials.

The wood used in construction is classified as either softwood or hardwood. Fig. 4-6. **Softwood** does not refer to wood that is soft; it refers to wood that comes from *coniferous* (evergreen) trees. Pine, fir, and spruce are some common softwoods that are used in construction. **Hardwood** is wood that comes from *deciduous* trees.

These trees shed their leaves each season. Oak, walnut, and maple are common types of hardwoods. Hardwoods are usually used for floors and for making cabinets, moldings, and other trim. Most of the lumber used in construction is softwood.

Lumber

Wood that is used in construction is called *lumber.* Two types of lumber that are commonly used in construction are dimension lumber and board lumber. **Dimension lumber** is lumber that measures between 2 and 5 inches thick. Dimension lumber is used to build framework for walls, floors, and roofs. Dimension lumber is classi-

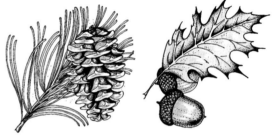

Fig. 4-6. Wood for construction comes from two types of trees. Softwood comes from coniferous, or evergreen trees. Hardwood comes from deciduous trees. Here, an evergreen is shown on the left. A hardwood is shown on the right. The inset above shows the needles and pine cone of the evergreen and the leaves and acorn of the oak.

1. Provide wood samples. Teach the students how to identify the varieties of wood commonly used in construction. Show students how to read the grade stamps found on lumber.

2. Divide the class into two groups. Ask each group to research and debate the question, ''Are our forests being destroyed by lumbering?''

fied by its size, or dimensions. For example, a piece of lumber that measures 2 inches by 4 inches is called a 2 × 4. Dimension lumber is generally available in even-numbered lengths, such as 8, 10, or 12 feet. Fig. 4-7.

Board lumber is lumber that measures less than 1½ inches thick and 4 or more inches wide. Boards are available in even-numbered widths, such as 2, 4, 6, 8, 10, and 12 inches. Like dimension lumber, all boards are generally available in even-numbered lengths.

It is important to realize that the stated size of lumber is not its actual finished size. For example, a 2 × 4 does not actually measure 2 inches by 4 inches. **Nominal size** is the size of the lumber when it is cut from the log. After it has been cut, the lumber is dried and then planed on all four sides to achieve smoothness. The finished size is therefore smaller than 2 inches by 4 inches. Table 4-A shows the nominal and actual sizes of softwood lumber.

Lumber is graded as it is cut from the log. The grade indicates the strength, usability, and appearance of the lumber. Table 4-B lists various grades of softwood lumber.

NOMINAL SIZE	ACTUAL SIZE
For Dimension Lumber:	
2 × 4	1½ × 3½
2 × 6	1½ × 5½
2 × 8	1½ × 7¼
2 × 10	1½ × 9¼
2 × 12	1½ × 11¼
For Board Lumber:	
1 × 4	¾ × 3½
1 × 6	¾ × 5½
1 × 8	¾ × 7¼
1 × 10	¾ × 9¼
1 × 12	¾ × 11¼

Table 4-A. The nominal and actual sizes of softwood lumber.

Wood Composites

Wood composites are those products that are made from a mixture of wood and other materials. Most wood composites are produced in large sheets, usually 4 feet wide and 8 feet long. Others, such as laminated wood joists and beams, are made to specification.

Plywood

One of the most commonly used wood composites is **plywood**. Plywood gets its name from its construction. It is made of several thin plies, or veneers, of wood that have been glued together. Each veneer is glued so that its grain is at right angles to the grain of the previous veneer. Fig. 4-8. The cross-layered grains make plywood very stable and strong.

Plywood is classified as *exterior*, for use outside, and *interior*, for use inside. The classification depends on the type of adhesive that is used to glue the veneers together. A waterproof glue must be used on exterior plywood. The glue that is used to make interior plywood is not waterproof, although interior plywood can withstand occasional moisture.

Fig. 4-7. Dimension lumber is used to frame walls, roofs, and floors.

1. Because lumber is a natural material, it is not uniform in strength or appearance. Thus, it must be graded. Show the class examples of defects such as warp, wind, knots, wane, and slope of grain.

2. Explain to students that wood composites are made to eliminate the defects that weaken regular lumber. They also provide wood products in unusual shapes and sizes.

BOARDS

APPEARANCE GRADES	Selects	B & BETTER (IWP — SUPREME) C SELECT (IWP — CHOICE) D SELECT (IWP — QUALITY)
	Finish	SUPERIOR PRIME E
	Paneling	CLEAR (ANY SELECT OR FINISH GRADE) NO. 2 COMMON SELECTED FOR KNOTTY PANELING NO. 3 COMMON SELECTED FOR KNOTTY PANELING
	Siding (Bevel Bungalow)	SUPERIOR PRIME

Table 4-B. Some common grades of softwood lumber.

DIMENSION/ALL SPECIES

Light Framing	CONSTRUCTION STANDARD UTILITY ECONOMY
Light Framing	SELECT STRUCTURAL NO. 1 NO. 2 NO. 3 ECONOMY
Appearance Framing	APPEARANCE
Structural Joists & Planks	SELECT STRUCTURAL NO. 1 NO. 2 NO. 3 ECONOMY
Decking	SELECTED DECKING COMMERCIAL DECKING
Studs	STUD ECONOMY STUD

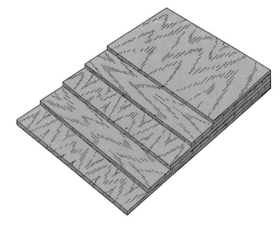

Fig. 4-8. Each ply of a piece of plywood is glued at right angles to the layers above and below it. This makes the plywood strong and resistant to warping.

Each side of a sheet of plywood is graded from A (highest grade) to D, according to the strength and appearance of its sides. Thus A-B plywood is plywood that has one excellent side and one side that has only a few minor flaws. Grades A and B are used when the plywood will be visible in the finished product. Grades C and D are used for general construction purposes. Table 4-C lists a few common grades and thicknesses of plywood.

1. Point out that one of the most important markings on construction plywood is the span indicator. For example, 24/16 tells the carpenter that the plywood may be put on roof trusses or rafters spaced up to 24 inches apart and on floor joists placed up to 16 inches apart.

Type	Description of Use		Grade of Plies		
		Face	Back	Inner Plies	
Interior					
A–A INT	For use where both sides will be visible, such as for cabinets, furniture, and partitions	A	A	D	
A–B INT	For use where two solid surfaces are needed, but the appearance of one of the sides does not have to be excellent	A	B	D	
B–D INT	For use as backing and sides for built-in cabinets, where only one side must be sound	B	D	D	
Exterior					
A–A EXT	For use on fences, signs, boats, and other items where both sides will be visible	A	A	C	
B–C EXT	For use in buildings, truck linings, as base for exterior finishes for walls and roofs	B	C	C	
MARINE EXT	For boat hulls and other items that will be exposed to water	A or B	A or B	B	

Table 4-C. Some standard grades of plywood.

Other Wood Composites

Several other types of processed wood composites are also used in construction. Fig. 4-9. Each has special properties that make it useful in some aspect of construction. The following list describes some of the most commonly used wood composites. All of these products are sold in 4′ × 8′ sheets.

- **Particleboard** is made of small wood chips that have been pressed and glued together. Particleboard is commonly used in houses as an underlayment between the subfloor and the floor.
- **Waferboard** is made of large wood chips that are pressed and glued together and then cured with heat. Waferboard is not quite as strong as plywood, but it can be used instead of plywood in many applications.
- **Hardboard** is made up of very small, thread-like fibers of wood that are pressed together.

Because the fibers are so small, when they are pressed together they form a very smooth and hard material. The fibers are held together by *lignin*, a natural adhesive found in the fibers. Hardboard is sometimes called *Masonite®*, after the man who invented it.

- **Fiberboard** is made from vegetable fibers, such as corn or sugarcane stalks. It is not very strong, but it has good insulating properties and therefore is used as insulation sheathing beneath the exterior siding of buildings.
- **Paneling** is the term used to describe hardboard or plywood panels that have been prefinished. Paneling is used as a decorative finish on interior walls. It is available in a wide variety of colors, patterns, and wood grains.

Laminated Beams and Joists

Beams and *joists* are the horizontal framing, or supporting, members of a building. These

1. Provide the class with samples of various kinds of wood composites with which they can become familiar.

2. Explain to students that when fiberboard or other insulating sheathing is used on exterior walls, diagonal bracing must be installed to give the walls rigidity.

Fig. 4-9. Some common wood composites. Top to bottom: particleboard, waferboard, hardboard (Masonite®), fiberboard, and a prefinished panel.

1. Mention that, because of the scarcity of large trees, some dimension lumber is being made of many layers of veneer glued together with the grain running in the same direction.

parts must be strong, because they support the weight of other building materials. In many cases, dimension lumber can be used for beams and joists. However, sometimes a beam or joist must be larger than is available in dimension lumber. In other cases, a beam must be curved to fit a specific application. One solution to these problems is to use glue-laminated lumber, such as *laminated beams* and *laminated joists*.

Laminated beams are long, thin strips of wood that have been glued together. Fig. 4-10. If the beam is to be curved, the wood strips are bent around a form and clamped until the glue dries. This process is repeated until the desired shape and thickness are reached. The resulting beam is strong and durable.

Laminated joists are made of three parts: two *flanges* and a *web*. Fig. 4-11. The flanges are at right angles to the web, forming a cross-section that looks like the capital letter *I*. Each part is made of several plies of wood. A laminated joist is lighter than a dimension-lumber joist, but it is just as strong. Another advantage of a laminated joist is that it does not warp or shrink as easily as dimension lumber.

Fig. 4-10. The laminated beams support the roof in this building.

2. Ask volunteers to experiment in making a laminated piece of lumber that might compare in strength with a piece of dimension lumber of equal size.

Fig. 4-11. This laminated floor joist is strong and lightweight.

||||| MASONRY

Masonry is the process of using mortar to join bricks, blocks, or other units of construction. These materials are used mainly for exterior walls on houses and buildings. Masonry walls have several advantages over other types of walls. They are naturally fireproof and waterproof. They are also very durable and require little maintenance. Fig. 4-12. Bricks and concrete blocks are the most common types of masonry units, but there are several other types, such as stone and tile.

Bricks

Bricks are masonry units made from clay or shale. After the clay or shale has been dug from the ground, it is finely ground. Impurities are removed and the remaining material is dried. Then it is pressed into molds to form long, rectangular-shaped bars. When the bars are removed from the molds, they are cut into individual bricks. Then the bricks are fired, or baked, in a kiln. Firing causes a chemical change in the brick that makes it hard and strong.

For Discussion

Is wood still a common building material in your community? For what types of buildings is wood most commonly used? What do you suppose are the reasons for this?

Fig. 4-12. The brick exterior of this building requires very little maintenance.

1. Explain to the students that, like concrete, masonry is very strong and rigid. Because it has very little flexibility, however, it cracks easily.
2. Discuss the different ways that a brick can be laid in a wall. Show some of the patterns that result.

Bricks are available in different sizes, shapes, textures, and colors. Fig. 4-13. Bricks may be solid or cored. *Cored* bricks are those that have holes. This reduces the weight of the bricks and provides an additional place to put mortar. Colors are determined by the type of clay or shale that is used and by the temperature of the firing process.

Did You Know?

In 1666, a great fire destroyed London. At that time, the city was built mostly of wood. As a consequence, the fire roared through the city, reducing more than four-fifths of London to ashes. After this fire, the city government drew up a plan for rebuilding the burned part of the city. To protect London against future destruction by fire, brick, rather than wood, was chosen as the main building construction material.

Concrete Blocks

Hollow concrete blocks are commonly used to construct walls. Concrete blocks have high compressive strength. This makes them especially good for use in walls that have to carry weight. Figure 4-14 shows typical shapes and sizes of concrete blocks.

Concrete blocks are made from a concrete mix that contains a small amount of water. The mix is placed into a block machine. In the block machine, the mix is squeezed and vibrated into molds to form the blocks. Most block machines can make about 15 blocks a minute. When the molded blocks emerge from the machine, they are placed in a kiln, where the concrete is cured. The temperature and humidity inside the kiln are carefully controlled, because the strength of the blocks depends on these factors.

Actual Dimensions			
	Width	**Height**	**Length**
Standard	3¾ "	2¼ "	8 "
Modular	3½ "	2⅙ "	7½ "
Roman	3½ "	1½ "	11½ "
Norman	3½ "	2⅙ "	11½ "
SCR	5½ "	2⅙ "	11½ "

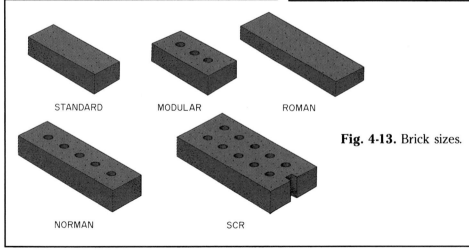

STANDARD   MODULAR   ROMAN

NORMAN   SCR

Fig. 4-13. Brick sizes.

1. Organize a field trip to a concrete block plant or a supplier of other masonry materials.
2. Refer students to Fig. 4-14. Explain where the various types of blocks shown there would be used in a block structure.

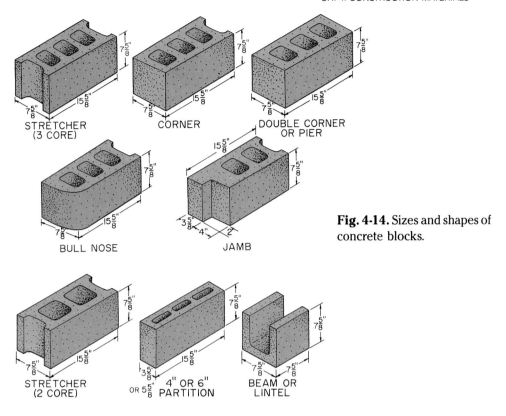

Fig. 4-14. Sizes and shapes of concrete blocks.

Mortar

All masonry units are held together with mortar. **Mortar** is a combination of masonry cement, sand, and water. **Masonry cement** is basically a commercially prepared mixture of portland cement and hydrated lime. The proportions of the ingredients in mortar vary according to its intended use. For example, the mortar used for an outside wall contains certain proportions of ingredients. Slightly different proportions of ingredients are used in the mortar for a wall that will not be exposed to water.

The mortar must be carefully mixed, because the strength of the finished product depends greatly on the strength of the mortar. If the wrong amounts of ingredients are used, or if the mixing time is too long or too short, the strength of the mortar is affected.

1. Demonstrate how mortar is mixed. Lay a few blocks and bricks so that the class can see how it is done.
2. Explain that every batch of mortar must be proportioned and mixed the same. If there are differences, the mortar will not be regular in appearance. This will spoil the appearance of the finished wall.

For Discussion

Have you ever seen stone walls in which the stones have been placed together without the use of mortar? How might the design of such a wall be different from the design of a wall in which mortar would be used? What difference would the use of mortar make in the way the stones could be placed?

 METALS

Almost every structure in our society has some metal in its construction. Steel, an alloy of iron and other metals, is used primarily as structural reinforcement. Fig. 4-15. Other metals, such as aluminum and lead, are also used in construction. Each of these metals has special properties that are helpful in building houses, offices, and other structures.

Steel

In construction, steel is used primarily to provide support to structures. Some construction projects, such as radio, television, and electrical transmission towers, are made completely of steel. Steel is also commonly used in homes and other buildings.

Fig. 4-15. Steel beams and columns make up the framework of this building.

1. Explain how structural steel can be fabricated using rivets, bolts, or the use of welding.

Structural Steel

Steel that is used to support any part of a structure is called **structural steel**. Horizontal steel *beams* and vertical steel *columns* can be fastened together to support walls, floors, and roofs. Structural steel can be processed into a number of different shapes and sizes. Fig. 4-16. These standard shapes and sizes are called **standard stock**.

Steel is classified according to the amount of carbon it contains. It becomes stronger and more brittle as its carbon content increases. Steel may contain from 0.15 to 0.65 percent carbon. Steel with a low percentage of carbon is used for buildings and bridges. High-carbon steel is used where the metal will be subject to extreme weather conditions or abrasion.

Special types of steel alloys have been developed to meet specific needs. For example, the outer layer of *weathering steel* is designed to rust. This layer of rust seals the steel from the atmosphere so that it cannot rust further. *Galvanized steel* is steel that has been coated with zinc to keep rusting to a minimum. *Stainless steel* has a chromium content high enough to allow chromium oxide to form on the outside of the steel. The chromium oxide protects the steel from rust.

Fig. 4-16. Common types of structural steel: I-beam, channel, angle, bars.

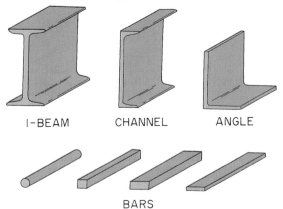

2. Discuss what must be done to a building with a steel skeleton if it is to be fireproof.

Fig. 4-17. Steel other than structural steel is used for many purposes in construction. These walkways are an example.

Bar Designation	Approximate Diameter (in inches)
#2	¼
#3	⅜
#4	½
#5	⅝
#6	¾
#7	⅞
#8	1
#9	1⅛
#10	1¼
#11	1⅜
#14	1¾
#18	2¼

Table 4-D. Sizes of reinforcing bars.

Did You Know?

The Eiffel Tower was constructed for the Paris Exposition of 1889. Nine hundred and eighty-four feet tall, the Eiffel Towel is nearly twice the height of the Great Pyramid. It was, however, built in just a few months. It was built at a low cost, using a small construction crew. The Eiffel Tower was an early and remarkable example of the uses of steel for building construction.

Miscellaneous Steel Parts

Besides structural steel parts, there are many other steel parts in a building. These miscellaneous steel parts include stairways, ladders, and open-grate flooring. Fig. 4-20. Low carbon content makes the steel workable so that it can be shaped more easily.

Steel-reinforced Concrete.

When concrete is used in a construction project, it is usually reinforced with steel. Steel makes the concrete less likely to break apart under stress. There are two methods of reinforcing with steel that are commonly used in construction. **Reinforcing bars**—or **re-bars**, for short—are steel bars that run through the inside of the concrete. Most reinforcing bars have ridges on them that help the concrete grip the bar. Table 4-D shows some sizes of the available reinforcing bars.

1. Have a student or group of students research what happens to reinforcing steel that is subjected to chemicals and severe weather conditions.
2. Explain why the placement of steel reinforcing in a concrete structure is critical. Mention that it imparts tensile strength.

Another kind of reinforcing for concrete is called **mesh**. Made from steel wire, mesh looks like a wire fence. Fig. 4-18. The wire is welded together in two different directions to make it strong. Mesh is specified by the size of the openings and the size of the wire.

Nonferrous Metals

Metals that do not contain iron are called **nonferrous metals**. Because nonferrous metals do not rust, they have many applications in the construction of buildings. The nonferrous metals that are used most often are aluminum, lead, and copper.

Aluminum is a relatively lightweight metal that is very weather resistant. Some of its uses are for window frames, rain gutters, and siding on the outside of buildings. Some air-conditioning ducts also are made from aluminum sheet metal.

Lead is one of the heaviest and most dense metals. Because of its denseness, lead has the ability to deaden sound. Therefore, in some buildings sheets of lead are used for soundproofing. Lead is also used to cover the walls of X-ray rooms in hospitals and clinics. The lead shield keeps the harmful X-rays from escaping.

Copper is very malleable: it can be shaped easily. For this and other reasons, copper sheets are sometimes used on the roofs of buildings. Pipes for plumbing and electrical wire are also made from copper. Fig. 4-19.

For Discussion

1. Have you ever watched a building being constructed? How many of the steel items identified in this section have you seen used? Have you seen reinforcing bars (rebar) or mesh?
2. Are any buildings in your neighborhood made from weathering steel? What appearance do these buildings have?

Fig. 4-18. Wire mesh reinforcement is placed inside the form before concrete is placed.

1. Explain why different types of metals should not be used together. Explain the possibility and effects of electroyltic action.

Fig. 4-19. Because copper can be shaped easily and is a good conductor, it is often used for electrical wire.

2. Discuss why lead is no longer used for water pipes. Mention that it has even been removed from the solder used to join copper water pipes.

Insulation

Walls and ceilings are insulated to reduce the transfer of heat. **Insulation** helps keep heat from penetrating the building in summer and cold from penetrating in winter. Insulation is usually made from spun glass, foamed plastics, or certain vegetable and mineral fibers.

Insulation is available in many different forms. The form used depends largely on the shape and size of the space to be insulated. The four most commonly used forms of insulation are reflective, rigid, loose fill, and batt or blanket insulation.

HEALTH & SAFETY

Asbestos is a mineral fiber that occurs in nature. It is found in rock and is released by crushing the rock. For years, asbestos materials were used in building construction for a variety of purposes. Because asbestos is nonflammable, it was widely used as an insulating material. It has now been discovered that asbestos is a cancer-causing substance. Today, the use of asbestos in building construction is restricted.

Reflective Insulation

Reflective insulation is unique in that the material itself is not necessarily an insulator. Reflective insulation relies instead on a reflective foil surface. The foil reflects heat away from the structure being insulated. Reflective surfaces can also be placed on traditional forms of insulation to increase their insulating abilities.

Rigid Insulation

Natural fibers or plastic foam can be used to make rigid sheets of insulation. Rigid insulation is used to sheath, or cover, walls quickly and easily. Fig. 4-20. It can also be used to insulate many other flat surfaces. Rigid insulation is usually nailed or glued into place. Some rigid insulation has a reflective outer coating to increase its insulating properties.

Loose Fill Insulation

Loose fill can be made of fibrous or granular materials. Fibrous loose fill is made from fiberglass, wool, or vegetable fibers. Granular fill is made from granulated cork or from perlite or vermiculite. Perlite is a lightweight volcanic glass. Vermiculite is a lightweight material made from mica, which is a mineral.

Fig. 4-20. Sheets of insulating material are commonly used to sheath exterior walls.

1. Explain that insulation qualities result from numerous small dead air spaces in a material that is a poor conductor of heat.
2. Discuss the social and financial implications of the use of asbestos insulation for the last seventy-five years.

Loose fill is usually blown into place through a special hose. It is used to insulate irregular surfaces that would otherwise be difficult to insulate. Fig. 4-21.

Batt or Blanket Insulation

The fibrous insulation materials contained in loose fill can also be formed into blankets and batts. *Blankets* are rolls of insulation designed to fit between framing members of a building. *Batts* are similar to blankets, except that they are not as long. Batts are made up to 8 feet (2.4 m) long, whereas blankets are available in rolls up to 24 feet (7.2 m) long. Batts and blankets are available in standard widths to fit between framing members set 16 or 24 (0.40 or 0.60 m) inches apart. Fig. 4-22. The insulation fits tightly so that pressure holds it in place. Sometimes the paper edge of the insulation is stapled to the wood to help hold it in place.

Fig. 4-22. Batts and blankets are designed to fit between framing members in wood-frame buildings.

Fig. 4-21. Loose fill insulation is used to insulate irregular surfaces.

1. Discuss which type of insulation would be best to use in each of the various parts of a house.

Vapor Barrier

The types of insulation described in the previous section are designed to keep excessively cold or warm air out of a structure. These types of insulation are not effective against moisture, however. As the warm, moist air inside a building meets cold air from outside, the warm air cools. As it cools, its ability to hold moisture decreases. As a result, water condenses inside the walls of the building.

A special **vapor barrier** is needed to prevent the water from condensing. The vapor barrier is placed between the inside wall of the building and the insulation. This keeps the warm, moist air inside the house so that it does not meet the cold outside air. Fig. 4-23. The vapor barrier can be made of plastic, foil, or asphalt. It should always be placed on the interior side of the insulation.

2. Explain that more than one vapor barrier should never be used. Each material outside of the vapor barrier should be five times as porous as the material next to it that is closer to the vapor barrier.

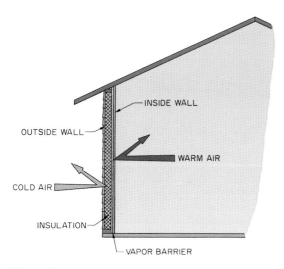

Fig. 4-23. A vapor barrier keeps water from condensing and building up inside walls.

Caulking

Although caulking is not in itself an insulating material, it does improve the performance of other insulating materials. Caulking is basically a gap-filling compound that is used to seal cracks and holes. Caulking helps to prevent unconditioned air from passing into or out of a home or building. A caulking gun is used to apply caulking around window trim, door trim, and other exterior and interior surfaces. Fig. 4-24.

Gypsum Wallboard

Gypsum wallboard is used to enclose interior walls and ceilings. This material is often called *sheet rock* or *drywall*. It is made of gypsum, a powdery mineral, sandwiched between sheets of special paper. The walls in most newer houses are covered with gypsum wallboard. Fig. 4-25.

Several types of gypsum wallboard are available. Regular wallboard has a smooth paper surface. After it is installed, it can be painted. Some wallboard is predecorated: a decorative finish is applied to it before it is installed. Fire-resistant wallboard is made with special additives that

Fig. 4-24. This person is using a caulking gun to apply caulking to cracks around window trim.

Fig. 4-25. Most interior walls are covered with gypsum wallboard.

1. Discuss the materials other than gypsum wallboard that are used for covering interior walls.

make it able to withstand fire longer than regular wallboard. Moisture-resistant wallboard is used in bathrooms and other high-moisture areas.

Pipes and Wires

Most structures that are designed for human habitation have utility systems. Utility systems usually include plumbing, electrical, gas, and sewer systems. Pipes and wires are commonly used in utility systems to conduct fluids and electricity from one place to another. Without pipes and wires, electricity and indoor plumbing would be impossible.

Pipes

Water and other fluids are carried in pipes. Many different kinds of pipes have been developed to meet construction needs. Each kind has both advantages and disadvantages. Copper pipe, although expensive, is often used in plumbing because it does not rust or corrode and because it is flexible. Galvanized iron and cast iron are used because iron is very strong. However, iron is also very heavy and rigid. Clay pipe is used for outdoor sewer lines. There is even a special glass pipe that is used in some factories to carry acid.

Plastic pipes made of polyvinyl chloride (PVC) or polybutadene (PB) have the advantage of being lightweight, noncorrosive, and easy to work with. Fig. 4-26. However, plastic pipes have two major disadvantages: they cannot withstand high heat, and they cannot support as much weight as metal pipes.

Wires

Wires are used in the electrical system of a building. The most common type of electrical wire is called *nonmetallic sheathed cable*, or *romex*. It is usually made of copper and is sheathed with insulation. Wire sizes are shown in Fig. 4-27. Wires that may be exposed to mois-

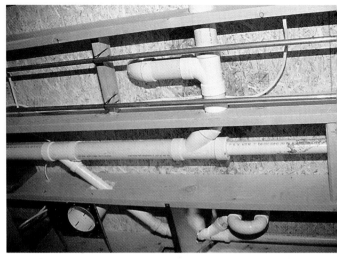

Fig. 4-26. Special connectors make plastic pipes easy to install.

Fig. 4-27. Standard wire sizes.

ture or to a harsh environment are protected by conduits. A *conduit* is a metal tubing that encases wires to protect them.

Asphalt Roofing

Asphalt is a petroleum product made from crude oil. Four kinds of roofing materials are made from asphalt. *Coatings and cements* are liquids and pastes that are used to help seal the roof against moisture. A second kind of asphalt product is called *felt*. Felt is a clothlike material that is saturated with asphalt. It is commonly used as an underlayment on a roof to help provide protection from the weather. Other roof-

1. Explain that plumbing, heating, ventilating, and cooling systems are also called mechanical systems.
2. Discuss how changes in piping systems have changed the plumber's job.

3. Assign a student or group of students to present a short report on the Smart House wiring being developed by the National Association of Home Builders.

Fig. 4-28. Asphalt shingles are installed over felt underlayment.

ing materials are installed over the felt. *Roll roofing* is similar to felt, but roll roofing is thicker. It has a coating of fire-resistant mineral granules to provide protection from fire and to disperse the heat from the sun. The fourth asphalt product is *shingles*. Fig. 4-28. Shingles are made from the same material as roll roofing, but shingles are cut into short strips. For example, one common shingle size is 12 inches by 36 inches.

Did You Know?

The first sources of asphalt were natural sources. Asphalt occurs in certain lakes and springs. There, it is believed to be an early stage in the breakdown of small marine animals into petroleum. It is known that natural asphalt was used as early as 2000 B.C. It was used then to help make a water reservoir leakproof. Today, asphalt is manufactured from petroleum.

1. Identify the materials that are used for roofing besides asphalt roofing products.
2. Discuss why many flat roofs have stone or crushed rock placed over the asphalt on the roof.

Flooring

Various kinds of **flooring**, or floor covering, are used in buildings. The floor covering that is used depends on the intended use of the area and the preference of the owner. Fig. 4-29.

Carpet is used in homes, stores, and offices to provide cushioning and an eye-pleasing effect. It is available in various styles and colors. The price range for carpet is wide enough to meet the needs of the majority of customers. Most carpet, however, shows wear quickly and must be replaced periodically.

Floor tile can be made of ceramic, asphalt, or vinyl. It is commonly used in areas where carpet is not practical. Floor tile is more easily cleaned and maintained than carpet and does not show wear as quickly. Some materials, such as vinyl, also come in 12-foot-wide sheets.

Wood floors are usually made of oak strips or squares and are very attractive. However, because oak flooring is expensive, it is not as commonly used as most other flooring materials. It is also relatively difficult to maintain.

3. Discuss how the development of synthetic fibers has increased the use of carpet. Mention that most carpets were once made from wool.

Fig. 4-29. Different types of flooring. Clockwise from top left: carpet, floor tile, oak flooring, and terrazzo.

Terrazzo is a special kind of concrete floor that has marble chips embedded in it. After the concrete has cured, the surface is ground and polished. This decorative flooring is very durable. Liquid epoxy can be poured over the concrete floor to make it very tough.

Adhesives

Adhesives are materials that hold, or bond, other materials together. In order to do this, adhesives must have both adhesion and cohesion. *Adhesion* is the ability of one material to stick to another. *Cohesion* is the ability of the materials to stick together. Several types of adhesives are used in the construction industry. The most common are wood glue, contact cement, and mastic.

Wood Glue

For the most part, wood glue is used to glue
1 wood materials together. There are many differ-ent types of wood glues that can be used in a wide variety of applications. Table 4-E lists the most common wood glues used in the construction industry.

Mastics

Mastics are thick, pastelike adhesives. They are often applied with a notched trowel or a caulking gun. Fig. 4-30. Mastics are very strong and often are used where it is difficult or inconvenient to use nails or other fasteners. For example, mastics are usually used to install wallboard, tile, and flooring materials over concrete or masonry surfaces.

Contact Cement

Contact cement is an adhesive that is applied to the surfaces of materials and then allowed to dry before the materials are combined. When the materials are finally combined, 2 the contact cement instantly forms a permanent bond. No clamping is necessary. This makes

Table 4-E. Common wood glues used in construction.

Adhesive	Advantages	Disadvantages
Polyvinyl-Resin (White Glue)	Strong Inexpensive Fast drying	Low moisture and heat resistance
Aliphatic-Resin (Carpenter's Glue, Titebond)	Strong Heat resistant Slightly moisture resistant	Low moisture resistance
Urea-Resin	Moisture resistant	Not waterproof Must be mixed before using Low heat resistance Expensive
Recorcinol and Phenol Resourcinol-Resin	Waterproof Resists high temperatures	Must be mixed before using Leaves visible glue line
Epoxy-Resin	Water resistant Fills gaps	Must be mixed before using Expensive

1. Explain that many adhesives do not have adequate cohesion to keep them from creeping due to shear. Such adhesives would not be adequate for gluing load-carrying members such as beams and trusses.

2. Explain that contact cement bonds instantly on contact. Demonstrate some ways in which two pieces can be aligned before the bond is made.

Fig. 4-30. This construction worker is applying mastic in preparation for laying ceramic floor tile.

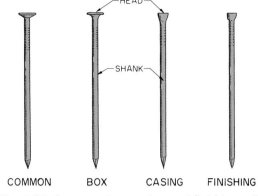

Fig. 4-31. Common, box, casing, and finishing nails are commonly used by construction workers. Notice the two main parts of the nail — the head and the shank.

contact cement a good choice for gluing large surfaces, where clamping would be difficult. Contact cement is used primarily for adhering plastic laminates to countertops and other surfaces.

Mechanical Fasteners

When you think of mechanical fasteners, you probably think of nails. However, there are also many other kinds of mechanical fasteners. Screws, nuts and bolts, and staples are a few of the most common. In this section you will learn more about the mechanical fasteners used in the construction industry.

Nails

Nails are probably the most commonly used mechanical fasteners in the construction industry. Many different types of nails are available. The most common are common nails, box nails, casing nails, and finishing nails. Fig. 4-31.

Nails vary both in length and in the diameter of their shanks. The word *penny* (abbreviated *d*) is used to describe the length of each type of nail. Because most nails are made from wire, the diameter of the shank is referred to by wire gage. Fig. 4-32.

Nails also vary in the materials from which they are made. Most nails are made of steel. However, because steel is susceptible to rusting, nails that will be exposed to moisture are *galvanized* (coated with zinc). Galvanized nails have much greater resistance to rusting than do non-galvanized, or *bright*, nails.

Common nails have large heads and diameters and are used mostly for rough framing work. *Box nails* are similar to common nails, except that box nails have slimmer shanks and thinner heads. Box nails are used for light framing work.

Casing nails and *finishing nails* are used mostly for trim work. They are less visible than common and box nails because of the shape of their heads. They are shaped so that the nail can be set beneath the surface of the wood with a nail set. A wood filler can then be applied over the nail to hide its location. Casing nails are larger than finishing nails and are used for heavier wood. Finishing nails are usually used for trim and molding on the interior of a building.

1. Provide students with samples of the various kinds and sizes of nails commonly used in the construction industry. Explain the uses of each type of nail.

2. Explain that there is a nail called a sinker. It is smaller in diameter than a common nail and larger in diameter than a box nail. Many carpenters prefer this type of nail because it splits the wood less.

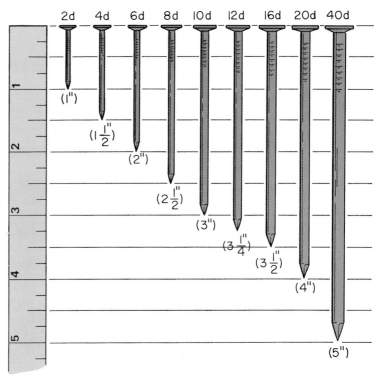

Fig. 4-32. Common nail sizes.

Many other special-purpose nails are also used in construction. For example, *scaffolding nails*, or *duplex-head nails*, are used for temporary structures, such as scaffolding and concrete forms. The double head on this kind of nail allows a worker to drive the nail into the wood to the first head. When the structure is disassembled, the nail can easily be pulled out using the second head. Special nails also have been developed for fastening drywall, flooring, rafters, shingles, and plywood. Fig. 4-33.

Screws

Screws are used to fasten wood, metal, and other materials together. *Wood screws* are designed to attach hardware or wood parts to wood. Although they are more difficult to use than nails, screws have more holding power.

They also allow the parts to be taken apart later without damaging the wood.

Drywall screws are used to attach wallboard or drywall to framing members. Drywall screws are installed with a special drill-like tool called a *power driver*. Fig. 4-34.

Like nails, screws are manufactured in many different lengths and diameters. The diameters are measured by gage numbers. The larger the gage number, the larger the diameter of the screw's shank.

Screws are also made with flat, round, or oval heads. Flat-head screws are designed to lay flush, or even, with the surface of the material. Round-head and oval-head screws are designed to extend above the surface of the material. Most screws are available with either a slotted head or a Phillips head. Fig. 4-35.

1. Demonstrate how wood screws require shank and pilot holes. Also illustrate the need for a countersink for flat and oval head screws and a counterbore and plug to hide screw heads.

2. Emphasize that drywall screws are self drilling and do not need pilot or shank holes drilled.
3. Provide the class with samples of various types and sizes of screws.

Scaffolding nail		Double head for easy removal from temporary wooden structures.
Plywood nail	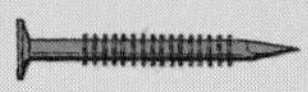	Slim shank has rings to hold plywood better.
Scotch truss nail	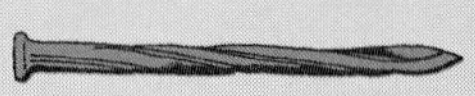	Ribbed shank has extra holding power.
Roofing nail	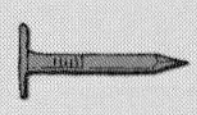	Short, thick shank is designed to hold roofing material; large head helps seal the hole in the roofing material.
Specialty power nail	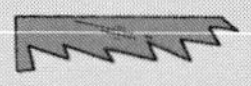	Shaped for use in power nailer.

Fig. 4-33. Specialty nails.

Fig. 4-34. A power driver and drywall screws.

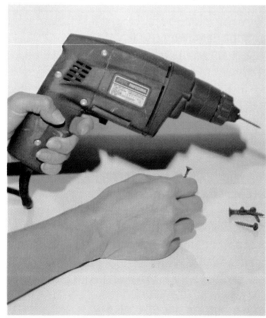

Fig. 4-35. Screws with flat, round, or oval heads are available with slotted or Phillips grips.

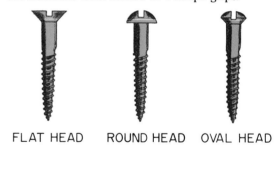

FLAT HEAD   ROUND HEAD   OVAL HEAD

SLOTTED   PHILLIPS

Other Fasteners

Many other types of mechanical fasteners are also used by construction workers. Three common types of bolts, for example, are shown in Fig. 4-36. *Carriage bolts* are used to fasten wood members together. *Machine bolts* are used to attach steel beams and other metal parts together. *Anchor bolts* are used to fasten wood plates to the top of concrete foundation walls. The bottom portion of the bolt is set in the concrete or in mortar in a concrete block. The top of the bolt is then fastened to the wood plate.

Framing anchors are used to strengthen framing joints. Fig. 4-37. A framing anchor consists of a piece of metal that has been bent to lay flat against both framing members. When a framing anchor has been nailed or bolted to both members, it helps support the joint.

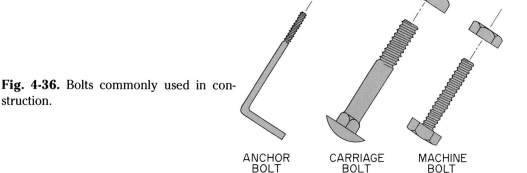

Fig. 4-36. Bolts commonly used in construction.

ANCHOR BOLT   CARRIAGE BOLT   MACHINE BOLT

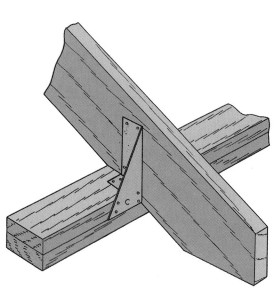

Fig. 4-37. A framing anchor strengthens a joint between framing members.

1. Discuss where framing anchors are used in construction. Explain why they would be necessary to fasten trusses to walls in areas where high winds are possible.

Power fasteners are often used to reduce the time it takes to fasten framing and other construction materials. Fig. 4-38. *Power nailers* and *power staplers* use pneumatic force to insert nails and staples at the pull of a trigger. Most power nailers use either box nails or special nails designed especially for power fastening.

1

For Discussion

Which of the various types of insulation have you seen? What do you suppose has caused people to pay more attention to providing good insulation in their homes?

Fig. 4-38. Power fasteners allow workers to install mechanical fasteners quickly and easily.

1. Assign students or groups of students to conduct more research into the various types of mechanical fasteners. Ask students to present written or oral reports.

Construction Facts

HOUSEWRAP

One of the biggest problems in making a house energy-efficient is controlling air infiltration. *Air infiltration* is the leakage of outside air into the air inside a house. Now a new material called *TYVEK® housewrap* can help control air infiltration.

TYVEK® housewrap is a flexible plastic sheet material. Made of very fine, high-density polyethylene fibers, it is very strong and will not rot. It is wrapped around the outside of the house just before the final siding or exterior covering is applied.

TYVEK® actually seals cracks and seams in the house. It blocks the air, yet allows the house to "breathe." In other words, moisture can escape, but there are no cracks for the wind to blow through. Reducing air infiltration can cut the cost of heating a home by approximately 25 percent. This can save homeowners a lot of money.

1. TYVEK® is a brand name. Explain that other house-wraps also are available.

CHAPTER **4**

R E V I E W

Chapter Summary

The construction of a building requires many different materials. They include concrete, which is a mixture of sand, rocks, and a binder. Wood is another material used in construction. For construction purposes, wood is classified as hardwood or softwood. Wood used in construction is called lumber. Wood composites are those products that are made from a mixture of wood and other materials. Wood composites include plywood, particleboard, waferboard, hardboard, fiberboard, and paneling. Masonry is the process of using mortar to join bricks, blocks, or other units of construction. Metals used in construction include steel, including structural steel and steel used to reinforce concrete. Metals that do not contain iron are called nonferrous metals. These include aluminum, lead, and copper. Insulation is used in a building to reduce the transfer of heat. Types of insulation include reflective insulation, rigid insulation, loose fill insulation, batt or blanket insulation, and vapor barrier. Gypsum wallboard, sometimes called sheet rock or drywall, is used to enclose interior walls and ceilings. Asphalt is a product commonly used in roofing products. There are various kinds of flooring, including carpet, floor tile, wood floors, and terrazzo. Adhesives are used to bond construction materials together. Mechanical fasteners include nails of various types and screws.

Test Your Knowledge   ₁

1. What are the main ingredients of portland cement concrete?
2. What is the main purpose of aggregate in concrete?
3. What is an admixture? Give an example.
4. What is the difference between softwood and hardwood?
5. Is most of the lumber used in construction made of softwood or hardwood?
6. Explain the difference between the nominal and actual sizes of a piece of lumber.
7. Name at least two types of wood composites.
8. Name two common types of masonry.
9. What is the purpose of mortar?
10. Name two types of steel reinforcers for concrete.
11. Name three common types of insulation material.
12. Name four kinds of flooring that are commonly used in buildings.

REVIEW

Activities

 1. Take a close look at your house or apartment. Make a list of the materials mentioned in this chapter that you think were used to construct it. (Hints: Is your house made of wood, brick, or concrete block? How are the inside walls finished? Is there any paneling? What types of flooring were used?)

 2. Visit a local do-it-yourself lumber supply store. With a ruler, measure the dimensions of 2 × 4s, 2 × 6s, 1 × 4s, 1 × 6s, and 1 × 10s. Compare your measurements with those listed in Fig. 5-8. What conclusion can you draw?

 3. Collect wood shavings from a pencil sharpener. Use the shavings and wood glue to make a 2″ × 2″ sheet of particleboard. Be prepared to explain how to make the particleboard. (How did you mold it into a 2″ × 2″ sheet?)

 4. Use thin balsa wood to create two sheets of plywood. Use wood glue to hold the plies together. In the first sheet, glue all of the plies with the grain in the same direction. In the second sheet, glue the plies at right angles, as described in this book. Test the strength of the two sheets. Be prepared to explain why plywood is constructed the way it is.

CHAPTER

5

CONSTRUCTION TOOLS AND EQUIPMENT

Terms to Know

arc welding machines	crawler crane	nail set	scraper
backhoe	crosscut saw	pavers	sledgehammers
backsaw	digital rules	Phillips screwdriver	spiral ratchet screwdriver
blind riveter	equipment	pipe wrenches	
brick trowel	excavator	pneumatic hammers	standard screwdriver
bulldozer	folding rules	portable circular saw	staplers
bull float	framing square	powder-actuated stud driver	surveyor's level
chalk line	front-end loaders		table saw
claw hammer	grader	power drills	tape measures
cold chisel	hacksaw	power miter saw	tower crane
compactor	hand tools	power screwdriver	transit
concrete pump	heavy equipment	pry bars	trencher
construction laser	laser-powered welder	radial arm saw	truck crane
conveyor	level	ripsaw	twist drill bit
cranes	miter gage	rotary hammer	water pumps
	nailers	saber saw	wood chisels

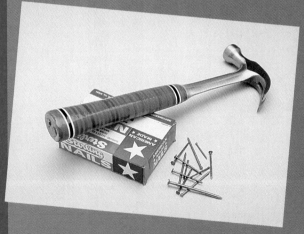

Objectives

When you have completed reading this 1
chapter, you should be able to do the
following:

- List the four categories of construction tools and equipment, and give two examples of each.
- Recognize and know the uses of various hand tools and power tools.
- Recognize and know the uses of various kinds of construction equipment.
- Describe three pieces of heavy equipment.

1. Resources:
- Chapter 5 Lesson Plan in the Teacher's Manual in this Teacher's Annotated Edition and in the Teacher's Resource Guide.
- Chapter 5 Study Guide in the Student Workbook.
- Chapter 5 Visual Master in the Teacher's Resource Guide.

Tools and equipment increase our ability to get a task done quickly and well. Tools and equipment are very important to the construction industry. Without them, construction projects would take a long time to complete, and some might never get done. Fig. 5-1.

You probably have heard the phrase "the right tool for the job." Each tool is designed to meet a certain need. For example, nails are driven by pounding them with a hammer. Screws are driven by twisting them with a screwdriver. You would cause damage and make little progress if you tried to pound a nail with a screwdriver or twist a screw with a hammer.

Sometimes a tool serves several purposes. For example, many hammers can be used both to drive nails and to pull nails. However, a tool should never be used to do a job for which it is not intended. Misusing a tool can result in damage to the tool, damage to the materials, and even injury to the person using the tool. For example, the delicate long-nosed pliers should not be used to apply force to a heavy object. Such abuse can easily bend the pliers' jaws out of line, making them useless for their intended purpose. Fig. 5-2.

The tools and equipment that are used in construction can be grouped into four categories:
- Hand tools
- Power tools
- Equipment
- Heavy equipment

Fig. 5-1. The interstate highway system is one project that might not have been attempted without today's advanced tools and equipment.

1. Ask the students to give examples of ways in which they have seen tools misused. Ask also for instances in which the misuse of a tool has caused an accident.

2. Ask each student to select a power tool or type of equipment. Ask them to research the development of that item and explain how its use has affected the construction industry.

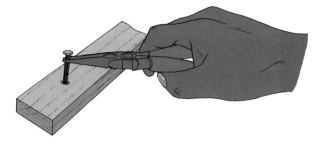

Fig. 5-2. Use long-nosed pliers and other tools only for their intended purposes. Misuse of tools can ruin them.

The construction industry requires many more tools than can possibly be described here. However, on the following pages you will find descriptions of some of the most common tools in each of the above categories.

 HAND TOOLS

Hand tools are tools that use power supplied by a person. Most hand tools are relatively small and can be carried around by the worker. Many kinds of hand tools are used in construction. Some are very specialized and can be used only by trained workers. Others, such as hammers, saws, and screwdrivers, are very common. Carpenters, electricians, plumbers, and other workers use both common and specialized hand tools.

Measurement and Layout Tools

1 Accurate measurement and layout are among the most important tasks of construction because

the rest of the construction process depends on them. No matter how well a structure is constructed, if it was laid out wrong, it will not meet the owner's requirements. Measurement and layout tools help surveyors lay out a site accurately. They also help carpenters and other workers build structures correctly according to the owner's specifications. Among the most common measurement and layout tools are those used for measuring distances, for squaring corners and framework, and for making straight horizontal and vertical lines.

Folding rules and **tape measures** are the most commonly used measurement tools. They are used to measure boards, pipe, wire, and many other construction materials. Tape measures are especially useful for measuring long or curved surfaces. **Digital rules** are used to measure relatively long distances, such as those in highway construction projects. Figs. 5-3, 5-4, and 5-5.

Another tool that is necessary to lay out a construction project is the **framing square**. Framing squares are used to measure 90-degree angles at the corners of framework and joints. They can also be used to measure cutting angles on dimension lumber. A framing square is made of a single piece of steel and marked with standard or metric units. Fig. 5-6.

A **level** is a long, straight tool that contains one or more vials of liquid. It is used to make

1. Teach students how to use rules and tapes. Emphasize the reading of feet, inches, and fractions of an inch. Also, explain the metric system and have them practice using metric rulers.

2. Show how the accuracy of any square can be checked by squaring off both directions from a straightedge.

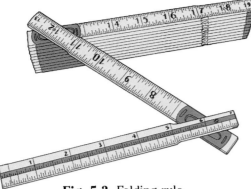

Fig. 5-3. Folding rule.

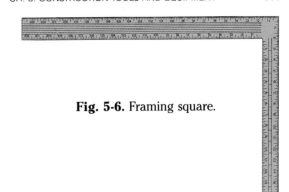

Fig. 5-6. Framing square.

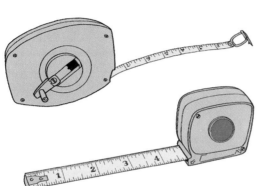

Fig. 5-4. Tape measures.

Fig. 5-7. Level.

sure that something is exactly horizontal (level), or vertical (plumb). When the level is exactly level or plumb, an air bubble in the liquid rests between two etched lines on each vial. Fig. 5-7.

Fig. 5-5. Digital rule.

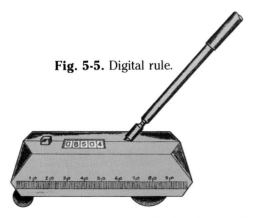

Did You Know?

The bubble level used by carpenters today was introduced in 1661. At first, it was used on telescopes and on surveying instruments. It was not used by carpenters until the middle of the nineteenth century, when such levels began to be manufactured in quantity in factories.

1. Demonstrate how a level should be handled, cared for, and used to level and plumb an object. Emphasize that great care must be exercised to keep a level accurate.

2. Show how to check the accuracy of a level. Take a reading. Turn the level end for end, and take another reading on the same bubble. These readings must be the same. Check each bubble in this way.

A **chalk line**, or chalk box, is used to mark a straight line. A chalk line consists of a line (string) that is contained in a housing filled with chalk. The chalk coats the line as the line is drawn out of the housing. To use a chalk line, you fasten the hook at the end of the line to one end of the surface to be marked. Then you pull the line taut across the surface. You make the mark by lifting the line away from the surface and then allowing it to snap back. When the line hits the surface, it leaves a chalk tracing. Fig. 5-8.

Did You Know?

The chalk line has changed little in 5,000 years. It was used by the ancient Egyptians to mark a straight line between two points. The only real change has been in the color of the line itself. The ancient Egyptians colored the line with wet red or yellow ocher. Ocher is an iron ore that was used as a color pigment. The ancient Greeks however, colored the line with white and red chalk, in addition to wet ocher. Workers today follow the Greek practice.

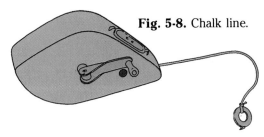

Fig. 5-8. Chalk line.

1. Demonstrate the proper use of a chalk line. Show how rapidly long straight lines can be made.

Hammers

Hammers are tools that are used primarily for pounding. They come in many different shapes, sizes, and weights, according to their intended uses. One of the most common types of hammer is the **claw hammer**. The *face*, or pounding surface, of the claw hammer is used to drive nails. Opposite the face is a V-shaped notch called a *claw*. The claw is used to remove nails from boards. Most claw hammers have 16-ounce *heads*. Their handles are made of wood, steel, or fiberglass. The lower portion of some claw hammers is covered with a rubber grip to help keep the tool from slipping in the worker's hand. Fig. 5-9.

Sledgehammers are heavy hammers that are used to drive stakes into the ground and to break up concrete and stone. The head of a sledgehammer is made of steel and comes in standard weights of 5, 10, 15, or 20 pounds. The handle is usually made of sturdy hickory wood. Fig. 5-10.

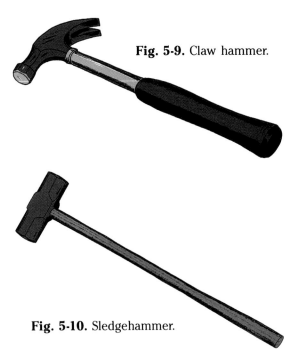

Fig. 5-9. Claw hammer.

Fig. 5-10. Sledgehammer.

2. As a safety tip, tell students never to pound the face of one hammer with the face of another hammer. The hammer faces are hardened steel. A chip can fly from one and injure the worker or someone nearby.

Pry Bars

Carpenters use **pry bars** to pry the boards used to form concrete away from the concrete after it has set. Pry bars come in many different styles. One of the most common has a chisel at one end and a chisel with a claw for pulling nails at the other end. Fig. 5-11.

Screwdrivers

The two most common types of screwdrivers are standard and Phillips screwdrivers. The **standard screwdriver** has a flat tip and is
1 designed to fit a standard slotted screw. The **Phillips screwdriver** has a tip shaped like an X. It is used to turn Phillips-head screws. The advantage of Phillips-head screws and screwdrivers is that the screwdriver grips the screw better. There is less chance of slipping. This reduces the chances of damaging the screwdriver, the screw, and the object being worked on. Figs. 5-12, 5-13.

A **spiral ratchet screwdriver** is one that relies on a pushing force rather than a twisting
2 force. The tips for a spiral ratchet screwdriver are interchangeable, so it can be used for Phillips-head or standard slotted screws. The spiral ratchet screwdriver is faster to use than ordinary hand-twisted screwdrivers. It is therefore used when many screws must be driven in a short time. Fig. 5-14.

Saws

Various types of handsaws are used to cut lumber. Most handsaws look basically alike. Fig. 5-15. The main difference among them is the type of blade the saw has and the way it is used.

Fig. 5-12. Standard screwdriver.

Fig. 5-13. Phillips screwdriver.

Fig. 5-14. Spiral ratchet screwdriver.

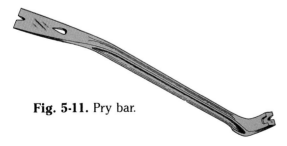

Fig. 5-11. Pry bar.

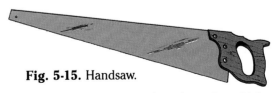

Fig. 5-15. Handsaw.

1. Safety tip: After driving a slothead screw, run the blade flat over the head to remove any burr. Never run your finger over the head first because a burr could cut you.

2. Explain that care must be taken when driving screws with a spiral ratchet screwdriver. The blade must not slip from the screw head. If it does, it can damage the surrounding material.

A **ripsaw** has chisel-like teeth designed for ripping, or cutting with the grain of the wood. Fig. 5-16.

A **crosscut saw** is used to cut across the grain of the wood. Its teeth are shaped and sharpened in such a way that it actually cuts two lines very close together and removes the sawdust between them. In this way it can achieve a smoother cut across the grain of the wood. Fig. 5-17.

A **backsaw** is a special kind of handsaw that has a very thin blade. The blade is reinforced with a heavy metal back called a *spine*. The spine keeps the thin saw blade from bending. As a result, the backsaw is used to make very straight cuts, such as those on trim and molding. Fig. 5-18.

A **hacksaw** is used to cut metal. Various types of hacksaw blades enable this saw to cut many different kinds of metal. Fine-tooth blades are used to saw thin sheet materials. Coarse-tooth blades are usually used for soft metals. Fig. 5-19.

Did You Know ?

A saw is a blade with teeth. The saw developed over a period of thousands of years. There were a number of problems in obtaining a workable saw. The blade had to be thin, yet strong enough not to buckle. It was, perhaps, the Romans who devised the technique of alternating the teeth of a saw from one side to the other. This allows the sawdust to be pulled from the saw cut. The alternation of teeth also reduced the friction of the saw blade in the cut. This made sawing easier.

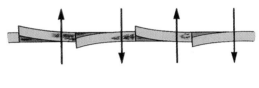

Fig. 5-16. Ripsaw blade. Top, top view. Bottom, side view.

Fig. 5-18. Backsaw.

Fig. 5-17. Crosscut-saw blade. Top, top view. Bottom, side view.

Fig. 5-19. Hacksaw.

1. Explain that bending the teeth of a saw in opposite directions is called giving the saw a set. This makes the groove that the saw cuts (the kerf) somewhat wider than the blade. This reduces drag on the saw.

2. Demonstrate the proper use of a handsaw. Show how to start a cut, how to make the cut, and how to finish the cut without splitting the material.

Chisels

A chisel is a tool with a wedge-shaped blade that is used to separate materials. **Wood chisels** are used to trim wood. They are used to pare or clear away excess material from wood joints. They are also used to remove wood to make gains (recessed areas) for hinges. Wood chisels are usually powered only by human muscle, but a *mallet* can be used to provide more force if necessary. Fig. 5-20.

Metal objects can be cut with a **cold chisel**. Cold chisels are made of solid steel. They can be used to cut sheet metal, round objects such as chain links, bars, bolts, and various other types and shapes of metal. A cold chisel is driven by hammer blows to its flat end. Fig. 5-21.

Specialized Hand Tools

In addition to common hand tools that almost all workers use, each type of worker uses specialized tools. These tools are designed to help the worker do tasks that are peculiar to his or her career. For example, carpenters use a **nail set** to drive finishing nails below the surface of wooden trim and molding. They can then fill the resulting holes with a wood filler. When a finish is applied to the surface, the finish nails are not visible. Fig. 5-22.

Plumbers use **pipe wrenches** to turn objects that are round, such as pipes. The most commonly used pipe wrench is the *Stillson wrench*. A plumber can adjust a Stillson wrench to fit a wide variety of pipe sizes by turning an adjusting nut on the body of the wrench. Fig. 5-23.

One hand tool that is universally used by masons is the **brick trowel**. Masons use brick trowels to place and trim mortar between bricks or concrete blocks. Brick trowels are usually made of steel and have handles of wood or sturdy, high-impact plastic. Fig. 5-24.

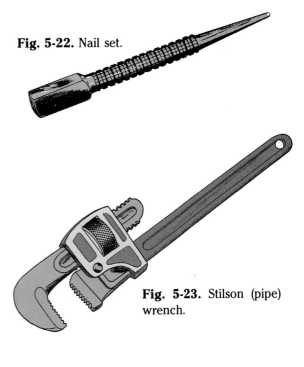

Fig. 5-22. Nail set.

Fig. 5-23. Stilson (pipe) wrench.

Fig. 5-20. Wood chisel.

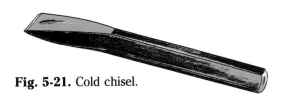

Fig. 5-21. Cold chisel.

Fig. 5-24. Brick trowel.

1. Demonstrate how to sharpen a wood chisel. Explain that dull wood chisels can be very dangerous because they cause the worker to use excessive force.

2. Safety tip: Use a grinding wheel to remove the mushroomed head of a cold chisel. Explain that if this is not done pieces may fly from the head, possibly injuring someone.

Cement finishers use a **bull float** to smooth the surface of wet concrete. The face of the float, the part that touches the cement, is made of soft-wood. As the softwood is swept across the top of the wet cement, it leaves a smooth, slightly textured finish. Fig. 5-25.

Sheet metal workers use a **blind riveter** to fasten pieces of sheet metal together. The advantage of a blind riveter is that the worker can do the entire riveting operation from one side of the sheet metal. Fig. 5-26.

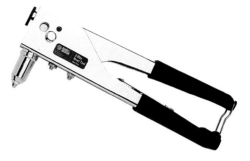

Fig. 5-26. Blind riveter.

For Discussion

Have you used any of the saws described in this section? Have you looked closely enough at the saws you use to see the way the teeth are arranged to cut effectively? Note that each tooth acts like a small chisel. How would this help in removing material?

Fig. 5-25. Bull float.

POWER TOOLS

Power tools are tools that are powered by forces other than human muscle. The power to operate most power tools is supplied by electric motors. A power tool usually provides more force than a person can. Therefore, with a power tool a worker can do a job faster and with less effort than by hand. Power tools often allow a worker to do a job more accurately, too.

The power that makes power tools so fast and efficient also makes them dangerous. Handle all power tools with respect. Be sure that you know how to use a tool *before* you use it. Follow all recommended safety precautions.

Power Saws

The many different cutting requirements for a construction project require several specialized types of saws. For example, a **radial arm saw** consists of a motor-driven saw blade that is hung on an arm over a table. This type of saw is used mostly for crosscutting 2×4's and other dimension lumber. It is also very good for cutting angles in rafters for roof frames. A radial arm saw is usually considered a *stationary* power

1. Safety tip: Some bull floats are made of magnesium or aluminum. Care must be taken that the handle does not contact any electrical wires.
2. Explain that power tools can be powered by compressed air, hydraulic power, and explosive power as well as by electricity.

tool. It is set up at one place on a construction site. The lumber is then brought there to be cut. Fig. 5-27.

Another stationary power saw is the table saw. A **table saw** consists of a blade mounted on an electric motor beneath a tablelike surface. Fig. 5-28. The blade sticks up through a slot in the table. The table saw is used for cutting large sheets of wood, plywood, and other wood products. It is also used for ripping lumber. The *fence*, or guide, is set at the desired distance from the blade. Once the fence has been locked in place, several pieces of lumber can be ripped to exactly the same width. Wood can be cut at an angle on a table saw by using an attachment called a **miter gage**. The miter gage can be adjusted to guide wood through the saw at an angle of up to 30 degrees. Portable miter saws also are available. Fig. 5-29.

Fig. 5-28. Table saw.

Fig. 5-27. Radial arm saw.

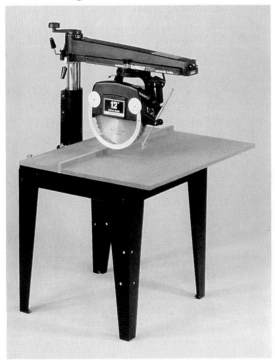

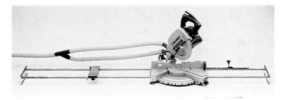

Fig. 5-29. Portable miter saw.

Construction workers also use several kinds of *portable* power saws. A **portable circular saw** is used to cut materials that are difficult to cut with stationary tools. Fig. 5-30. For example, a portable circular saw can be used to cut the ends off rafters after they have been assembled. A **power miter saw** is a circular saw mounted over a small table. Fig. 5-31. The saw pivots to enable the worker to cut various angles in wood.

1. Prepare and hand out a list of safety rules for both the radial arm saw and the table saw. Review these rules. Then demonstrate the operation of each tool.

2. Demonstrate the safe use of the portable circular saw, the power miter saw, and the saber. Review the safety rules that have been developed for their use.

A power miter saw is used to cut precise angles in wooden molding and trim. A **saber saw** has a small knife-shaped blade that reciprocates (moves up and down) to cut curves. Workers such as plumbers and carpenters use saber saws to cut holes in floors and roofs for pipes. Fig. 5-32.

Fig. 5-30. Portable circular saw.

Fig. 5-31. Power miter saw.

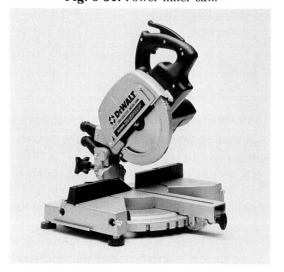

Power Drills and Screwdrivers

Power drills are used for drilling holes in wood, metal, and concrete. The size of a drill is determined by the chuck size and the power of the motor. The *chuck* is the part of a drill that holds the **twist drill bit**, or *bit*. A ½-inch drill will hold a bit of any size up to ½-inch in diameter. Some drills have reversible motors so that they can turn forward or backward. Some are even battery powered for use in places where there is no electrical service. Fig. 5-33.

A **power screwdriver**, or *screwgun*, is used to install and remove screws. It is similar to an electric drill. However, instead of a twist drill bit, a power screwdriver has a special screwdriver bit. The screwdriver bit fits into the head of the screw just like a screwdriver. Drywall installers use a power screwdriver to fasten wallboard to wall studs. Fig. 5-34.

Power Hammers

Power hammers are tools that strike with great force. **Pneumatic hammers**, or *jackhammers*, are used to break up concrete or asphalt paving. You have probably seen — and heard — one

Fig. 5-32. Saber saw.

1. Demonstrate how to install drill bits and safely use the power drill. Review any safety rules that have been developed.
2. Safety tip: Be sure to use hearing protection when working with or nearby a pneumatic hammer.

being used. An air compressor nearby supplies air at high pressure. A hose carries the air to the tool. The compressed air provides the power to move the bit, or chisel, up and down as it breaks into the paving. Fig. 5-35.

Another type of power hammer, the **rotary hammer**, looks like an electric drill. A rotary hammer operates with both rotating and reciprocating action. It is used to drill holes in concrete. Fig. 5-36.

Fig. 5-35. Pneumatic hammer.

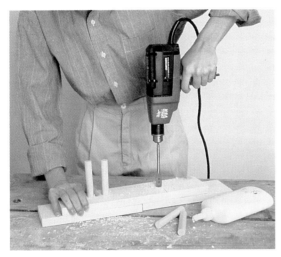

Fig. 5-33. Power drill.

Fig. 5-34. Power screwdriver.

Fig. 5-36. Rotary hammer.

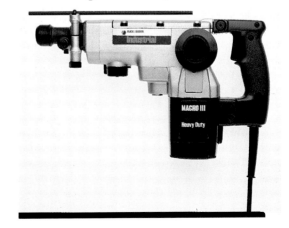

1. Explain that, in order to operate properly, pneumatic tools must have an air supply that is filtered, free of condensation, lubricated, and pressure controlled.

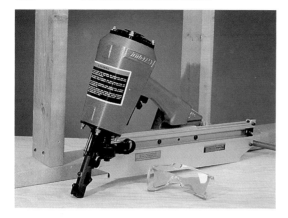

Fig. 5-37. Pneumatic nailer.

Fig. 5-38. Powder-actuated stud driver.

Power Nailers and Staplers

Nailers and staplers are power tools that fasten materials together. **Nailers** are sometimes called "nail guns" because they "shoot" nails. Most nailers are pneumatically powered. When the trigger of a nailer is pulled, air from an air compressor applies a strong force to the nail. Lumber can be nailed easily with a nailer just by aligning the boards and pulling the trigger. One pull on the trigger drives a nail all the way in. Fig. 5-37.

One specialized kind of nailer is a **powder-actuated stud driver**. It is powered by a 22-caliber cartridge that contains gunpowder. A special nail or fastener is put into the barrel, and the tool is loaded with a cartridge. The gun is pressed against the parts to be fastened, and the trigger is pulled. The powder-actuated stud driver can drive ½-inch- to 3-inch-long pins into wood, steel, or concrete. Carpenters use it to fasten 2 × 4's to concrete walls. It is also used to fasten metal door frames to concrete walls. Fig. 5-38.

Staplers work like nailers, but they are loaded with U-shaped staples instead of nails. Some are pneumatic, and others use electricity. Roofers use staplers to fasten roof shingles to decking. Carpenters use them to staple insulation into place. Fig. 5-39.

Fig. 5-39. Stapler.

1. Safety tip: Charges for driving powder-actuated fasteners are made in various strengths. Use the lightest charge possible for the job.

2. Safety tip: When using powder-actuated fasteners in closed places, hold your mouth open. This will equalize the pressure on both sides of your eardrums.

W.H.T.C. LEARNING RESOURCES CENTRE

For Discussion

The advantages of using portable power tools are obvious. Can you list a few ways in which the use of portable power tools has affected the construction industry.

⦀ EQUIPMENT

Equipment is a term that refers to large, complex tools and machines. Each type of equipment is designed to do a certain job. Most of the equipment that is used in construction falls into one of the following categories: surveying equipment, pumps, conveyors, and welding machines.

Surveying Equipment

Surveying equipment is used to measure land size and elevation. A survey is needed to begin almost any construction project. Surveyors mark off property boundaries and other important lines for construction workers. To do this, surveyors need accurate equipment.

A **transit** measures horizontal and vertical angles. Fig. 5-40. Surveyors use it to measure relative land elevation. They use a **surveyor's level** to find an unknown elevation from a known one. Fig. 5-41. A **construction laser** is a versatile instrument that can be used as a level or as an alignment tool. It flashes a narrow, accurate beam of light that workers can use as a baseline for additional measurements. Fig. 5-42.

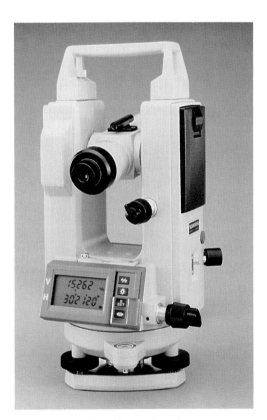

Fig. 5-40. Transit.

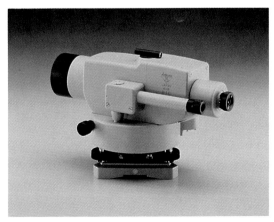

Fig. 5-41. Surveyor's level.

1. Demonstrate the use of a transit. Emphasize the care that must be taken in setting up and handling the instrument.

2. Explain the difference between a transit and a surveyor's level.

3. Assign a group of students to study and report on the use of laser instruments in the surveying and construction industries.

Fig. 5-42. Construction laser.

Pumps

The two kinds of pumps that are most commonly used in construction work are water pumps and concrete pumps. **Water pumps** are used to pump water out of holes in the ground so that work can be done. These pumps are usually powered by small gasoline engines. Because they do not require electricity, they are considered very portable. Fig. 5-43.

A **concrete pump** is used to move concrete from the concrete mixer to the concrete form efficiently. The pump is usually mounted on a truck. It has a *boom*, or long arm, that can be pointed in any direction. The boom holds and directs a hose through which the concrete is pumped. Fig. 5-44.

Fig. 5-43. Water pump.

Did You Know?

The Sumerians were an ancient Middle Eastern people. There is evidence that they practiced land surveying. Clay tablets from their culture record land measurements. Also, boundary stones used to mark land plots have been found. The ancient Egyptians also practiced land surveying. A drawing on the wall of a tomb at Thebes, in Egypt, shows two men measuring a field with what seems to be a rope marked at regular intervals. In fact, surveying may have begun in ancient Egypt. The Great Pyramid, which was built around 2700 BC, is accurately square. This indicates that the builders had a good knowledge of surveying.

1. Explain why a water pump requires less power to operate than a concrete pump.
2. Guide students in a discussion of how the development of the concrete pump has reduced the amount of work that crews have to do on high-rise buildings.

Fig. 5-44. Concrete pump.

Conveyors

Materials other than fluids are often moved on a **conveyor**. You have probably seen conveyors in a supermarket or an airport. At the supermarket a conveyor automatically moves the groceries placed on it forward to the cashier. At the airport a conveyor moves luggage from ground level to a compartment in an airplane.

A similar type of conveyor is used in construction to speed the movement of materials. Roofers, for example, use conveyors to carry heavy bundles of shingles and other materials from the ground to the roof of a building. This allows the roofers to stay on the roof instead of spending time climbing up and down ladders. It also reduces the chances of workers being injured while climbing ladders. Fig. 5-45.

Fig. 5-45. The roof of this building covers over 3 acres (1.2 ha). In roofing such large buildings, contractors sometimes use conveyors to transport materials onto the roof.

1. Safety tip: Conveyors are usually built so that there may be pinch points present. All guards must be left in place.

2. Ask the class to study back issues of *Heavy Equipment* magazine and other trade publications. Ask them to report on ways in which conveyors are used to move massive amounts of material.

Welding Machines

Ironworkers use **arc welding machines** to weld materials such as steel beams at construction sites. An arc welding machine, or *arc welder*, uses an electric arc to melt portions of the metal beams and thus the beams weld together. A gasoline engine powers the machine. The engine turns an electrical generator, which provides the electric arc. Fig. 5-46.

Another type of welding machine that is used in special situations is a **laser-powered welder**. A concentrated laser beam can heat metal to temperatures over 10,000 degrees Fahrenheit (5,540 °C). This makes the laser an ideal heat source for welding hard-to-melt metals, such as heat-resistant types of steel. Fig. 5-47.

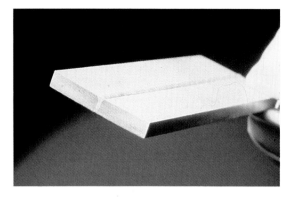

Fig. 5-47. The weld that joined two pieces of metal was made by a laser-powered welder.

Fig. 5-46. Arc welding machine.

HEALTH & SAFETY

The use of any type of tool carries with it the risk of injury. In the United States, most states enacted some type of employer liability law between 1885 and 1910. Later, workmen's compensation laws were passed. These laws allow workers to recover damages when the disease or accident arose in the course of employment. Such laws now cover employment in most areas of business, not only in occupations commonly thought of as hazardous.

HEAVY EQUIPMENT

Some machines used in construction are very large and powerful. Such machines, called ² **heavy equipment**, are designed to do jobs that might be impossible to do by hand. Heavy equip-

1. Safety tip: Whenever one is present where arc welding is being done, care must be taken not to look at the arc unless eye protection is being worn.

2. Ask the class to trace the development of ways to power heavy equipment. They should discuss the use of steam, gasoline, diesel, diesel electric, and diesel hydraulic powering systems.

ment is expensive to buy and operate. It saves money in the long run, however, because it helps people do the work quickly and efficiently. Heavy equipment is used for jobs such as lifting and moving earth or other heavy materials. Can you imagine moving all the earth for an interstate highway using only shovels and wheelbarrows? That job would take a lifetime or more to complete without heavy equipment.

Heavy equipment includes machines such as cranes, excavators, bulldozers, and loaders, as well as equipment that is used in highway construction. There are several variations of each of these types of equipment. Each variation has been developed to meet specific needs on the construction site.

Cranes

Cranes are machines that lift large and heavy loads. They can also move loads horizontally by carrying them along a radius. Cranes are classified according to the weight they can lift safely. For example, a 50-ton crane can lift 50 tons or 100,000 pounds.

All cranes have similar basic parts. A *cable* is used to attach the object to be lifted to the hoist. The *hoist* is the mechanism that winds up the cable and does the lifting. The **boom** is the long arm of the crane that directs the cable. Several different kinds of tools can be put on the end of the cable to do specific jobs. The two most commonly used are the hook and the bucket. A *hook* is for general lifting. A *bucket* is used for digging and carrying. Fig. 5-48.

Most of the cranes in use today are *hydraulic*. These cranes have solid booms that telescope and extend hydraulically. *Mechanical* cranes are those with the familiar gridwork booms. Many different kinds of cranes have been developed for special purposes. Fig. 5-49. A **crawler crane** is mounted on metal treads so that it can move over rough terrain at a construction site. A **truck crane** is mounted on a truck frame so that it can be driven to the site.

A **tower crane**, or *climbing crane*, has a built-in jack that raises the crane from floor to floor as the building is constructed. A tower crane is used in the construction of tall buildings. It is usually positioned in the elevator shaft. When its job is done, another crane is used to remove the tower crane from the building.

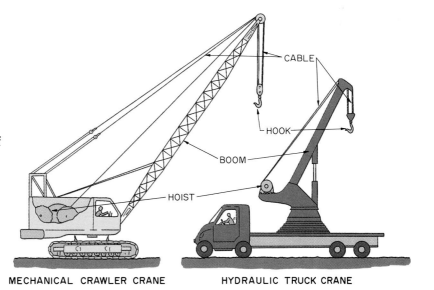

Fig. 5-48. The main parts of cranes.

CABLE

HOOK

BOOM

HOIST

MECHANICAL CRAWLER CRANE   HYDRAULIC TRUCK CRANE

1. Cranes swing loads to one side or the other. Thus, the crane must be stabilized on either side with outriggers. Explain that these outriggers must rest on a solid base. Otherwise, the crane can be tipped over.

2. Explain that crane booms, cables, and loads must be kept at least ten feet away from any electrical wires to safeguard the operator and other workers.

Fig. 5-49. A 640-foot (195-meter) crane.

Excavators

An **excavator** is a machine that is used for digging. It scoops up earth from one place and deposits it in another. Excavators are among the most common types of construction equipment because almost every construction job requires some excavation.

A **backhoe** is a type of excavator that is used for general digging. It is usually mounted on either a crawler or a truck frame. A dipper bucket is attached to a boom that is operated by hydraulic cylinders. The bucket is designed to dig toward the machine. The backhoe can dig below the surface on which it stands, so it is often used for digging holes. The size of the hole that is dug depends on the size of the bucket that is used. Fig. 5-50.

A **trencher** is a special kind of excavator that is used to dig *trenches*, or long, narrow ditches, for pipelines and cables. This machine is made of a series of small buckets attached to a wheel or chain. As the wheel or chain rotates, each bucket

Fig. 5-50. Backhoe.

1. Explain that cranes using dragline buckets can be used for excavating.
2. Explain that, if large amounts of soil are to be excavated, provisions must be made for moving the soil away from the excavation.

3. Emphasize the dangers of working in trenches that have been dug in all but the most stable soils.
4. Explain the use of shoring, bracing, and cribbing.

Fig. 5-51. Trencher-excavator.

digs a small amount of earth. The operator controls the depth and length of the trench. Trencher-excavators are also used for trenching. Fig. 5-51.

A *front-end loader* is sometimes used for excavation.

Front-end Loaders

Machines with large scoops used for shoveling are called **front-end loaders**. These machines are used to scoop up and deposit dirt or other materials. Loaders are often used to load trucks. Because a loader is mounted on a truck frame or a crawler, it can move small amounts of earth over short distances. Loaders have many other uses as well. For example, they are used to excavate basements, to backfill (fill in) ditches, and to lift and move construction materials. Front-end loaders are also called *scoop loaders* or *tractor shovels*. Fig. 5-52.

Fig. 5-52. Front-end loader.

1. Discuss what bulldozers and front-end loaders have in common and also how they differ.
2. Discuss the function of the steel cage that surrounds the operator on some front-end loaders.

Bulldozers

A tractor equipped with a front-mounted pushing blade is known as a **bulldozer**, or "dozer". The bulldozer is one of the most basic and versatile pieces of construction equipment. One of its primary parts is the blade, which is attached to the frame of the machine. Powerful hydraulic cylinders can move the blade up or down a short distance. Different blades are used for specific purposes. Many workers consider the straight blade to be the most useful. This blade is used to move earth over short distances. Another commonly used blade is slightly curved. It is designed for clearing land of bushes and trees. Fig. 5-53.

Most bulldozers are really crawler tractors. The steel tracks of the crawlers give excellent traction. This keeps the bulldozer from slipping when it pushes heavy loads. Other bulldozers have large rubber tires instead of crawlers. The rubber tires enable these machines to travel longer distances at higher speeds than crawler tractors.

Highway Construction Equipment

Highway construction requires a unique range of equipment, including some machines not used in any other form of construction. Most highway construction is done with four basic

Fig. 5-53. Bulldozer.

1. Explain that bulldozers and front-end loaders with steel tracks should not be used to compact loose earth because the weight on the tracks is not sufficient.

2. Ask individual students to study and report further on individual types of heavy equipment.

Fig. 5-54. Scraper.

kinds of machinery: scrapers, graders, compactors, and pavers. The many variations on these basic machines enable workers to adapt to local weather and soil conditions.

A **scraper** is a machine that is used for loading, hauling, and dumping soil over medium to long distances. Fig. 5-54. A **grader** is an earthworking machine that is used to grade, or level, the ground. It is used to prepare roadways and parking lots for paving. Fig. 5-55. A **compactor**, or *roller*, is used to compact the soil of a roadway just before the road is paved. Fig. 5-56.

Fig. 5-55. Grader.

1. Explain that, to be properly compacted, soil must not be too dry or too wet. Improperly compacted soil will not give good support.
2. Explain that compaction must take place in lifts or layers. These may vary from several inches to a foot thick.

Fig. 5-56. Compactor.

Types of compactors include steel drum rollers, tamping-foot rollers, grid or mesh rollers, and rubber-tired rollers. **Pavers** were developed to help in the construction of highways, parking lots, and airports. These machines place, spread, and finish concrete or asphalt paving material. Paving can be done very quickly using these machines. Fig. 5-57.

For Discussion

Are there any interstate highways near your city or town? What effect has the presence of such a highway had on building in your city or town, and especially near the interstate. Have you noticed that any particular type of building has been constructed?

Fig. 5-57. Paver.

1. Discuss the importance of properly maintaining construction equipment. What is preventive maintenance? How does it help speed construction?

Construction Facts

JUMBO

The *jumbo* is a special piece of heavy equipment that was used in the construction of the Daniel Johnson Dam in Quebec, Canada. It is the world's largest hydraulic rock excavator, a monster machine weighing approximately 100 tons (91 metric tons). The jumbo has seven booms, each 12 feet (3.6 m) long. A hydraulic drill is located at the end of each boom. These drills were used to drill holes quickly in the hard Canadian granite. Dynamite was then placed in the holes to blast the rock apart. Because the jumbo could drill so many holes at the same time, the blasting work could be done much faster than with an ordinary excavator.

During the construction of the dam, extra care was taken to keep the jumbo in good working condition. Each day the machine was repaired and carefully maintained to prevent future problems. The repairs were made inside a specially built, heated garage for protection from the harsh Canadian winter with its −60 °F. (−51 °C.) temperatures. The preventive maintenance paid off. The machine did not lose a single day of work due to equipment breakdown — an impressive record for such a complex machine.

The Daniel Johnson Dam was completed faster and more accurately because of the jumbo. It was an expensive piece of heavy equipment, but the $2.5-million monster shortened a two-year project to just eight months. The jumbo was definitely the right tool for this job.

1. Explain that specialized machines are being developed for specific jobs. Explain how this makes larger and more difficult construction projects possible.

REVIEW

Chapter Summary

Tools and equipment increase our ability to get a job done efficiently and quickly. Hand tools use power supplied by a person. These include measurement and layout tools, as well as hammers, pry bars, chisels, saws, and specialized hand tools. Power tools are tools powered by forces other than human muscle. Power tools include power saws, power drills and screwdrivers, power hammers, and power nailers and staplers. The term *equipment* refers to large complex tools and machines. These include surveying equipment, pumps, conveyors, and welding machines. Heavy equipment is designed for jobs that might be impossible to do by hand. Heavy equipment includes machines such as cranes, excavators, bulldozers, and loaders, as well as the equipment used in highway construction.

Test Your Knowledge ¹

1. Name three problems that can occur when a tool is misused.
2. What are the four main categories of construction tools and equipment?
3. Name three common hand tools that are used by most workers on a construction site.
4. For what type of job can a backsaw be used?
5. What type of saw consists of a motor-driven saw blade that hangs on an arm over a table?
6. What two power tools mentioned in this chapter are considered stationary power tools?
7. Name two types of power tools that are used to fasten materials together.
8. What is meant by *equipment*?
9. Why are water pumps commonly needed on a construction site?
10. What type of welding machine can be used to weld heat-resistant metals? Why is this machine capable of welding such metals?
11. Name four types of heavy equipment that are used in construction.
12. Name four kinds of heavy equipment that are used specifically for road and parking lot construction.

REVIEW

Activities

1. Visit a nearby construction site. Observe the tools and equipment being used. Make a list of tools and equipment that you recognize from each category named in this chapter.

2. Look in a tool catalog to find five power tools. Then, for each power tool, find a hand tool that can do the same job. On a piece of paper, list each tool and its price. Then explain the advantages and disadvantages of using power tools and of using hand tools.

3. Go to a hardware store or lumberyard and identify five tools that are not described in this chapter. List and describe the uses of these tools on a piece of paper.

4. Select a career related to construction. Research the career and prepare a list of the tools and equipment that people in the career most commonly use. Research the career and prepare a brief report on how job skills and responsibilities may have changed over the last one hundred years.

5. Tools must be properly maintained and serviced. For example, a grinding wheel should be used to remove the mushroomed head of a cold chisel. Also, wood chisels should be kept sharp. Research the maintenance of small hand tools. Then prepare a short written report on common maintenance practices that will make hand tools more effective and safer to use.

CHAPTER

6 CONSTRUCTION FRONTIERS

Terms to Know

Com-ply®
computer-aided
  design (CAD)
geotextiles
materials
Micro-lam®

modular
  construction
module
oriented-strand
  board
prefabricated units

Objectives

When you have completed reading this 1
chapter, you should be able to do the
following:
- Describe several new construction materials.
- Describe several new construction methods.
- Describe how computers are being used in construction.

1. Resources:
- Chapter 6 Lesson Plan in the Teacher's Manual in this Teacher's Annotated Edition and in the Teacher's Resource Guide.
- Chapter 6 Study Guide in the Student Workbook.
- Chapter 6 Visual Master in the Teacher's Resource Guide.

We live in a changing world. The goal of change is improvement—to be or do something better than before. Examples of change are all around us. Think of the changes in medical care and treatment in the last 50 years. Human heart transplants can now be done successfully. Even artificial hearts are in the realm of the possible. Think of the changes in transportation. Airplanes were invented less than 100 years ago, yet now we can fly almost anywhere in the world in less than one day.

The construction industry is changing, too. New materials and methods can help contractors do their work more quickly, accurately, and safely. Because of new materials and techniques, workers are becoming more productive.

Although no one can accurately predict the future, it is possible to make educated guesses about what could happen in the years ahead. By looking at recent developments, we can see the kinds of changes that might take place. This chapter will introduce you to some of the new materials and processes that are used in the construction industry today.

||| NEW MATERIALS

Progress is made when people develop new, better materials to use and better ways in which to use them. **Materials** are the substances from which products are made. The materials used in construction must be durable, affordable, and easy to use. Some companies that manufacture building products hire researchers to search for and develop new materials. Their goal is to find better products and techniques that will make construction both safe and economical.

After an idea has been developed, the manufacturer must work to get it accepted by builders and by the general public. Several materials that were developed only recently are already being used in construction work. New types of adhesives, plastics, and wood composites are examples of such new materials.

Adhesives

An adhesive is any substance that can be used to *adhere*, or bond together, two objects. We think of adhesives in connection with paper, fabrics, glass, and, in some cases, wood. Now new, stronger adhesives are being used and perfected that can bond almost any material to almost any other material. Fig. 6-1. In construction, adhesives are being used more and more

Fig. 6-1. These concrete bridge segments are bonded together with an adhesive.

1. Discuss why improvements in technology that increase productivity also tend to raise the level of education needed by the workers involved.

2. Ask students to pretend that a material has been developed to replace glass. Ask them what questions would need to be answered about the material before people would be willing to consider its use.

frequently instead of nails. Adhesives save time on a construction job. For example, drywall can be fastened to studs more quickly with adhesive than with nails.

Did You Know?

Adhesives have become important in construction. They are also important in joining pieces to make various objects of wood. Adhesives were used in ancient times. For example, some Egyptian carvings over 3,000 years old show a piece of veneer being glued to a wooden plank. In ancient times, glues were obtained from natural sources. The sticky resin obtained from some trees was used as a glue. Today, many glues are based on synthetic resins, which are products of the laboratory.

Plastics

Plastics have been used in many areas of construction for several years. New applications for plastics are being discovered almost daily. In fact, it is possible that plastics will someday replace most of the materials with which we now build. Some of the newer applications of plastics include products such as liquid storage tanks, roofing, and protective coatings. Waterproofing materials, engineering fabrics, and fasteners are also being made out of plastic.

Engineering fabrics are also called **geotextiles**. Geotextile material is like a large piece of plastic cloth. This fabric can be spread on the ground as an *underlayment*, or bottom layer, for roadbeds or slopes along a highway. Fig. 6-2. It is used to keep soil in place and to prevent erosion.

Structural shapes are another new application for plastics. Structural shapes made of fiberglass are now available for use where structural steel is not practical. For example, structural fiberglass can be used to build structures such as chemical plants, where steel would rust or corrode. Fig. 6-3.

Fig. 6-2. Geotextiles are used to stabilize soil. Here, geotextile is in place on a new road and paving is about to start.

1. Ask students to list those places in the school building where adhesives might be used for fastening.
2. Explain the following terms: shelf life, pot life, setting time, and curing time.

3. Discuss with students the materials used to produce plastics. What implications does this hold for the future cost of plastics?
4. Provide samples of geotextiles and other plastic construction materials.

Fig. 6-3. Fiberglass structural shapes can be used to build structures in hostile environments. Because of their resistance to rust and corrosion by salt water, fiberglass bolts are used on this tower.

Did You Know?

The Amazon river basin in Brazil contains the largest tropical rain forest in the world. Covering hundreds of thousands of square miles, it contains hundreds of varieties of trees. As an example, more than 100 species were counted in one-half a square mile. In recent years, vast areas of this forest have been cleared. Millions of trees have been destroyed and thousands of Indians displaced. The forest has been cleared to provide farmland and to harvest timber. However, as farmland, the land is poor. Very few trees are being planted to replace the timber that has been cut down. A rain forest, which takes thousands of years to develop, is being destroyed.

Oriented-strand Board

Oriented-strand board is made from small, crooked trees that otherwise would be unprofitable to harvest. About 60 percent of the product is made from pine. Hemlock and poplar make up the remaining 40 percent. All three woods are mixed together to make panels. Oriented-strand board can be used almost anywhere that plywood can be used.

Wood Materials

Even allowing for conservation and the replanting of trees, our timber supply is slowly being exhausted. Thus, it has become necessary to develop new ways of using our valuable wood resources. One of the first developments was plywood. Plywood has proved to be a popular and very useful building material. Other wood products are now being used in combination with wood and plywood. Some of the newest building materials made of wood are oriented-strand board, Com-ply®, and Micro-lam®.

Did You Know?

There are many types of plywood. Plywood is made from veneer. A veneer is a sheet of wood of even thickness. All plywood is made by gluing together a sheet of veneer to other sheets of veneer or to a solid wood core. It was the invention of modern wood glues that allowed the large-scale production of plywood.

1. As more of the wood from a tree is being used, our forest resources are being stretched. With the students, discuss ways in which the forests can be made to produce for generations to come.

2. Discuss how we can persuade other countries to conserve their timber resources.

Com-ply® and Micro-lam®

Com-ply®, or composit-ply, is made of several plies of veneer strips laminated to a core of particle board. **Micro-lam®** is made of pieces of veneer that have been laminated in a parallel direction. Fig. 6-4. Thin, dried veneer is coated with waterproof adhesive and bonded under heat and pressure. Micro-lam® is up to 30 percent stronger than comparable lumber. In addition, it uses 35 percent more of each tree than does regular lumber. The Micro-lam® process virtually eliminates warping, twisting, and shrinking.

New materials are not always accepted immediately. People tend to buy products they have used in the past—the ones they know will work. However, to meet the new and different construction needs of the future, builders, lawmakers, and consumers must sooner or later accept new ideas. To be sure that new materials are worthy of the people's trust, researchers test new materials extensively before putting them on the market. After a new product has been tested, building codes must be changed to include it so that contractors can legally use the material. This process takes time. However, new materials are usually approved and accepted by the people as the need for the new materials arises.

For Discussion

Adhesives are mentioned as being very useful in modern construction. You have probably seen adhesives used in the home. Do home uses for adhesives suggest to you any uses for adhesives in construction?

Fig. 6-4. This Micro-lam® beam was manufactured by gluing thin layers of wood together.

1. Explain that building codes can be written in two different ways. A specification-type code tells what materials can be used for what purposes. A performance-type code states that a material must perform in a particular way. It is much easier to have materials approved under a performance code. Ask the class to find out which type of code is used in your locality.

NEW METHODS

New methods or processes of construction are developed mostly by construction engineers and by supply companies. Once developed, the new processes are tested thoroughly in laboratories before they are used in the construction industry. Many of these new methods have been approved and are now being used by more and more construction companies. Laser technology and prefabrication are two examples. Modular construction, another promising new construction technique, is still being developed in laboratory settings.

Laser Tools

Many uses have been found in the construction industry for lasers. The laser *emits*, or gives off, an absolutely straight beam of light. Its most obvious use is as an alignment tool: lasers are used to mark elevations in construction projects.

In addition to marking elevations, lasers can help construction crews maintain elevations. For example, a laser is mounted on a tripod at the construction site. An electronic receiver is then attached to the blade of a grader. The laser automatically controls the height of the grader blade. This enables the grader to achieve an exact elevation. Fig. 6-5. Lasers can guide paving machines and trenching machines in a similar way.

A concentrated laser beam can reach very high temperatures. Therefore, lasers can be used to weld heat-resistant metals. For example, some types of structural steel can benefit from laser welding techniques. On a similar principle, lasers can be used to drill holes in very hard surfaces.

HEALTH & SAFETY

Some lasers are extremely powerful. These lasers can produce serious injury. Most lasers, however, are low-power. Such lasers do not produce a light as intense as that produced by more powerful lasers. Even with these lasers, however, you should not look directly into the laser beam or into any reflection of the laser beam.

Fig. 6-5. The electronic receivers on this grader blade receive a signal from the laser. The laser controls the height of the blade, making the correct elevation easier to accomplish.

1. Explain that a laser beam can be used as a reference point in the layout of a building. The laser is set in the basement. A hole is left in each floor for the laser to shine through. All measurements are taken from this laser beam.

2. Discuss how the development of the laser has enabled some construction processes to be done more accurately.

Prefabrication

Components of structures and even whole structures are now being built in factories and shipped to the building site. Fig. 6-6. Such buildings are called **prefabricated units**. The units are shipped complete. They include the trim, plumbing, insulation, doors, and even molded-plastic bathrooms. The units are assembled at the construction site. This method is a quick and efficient way to construct a building. Fig. 6-7.

Modular Construction

Another method of construction that falls somewhere between prefabrication and traditional construction is called **modular construction**. In this method, a building is designed to be constructed with modules. A **module** is simply a standard unit that has been chosen by a manufacturer, such as 4 inches. Modules allow the material supplier to stock pieces in standard sizes. When the building is to be con-

Fig. 6-6. This factory manufactures prefabricated housing units. These units are delivered to the site almost complete.

1. Assign the class to research periodicals from the early 1970s for articles on Operation Breakthrough. This was the first national effort to find new and more efficient methods of constructing housing. Post copies of articles on the bulletin board. Compare what was happening then with recent developments in prefabrication and modular construction. Acceptance then was weak because marketing was usually poor.

1 structed, the contractor orders all the parts, which have already been cut to size in the factory. The builder needs only to assemble the 2 pieces. Little or no cutting is needed at the site.

Did You Know?

Large stone blocks were used to build the pyramids of ancient Egypt. Archeologists have found evidence that indicates that these large blocks were cut to roughly the needed shape at the quarry. They were then cut to exact size just before they were placed on the pyramid. Strictly speaking, this was not prefabrication. It was, however, precutting, which is a step in prefabrication.

Fig. 6-7. This motel was made from prefabricated units.

1. Explain that modular construction as discussed in the text differs from the prefabrication of modular or boxlike units that can be built in a factory, transported to the job site, and assembled to form a completed building.

2. Discuss the advantages and disadvantages of using prefabricated modular units.

For Discussion

You may have seen prefabricated buildings being constructed in your city or town. What advantages do you think there are to constructing a prefabricated building? Can you think of any disadvantages?

||||COMPUTERS

Computers are now found in most businesses, and construction is no exception. Computers are used for both designing and engineering. Sometimes computers are even used to help run construction companies.

Computer-aided Design

The use of computers for designing and engineering construction projects has become 1 common. **Computer-aided design (CAD)** speeds up the designing and engineering work of a project. CAD also provides great accuracy in design calculations. Fig. 6-8.

The drawings and specifications for a project can be made easily and quickly using a computer. A CAD graphics program connected to a plotter can be programmed to draw a plan in just a few minutes. Specifications are prepared using a word processing program and a printer.

Computers and Construction Management

Computers are used not only for design and engineering, but also in the management of the construction firm. Computers are used for estimating the costs of a project. They are also used to schedule the many tasks involved in a project and to keep track of the schedule. Fig. 6-9. Computers are used to keep track of material and labor costs. Of course, computers are also used for the recordkeeping tasks that are part of any business. Such tasks include payroll, inventory, and billing.

By using computers, construction managers are able to receive detailed reports of every phase of a project in a short time. Project reports help managers find opportunities to improve productivity at the job site. Using a computer helps a 2 contractor stay in control of costs and scheduling. In effect, the computer helps a construction company compete more effectively with other firms.

Fig. 6-8. A plotter connected to a computer can draw plans very quickly.

1. Take the class to visit a CAD facility or show an audiovisual presentation of how CAD is used in architecture.

2. Explain that there are computer programs that take a great deal of the monotony out of estimating and scheduling construction projects. They can measurably reduce the amount of labor required for such tasks.

For Discussion

Computer-aided design (CAD) is now being used more often. Certain other uses for a computer in construction management are mentioned in the text. Can you think of any other uses?

Fig. 6-9. A computer can help managers keep projects on schedule.

THE FUTURE

What will the future hold for construction? There will be changes in every area, from the appearance of structures to the skills of the people that build them. New equipment will be developed that can do jobs more quickly and efficiently. Equipment will be more powerful and efficient than that which is used today. More tools will be created to do specific jobs. The need for unskilled labor may decrease. Instead, there will be a need for people who know specific skills. New materials will create a need for people specially trained to handle them. Some workers will have to be retrained as new materials and processes are introduced.

Space Habitats

In the future, a construction crew may be called upon to build a space station several hundred miles into space. Fig. 6-10. Such a structure would have to be self-contained. It would have to have its own atmosphere, temperature control system, and, perhaps, a gravity system.

1. Discuss the general skills that will make a person in the construction industry flexible enough to keep up with changes in the tools, processes, and materials of construction.

Such a space station would be known as a space *habitat*. As we continue to expand our horizons, we will have to create new designs and building techniques to meet special needs. One element, however, will remain the same: construction will continue to be the interesting challenging industry it is today.

For Discussion

The construction of a space station would face certain problems. Among the problems would be that of working in an environment without gravity. How would such an environment affect work practices? What unusual precautions would need to be taken?

Fig. 6-10. Someday structures may be built in space.

1. Ask students if they would expect people building construction projects in space to have the same level and type of education as those building a house on earth. Discuss their answers.

Construction Facts

INTELLIGENT BUILDINGS

New electronic technology has allowed buildings to become "intelligent." Building intelligence refers to the capabilities of electronic equipment and systems that are built into a building.

The basic idea of a smart building is that a network of sensors gathers data about the building environment. A computer uses the information from the sensors to adjust the building controls to meet changing conditions. Such a system can control the mechanical, fire and life safety, security, and energy management systems. It can also control elevators, on-site data communications, and telecommunications.

One example is a system that saves energy by sensing occupancy of rooms in the building. In this sytem, special sensors mounted in the ceiling are wired to the lights. When a sensor detects human body heat, it causes the lights in that room to turn on. The lights turn off 12 minutes after a room has been vacated. This system can reduce a monthly electric bill by about half.

Smart buildings are becoming more and more popular. Many existing buildings are being retrofitted for high-tech electronic systems that will make them smarter. Electronic systems are also easy to include in designs for new buildings. Research is now being done on other electronic systems that may make buildings even smarter in the future.

1. Discuss how the smart buildings mentioned in the text can help with energy conservation. How would one calculate how much energy must be saved before the added cost has been recouped?

2. Get information from the National Association of Home Builders in Washington, D.C., about the Smart House that they are developing. Assign a student to report on the project.

CHAPTER 6

R E V I E W

Chapter Summary

There are many new developments in construction technology. New materials are frequently being introduced. Materials are the substances from which products are made. An adhesive is a substance that can be used to bond two materials. Plastic materials are finding new applications in construction. Several new products have been developed, including oriented-strand board, Com-ply®, and Micro-lam®. New construction methods have also been introduced. These include the use of lasers in surveying and welding. Prefabricated units and the use of modular construction have made building easier. Computer-aided design (CAD) speeds up the design work needed for a construction project. Computers can also be used in accounting, billing, and material ordering.

Test Your Knowledge

1. What is one advantage of using adhesives instead of nails for some construction tasks?
2. Name at least four new applications for which plastic is now being used.
3. What is oriented-strand board?
4. What are three advantages of using Micro-lam® instead of lumber?
5. What are two uses for geotextiles?
6. Name three uses for lasers in construction.
7. What are prefabricated units?
8. What method of construction allows builders to order parts of a structure ready-made so that little or no cutting is needed at the site?
9. Name two advantages of using CAD in construction design and engineering.
10. Name four ways in which computers can be used to help manage a construction company.

REVIEW

Activities

1. Walk around your home or another building. Make a list of the things made of plastic that are used in the building's construction. What would have been used in place of plastic if the building had been constructed fifty years ago?

2. Find an old building in your community. Write a report describing how the building could be renovated. Tell what you think the renovated building might be used for.

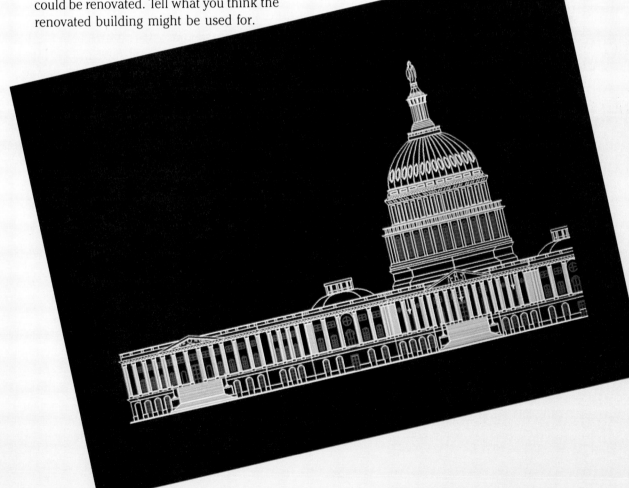

ACTIVITIES

Activity 1: Measuring an Incline Using an Inclinometer

Objective

After completing this activity, you will know how to construct and use a simple inclinometer. This can be used to measure the degree of slope for a driveway, patio, or other land forms.

Materials Needed

- 10 sheets of grid paper (10 squares per inch)
- 1 piece of $5/8'' \times 24'' \times 36''$ plywood
- 1 piece of $22'' \times 28''$ white posterboard
- 1 piece of strong nylon fishing line 24" long
- 1 lead fishing weight with attachment eye
- 1 small, clear protractor
- 1 wood screw, 1" long

Your teacher will guide you through the construction and use of your inclinometer. He or she also will provide the following items:

- adhesive to attach posterboard to plywood
- overhead projector
- fine-point permanent marker
- 6' tape measure
- 18" metal straightedge
- screwdriver, level, scissors, and other necessary tools.

Steps of Procedure

1. Your first step is to construct a large cardboard protractor. This can be done by projecting a clear protractor onto a $22'' \times 28''$ piece of white posterboard with an overhead projector. The projected protractor should not be larger than 26" wide and 13" high.

2. Accurately trace the shape of the protractor and the individual degree markings with a pencil. Go over the markings with a fine-point permanent marker. Label the degree markings as shown in Fig. A. Next, trim the piece of posterboard so it will easily fit onto the $24'' \times 36''$ piece of plywood.

3. Now measure over 18" from one end of the long side of the plywood board. Use a carpenter's square to mark a straight line down from the top, passing through the 18" mark. This represents the middle of the board. Measure 2" down from the top of the board. Place a mark on the line you have just drawn. This locates the position where you will place the 1" wood screw. In placing the screw, make certain it is straight and not turned all the way through the plywood.

4. Wrap one end of the nylon fishing line around the projecting portion of the wood screw. Tie the line securely. Place the other end of the line through the eye of the fishing weight. Adjust the length of the line so the weight is at least 3" above the bottom edge of the board. Tie the weight securely. Cut off the excess line.

5. Use a carpenter's level to find a flat surface that is exactly level. Now place the bottom edge of the plywood on this surface. Allow it to remain in this position until the fishing weight stops moving. Now mark the exact position of the line on the board just above the weight. Use a metal straightedge and pen-

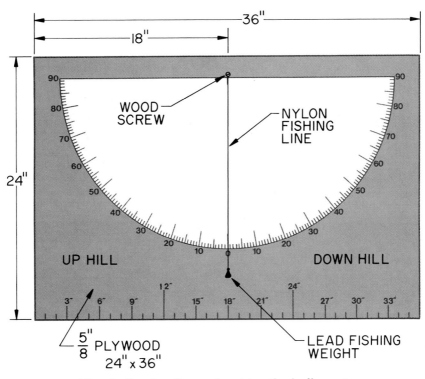

Fig. A. Constructing and making the inclinometer.

cil to extend this mark up to the center point of the wood screw.

6. Next, place adhesive on the back of the protractor. Position the protractor on the board so the center mark along the straight portion of the protractor is against the midpoint of the wood screw. The 0° mark should be placed exactly on the line you have just marked near the bottom of the board.

7. You can also make your inclinometer into a measuring board by creating a simple ruler along the bottom edge. Refer to Fig. A to see how the board is marked with a fine-point permanent marker. This scale will be useful when you begin using your inclinometer.

8. You are now ready to measure the incline of one or more driveways in your neighborhood. Beginning at the street, with the scale facing you, place the left end of the board at the very end of the drive. The weight will swing to a position on the protractor. If the drive slopes uphill, the line will be to the

ACTIVITIES

left of the 0° mark. If the drive slopes downhill, the line will be to the right of the 0° mark.

9. When the line stops moving, read and record the degree of incline. This represents the degree of incline in the first three feet of the driveway. Move the left end of the board forward to the point at which the right end was located for the first measurement. Once again, read and record the degree of incline. Repeat this procedure for the entire length of the driveway. Fig. B.

10. The data you have collected can be graphically shown on a sheet of graph paper. Begin by drawing a straight line the length of your grid paper. Let four squares represent one foot. Place a mark every three feet along the line. Now place the protractor on the pencil line with the midpoint on the beginning of your measurement. Next, refer to the data to see what the first degree of incline was. In the example provided it was 12°. Place a small mark to indicate the 12° position.

11. Use a straightedge to project this back toward the beginning point and directly over the 3″ mark. Then move the protractor and locate its midpoint directly on the mark you have just made. If there was an incline in the first 3″, this means your protractor will be slightly above the straight line you began with. Repeat this process using all the data you have collected.

12. What would you conclude if you discovered the incline of the driveway sloped toward the garage door?

Other Applications

1. Patios should slope away from the house and not have small dips. This will avoid water damage to the house or standing pools of water. The inclinometer can be used to check the degree of slope the patio has before pouring concrete or laying patio bricks. This check is best done by using the inclinometer along a long, straight 2″ × 4″ board placed on the ground.

2. An inclinometer of this design can also be used to conduct studies of lake and ocean beaches. It may be used to measure the degree of beach incline. This might then be related to the type of vegetation and animal life found in each measured sector.

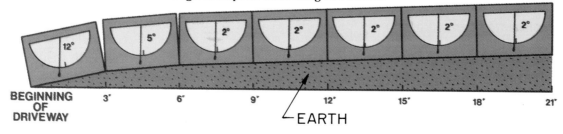

Fig. B. Steps in measuring the incline.

Activity 2: Emphasizing Construction Safety

Objective

After completing this activity, you will know how to inform others of the safety hazards that exist in construction.

Materials Needed

- 100 sheets of plain white paper
- colored markers or crayons
- 12 scissors

Steps of Procedure

1. Your teacher will divide the class in half. One group will study safety practices as they apply to the construction of the substructure. The other group will study safety practices as they apply to the construction of the superstructure.

2. A symbol is a sign used to represent something else. Fig. A. Discuss the qualities a symbol must have if it is to be recognizable to all. Discuss the importance of color and design. You should remember the important points of this discussion when you begin to design your own safety sign.

3. Each student should draw two different and original safety signs. The signs should apply either to the substructure or the superstructure, depending on the group to which the student is assigned. Examples of these signs can be found at construction sites. Because each sign is the work of a different student, each sign will be different. Some of the signs may resemble in shape, color, and symbol — the signs actually used in the construction industries. Other signs will be different.

4. Tack up these signs around the classroom or lab area.

SAFETY GLASSES

CAUTION

Fig. A. Some common safety signs. Note the way in which the symbol is used to promote quick understanding of the message of the sign.

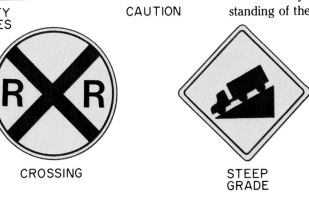

CROSSING

STEEP GRADE

SECTION

III

THE CONSTRUCTION COMPANY

Chapter 7: Organization of Construction Enterprises
Chapter 8: The Business of Construction

CHAPTER 7

ORGANIZATION OF CONSTRUCTION ENTERPRISES

Terms to Know

board of directors
construction
  management
  companies
construction
  superintendent
corporation
field engineer
field office

general contractor
home office
joint venture
partnership
project manager
proprietorship
specialty contractor
stock
stockholders
subcontractor

Objectives

When you have finished reading this 1
chapter, you should be able to do the
following:

- Define and explain the types of business ownership.
- Explain the difference between a general contractor and a construction management company.
- Describe the relationship between the general contractor and subcontractors.
- Explain the organization of a typical construction company.

1. Resources:
- Chapter 7 Lesson Plan in the Teacher's Manual in this Teacher's Annotated Edition and in the Teacher's Resource Guide.
- Chapter 7 Study Guide in the Student Workbook.
- Chapter 7 Visual Master in the Teacher's Resource Guide.

Construction companies have many responsibilities in addition to the actual construction work. To carry out these responsibilities efficiently, a construction company must be well organized. First the type of company ownership must be decided and a chain of command must be established. If the company intends to specialize in a certain kind of construction, the specialization must be defined. Also, provisions must be made for hiring workers. The responsibilities of the workers must then be determined. As you can see, many factors affect the organization of a company. In this chapter, you will explore some methods of organization of construction companies.

For Discussion

The text mentions a few of the things that a construction company must consider when hiring workers. Can you think of some others?

TYPES OF OWNERSHIP

Ours is a *free enterprise system*. This means that businesses compete against one another for profit. Anyone is free to start their own business.

Construction is basically a business. The business is that of building structures. In this sense, a construction business is unique. However, a construction business has elements in common with other types of businesses. One such element is company ownership. There are three basic types of company ownership for any business: proprietorship, partnership, and corporation. Each of these has unique advantages and disadvantages.

Proprietorship

A company that is owned by one person is known as a **proprietorship**. This type of business can be called a one-person operation. Fig. 7-1. Usually the *proprietor*, or owner, uses his or her own money to get the company started. The proprietor makes all the decisions and has the sole responsibility for every part of the business. This includes buying materials, hiring workers, and seeing that the work is done. The proprietor is also responsible for all of the bookkeeping and accounting.

In a proprietorship, the owner keeps all the profit. However, if the company fails, the propri-

Fig. 7-1. The owner of a proprietorship makes all the final decisions. A proprietor assumes complete responsibility for all aspects of the operation of the company.

1. Ask students to identify the responsibilities of a construction company. Do this again at the end of the chapter to see how their perception of a construction company's responsibilities has grown.

2. If a proprietorship grows to the point where many employees are involved, how can the owner get and keep employees who will manage the business with the same vigor as the owner? Discuss this.

etor is personally responsible for its debts. If the company cannot pay its bills, the creditors (people to whom money is owed) can demand that assets, or property, be sold and the money given to them. If the company assets are not enough, the proprietor may have to sell personal assets to pay the creditors. That means the proprietor may have to sell a house, a car, or furniture.

Partnership

Two or more people can form a business known as a **partnership**. Fig. 7-2. Sometimes a partnership is formed when a proprietorship expands or when a parent brings a son or daughter into the business. Other partnerships may be formed by people who have similar interests in a certain type of business.

Most partnerships have a legal contract to protect the partners. This contract states the rights and responsibilities of each partner. Partners may divide the responsibilities in any way they wish. For example, one partner may supply the capital. Another may be responsible for the daily operation of the company. The partners can divide profits and responsibility for financial losses in any way they wish. If a formal agreement is not specified, all partners are assumed to be equally responsible.

Partnerships have several advantages over proprietorships. They offer additional financial resources and a wider range of skills. They retain the simplicity of a proprietorship. The financial responsibility in a partnership is not as great as that of a proprietorship. This is because more than one person is responsible for the company debt. However, in a partnership, authority may be divided. When the partners disagree on a major decision, they must be able to work with each other to resolve the problem.

Corporation

A **corporation** is a company that is owned by many people. Fig. 7-3. These people buy ownership of the company by purchasing shares of ownership called **stock**. The stock is sold in the form of *stock certificates*. Fig. 7-4. The more stock an individual owns, the more ownership

Fig. 7-2. These two people have formed a partnership. Together they own and operate their company.

1. Discuss what a business person should look for when selecting a person or persons to form a partnership.
2. List and discuss items that should be agreed upon and spelled out in a partnership agreement.

3. Emphasize that the skills needed to solve disagreements are being developed in the student's present relationships. Explain to the students that they should attempt to develop these skills.

Fig. 7-3. A corporation is owned by many people. This annual stockholders' meeting gives the owners an opportunity to voice their opinions.

he or she has in the company. The individuals who own the stock are called **stockholders**.

Even though a corporation is owned by many people, it is legally recognized as an individual. The law treats a corporation just as it would a person. A corporation can apply for loans, sign contracts, and sell merchandise just like a person.

The people who decide to start a corporation are called *incorporators*. Fig. 7-5. To start a corporation, the incorporators send an application to their state government for approval. This special application is called *articles of incorporation*. It lists the names and addresses of the incorporators. It also describes the proposed business, its location, and the number of shares of stock to be sold. After the articles of incorporation are approved, stock can be sold. A **board of directors** is elected by the stockholders to run the company.

Fig. 7-4. A stock certificate represents shares of ownership in a corporation. (*Goes Lithographing Co.*)

1. Emphasize that the ownership in a public corporation may change from day to day as people buy and sell stock in the corporation.

2. Ask students what effect might result if a large corporation bought out all of its competition. Is this in the best interest of the public?

Fig. 7-5. These incorporators are discussing how to organize their new corporation.

The board of directors sets goals and makes policy decisions. Fig. 7-6. It also hires managers to take care of the daily business of the company.

Fig. 7-6. The board of directors meets periodically to set goals and company policy.

Did You Know?

The incorporation of businesses began in England in the early 1600s. At that time, businesses began to build up cash reserves. Looking for a place in which to invest it, some of them decided on the New World. Many of the companies that helped settle North America were, in fact, corporations. One example was William Penn's "Free Society of Traders," which helped settle what is now Pennsylvania.

A corporation has several advantages over either a proprietorship or a partnership. One advantage is that the owners have greater financial protection. If the corporation cannot pay its bills, it may declare *bankruptcy*. In bankruptcy, the company assets are sold to pay the debts. The stockholders lose the money they have invested. However, they do not lose their personal assets, such as homes and cars.

1. Discuss why a corporation might seek to be incorporated in a state different from the state in which it does most of its business.

Another advantage of a corporation is that money can be raised at almost any time by selling additional shares of stock. The money from the sale of the stock is usually used for assets such as new equipment or an office building. The company thus becomes bigger and stronger.

A third advantage of a corporation is that it is legally recognized as an individual. Thus, it can exist beyond the lifetime of any single owner. The ownership of a corporation can be transferred easily without disrupting the business.

Corporations also have some disadvantages. For example, a corporation can only engage in business that is either stated or implied in its articles of incorporation. For example, a corporation that sells typewriters cannot suddenly decide to manufacture typewriters unless manufacturing is included in the articles of incorporation. Instead, the corporation would have to amend the articles of incorporation to include manufacturing before it could legally manufacture typewriters.

One of the biggest disadvantages of a corporation is the heavy taxes that are levied against it. A corporation must pay federal income tax. Then, after dividends are paid to stockholders, the stockholders must pay income tax on them. In effect, the profit of a corporation is taxed twice. In addition to income tax, corporations must also pay a franchise tax in some states. A *franchise tax* is a tax levied by a state for the privilege of operating as a corporation in that state.

Joint Venture

In the construction business, two companies sometimes combine into one for the purpose of working on a certain project. This type of ownership is called a **joint venture**. Fig. 7-7. For a specific period of time and for a specific purpose, the two companies agree to be known as a single company.

A joint venture benefits both companies. It gives them business that neither company alone would have been able to handle. By combining the forces of the two smaller companies, the larger company is able to handle a larger project. Both companies sign a contract that specifies all the details of the business. The contract defines the responsibilities of each company and the percentage of profits that each company will receive.

Did You Know?

The Chunnel is a 31-mile tunnel being constructed beneath the English Channel. The Chunnel will connect Great Britain and France. The Chunnel is being built by two companies. One company is an English company. The other company is a French company. To build the Chunnel, these two companies have formed a single company. The total cost of the Chunnel is huge—nearly $6 billion. There also are a number of construction engineering problems. In fact, the Chunnel is the largest civil engineering project in the history of Western Europe. Because the project is so large, it is more easily handled by two companies working closely together as a single unit.

1. What disadvantages might result from a joint venture? Why should a company be very careful about choosing a company with which to enter a joint venture?

2. Ask the class to look through construction-related periodicals for articles describing joint ventures. Have each student write a short paper describing the joint venture.

Fig. 7-7. The Chunnel is an enormous construction project. It is a tunnel beneath the English Channel. It will link England with France. This massive project is a joint venture of two companies, one English and the other French.

For Discussion

This section has discussed the three basic types of company ownership: proprietorship, partnership, and corporation. If you were setting up a construction business, which type of company ownership would you prefer? Give reasons for your choice.

1. Have a student or group of students look up recent articles on the Chunnel project and report on its progress.

TYPES OF CONSTRUCTION COMPANIES

Most construction companies specialize in one type of construction, such as the building of highways. Other companies are very specialized. They do only one type of work, such as plumbing or landscaping. Still other companies specialize in management of construction projects.

General Contractors

A **general contractor** is a company that undertakes an entire construction project. Fig. 7-8. For example, a general contractor may undertake to build a building, a bridge, a power plant, or a highway. Whatever the project, the general contractor is responsible for all of the work that is done from start to finish.

A general contractor usually has an established crew of construction workers. In addition to these workers, most general contractors hire subcontractors for specific jobs. Together, the general contractor and the subcontractors are able to complete the project.

Specialty Contractors

Some construction work is done by companies that specialize in one type of construction job. They do only one kind of work, such as painting, electrical wiring, or paving. Such construction companies are called **specialty contractors**. Fig. 7-9. Specialty contractors provide a wide range of construction services to individuals as well as general contractors. For example, if you needed a new roof put on your house, you might call a roofing contractor.

When a general contractor hires a specialty contractor, the specialty contractor is known as a **subcontractor**. The general contractor sub-

Fig. 7-8. The construction project in the background is being built by a general contractor.

1. What would be the advantages of using subcontractors to do all the work on a project if the project is located hundreds of miles from the general office of the company?

2. Discuss the advantages and disadvantages of being a subcontractor. How might these change as a business grows?

Fig. 7-9. Hanging wallpaper is a specialized type of work. It is usually subcontracted to a company that specializes in hanging wallpaper.

contracts, or hires out, a specific construction job to the subcontractor. A general contractor might typically hire subcontractors to do electrical wiring and painting. Other subcontractors might be hired to install plumbing systems, piping, and heating, ventilating, and air conditioning (HVAC) systems. Fig. 7-10. The landscaping work is usually done by a subcontractor that specializes in landscaping. Carpeting and other flooring materials are usually installed by subcontractors that specialize in flooring. Even elevators are installed by specialty contractors.

Although the general contractor hires the subcontractor to do a specific task, both companies are actually working for the owner of the property. The owner relies on the general contractor to act as the agent to hire the specialty contractors. The general contractor makes sure that the subcontractors do their work correctly and on schedule. The owner holds the general contractor responsible for the finished project. It is therefore to the contractor's advantage to see that the subcontractors do their work well.

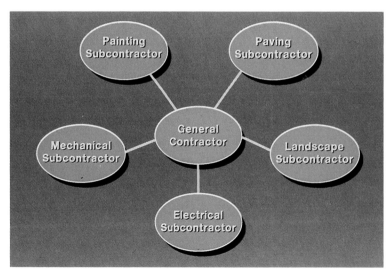

Fig. 7-10. The general contractor usually relies on subcontractors to do specialized work. These include the painting subcontractor, mechanical subcontractor, electrical subcontractor, landscaping subcontractor, and paving subcontractor.

1. Point out that some subcontractors, such as plumbers, require extensive training, guided work experience, and testing before they can be licensed to operate a business.

2. Discuss this situation. You own a building under construction. You do not like the way the subcontractor is installing the plumbing. What leverage is available to you to get the job done correctly?

Did You Know?

A canal is a specialized construction project. The Suez Canal provides a short route between the Mediterranean Sea and the Indian Ocean. The person mainly responsible for its construction was Ferdinand de Lesseps, a French diplomat. In building the canal, de Lesseps overcame a number of difficulties. After his success in building the Suez Canal, de Lesseps attempted to build a canal across the Isthmus of Panama. Here, however, he met with difficulties. Construction was halted. The canal was finally finished in 1914 by the United States.

For Discussion

What are the advantages in a general contractor hiring a specialty contractor to perform certain work on the project?

COMPANY ORGANIZATION

Every business must have some type of organization if it is to function efficiently. Construction businesses undertake two completely

Construction Management Companies

Construction management companies
1 are those that manage construction jobs without doing any of the physical construction. A construction management company hires separate contractors to do each part of the work. Then it schedules and coordinates the work among the various contractors. Fig. 7-11. The construction management company is also responsible for overseeing the construction. It
2 checks on the progress and makes sure the work is done properly.

Fig. 7-11. The construction manager coordinates all the work being done by the various contractors.

1. With the class, discuss whether a construction company could be both a general contractor and a construction manager. What would be the difference in the amount of risk and profitability?

2. Discuss the following. You want to construct a building. You can oversee the construction yourself, give the job to a general contractor, or have a construction management firm do it. Which option would you choose and why?

different kinds of work: office work and physical construction work. Most construction companies have found it convenient to maintain a permanent business office as well as an office at the site of construction. Therefore, construction companies are usually organized around two distinct offices: the home office and the field office. All of the organizational and business work is done at one of these two offices.

The Home Office

The **home office** is the company headquarters. Fig. 7-12. Most of the general work that is not actually physical construction is done at the home office. The home office is usually organized into three divisions: business administration, engineering, and construction.

Business Administration

The business administration division is responsible for business and financial operations. Fig. 7-13. Administrators are responsible for marketing, deciding which jobs to accept, and signing contracts and other legal documents. They also deal with labor relations and other personnel matters. In personnel management, the administration must be aware of any problems caused by job-related stress. They should be alert to ways of minimizing such stress. In addition, the business administration division is usually responsible for payroll preparation and accounting.

Engineering

The engineering division of the company is concerned with designing the structure of a

Fig. 7-12. The company headquarters is located at the home office.

1. Some decision-making is involved in each division of the home office. Discuss how employees should have prepared themselves to make intelligent decisions.

2. Trace the movement of a material order from the time that it is written until the invoice has been paid. This will help the class understand the division of duties between the home office and the field office.

Fig. 7-13. Business administrators keep the company running smoothly.

project on a given site. The **field engineer** oversees the project and makes certain that the building is laid out properly. Engineers also design the electrical and mechanical systems for a project according to the specific requirements of the owner. The engineering staff orders and supervises field surveys and helps develop the plans for the project. Estimators in the engineering offices estimate how long the job should take to complete, as well as the total cost of the job. Fig. 7-14.

Construction

The construction division of the company supervises the projects being built. This division is responsible for keeping track of the materials used and the actual amount of time spent on a project. Such work is called *project accounting*. The yards and shops are under the control of the construction group. The *yards* are where the company equipment is stored, and the *shops* are where it is maintained. The construction division also includes the project manager. The **project manager** is the person in the home office who is directly responsible for a certain construction project. Fig. 7-15.

Fig. 7-14. Estimators, working in the home office, determine how much work must be done to complete a project. They estimate what the project will cost.

1. Emphasize the need for good written communication between the home office and the field office. What implications does this have for the education of a person who will work in these occupations?

2. Explain that the project manager must know the status of each job. He or she must allocate the equipment and personnel to each job in such a way that all of them will progress as desired.

Fig. 7-15. At the home office, a project manager may keep track of several projects at the same time.

The Field Office

The **field office** is a temporary office that is established at the construction site. It is usually a small building or a trailer. This office serves as the center of operations at the site. A clerk or secretary at the field office takes care of timekeeping reports, payroll, and other general paperwork. If the building project is large, the field engineer also has a desk at the field office.

The field office also serves as the home base for the construction superintendent. The **construction superintendent** is the person in

charge of all construction proceedings. He or she is responsible for seeing that the construction work gets done correctly and on schedule. To keep the construction on schedule, the superintendent coordinates the efforts of the workers at the job site. Each of the different groups of workers has its own supervisor. Fig. 7-16. Each supervisor receives instructions and schedule information directly from the construction superintendent.

For Discussion

The home office is organized into three divisions: business administration, engineering, and construction. In order for the home office to operate efficiently, what qualities would be needed in the people working in the three divisions?

Fig. 7-16. The workers on a job can be more efficient if they are organized. The supervisor tells each worker what to do.

1. Discuss the human relations skills that a successful superintendent or supervisor must have. What kind of person would you work the hardest for? How can these qualities be developed?

2. With students, discuss what can be done to raise the percentage of contracting work done by minority-owned construction companies.

Construction Facts

CONSTRUCTION BOSS

Mary Smith, a 43-year-old single mother,
1 has turned a borrowed $1,000 into a construction company that now does almost a million dollars' worth of business a year. Ms. Smith is the president of her own construction company. She is one of a small number of black women who head construction companies. How did she get into the construction business?

In 1987, she was laid off from her job as a waitress. Determined to provide for her family, she borrowed $1,000 from her uncle. With this money and the cooperation of a few other people, she incorporated her company.

At first she encountered resistance everywhere she turned. The Small Business Administration turned down her loan applications. People simply could not understand why a former waitress would want to operate a construction company. Her persistence, however, has paid off.

Now her company does both general contracting and subcontracting. The company has renovated several apartment buildings under contracts of up to $150,000. Her company has also worked as a painting subcontractor for other construction companies.

People thought that Mary Smith was crazy to get into the construction business. Nevertheless, through her determination and hard work she has built a company that now has 17 employees.

1. Emphasize that one purpose of the class is to give a better understanding of construction early enough to enable students to make construction a career option and plan their education accordingly.

CHAPTER **7**

R E V I E W

Chapter Summary

Construction is a business. Company ownership can be organized as a proprietorship, partnership, or corporation. There are advantages and disadvantages in each type of ownership. A joint venture is another type of ownership. A general contractor is a company that undertakes an entire construction project. A specialty contractor specializes in one type of construction job. Construction management companies manage construction projects without doing any of the work. The field engineer oversees the construction project. The construction superintendent is the person in charge of all construction proceedings.

Test Your Knowledge

1. In a proprietorship, how many owners does a company have?
2. Who is responsible for company debts if a partnership fails?
3. What is the name of the type of company that sells shares of ownership to many different people?
4. What is stock?
5. What is the name of the type of construction company that is formed from two smaller companies for the purpose of doing a specific project?
6. What is the difference between a general contractor and a subcontractor?
7. Which type of company is responsible for seeing that the project is completed properly but does not take part in the actual construction?
8. What are the two kinds of construction company offices?
9. Name two responsibilities of the field engineer.
10. What person is responsible for coordinating the work of the subcontractors and seeing that the work runs smoothly?

1. The answers to the Test Your Knowledge questions are in the Teacher's Manual at the front of this Teacher's Annotated Edition.

REVIEW

Activities

1. Look under the heading *Construction* in the Yellow Pages of your telephone book. From the company names that are listed, see if you can guess whether each one is a proprietorship, partnership, or corporation.

2. Most construction projects have a large sign posted near the front of the site. Visit a construction site. Locate the field office and look at the sign. Answer the following questions:

   a. Is a general contractor or a construction management company in charge of building the project?

   b. In what city is the home office of the general contractor or the construction management company?

CHAPTER

8

THE BUSINESS OF CONSTRUCTION

Terms to Know

bar chart
bids
bond
construction
  superintendent
contract
cost accounting
cost-plus contract
critical path method
  (CPM) chart

incentive contract
lump-sum contract
negotiate
overhead
payment bond
performance bond
project accounting
project control
project manager
unit-price contract

SUPER INSULATED HOME
sensible solar homes
■ DOUBLE EXTERIOR WALL R-38   ■ SOFFIT/RIDGE VENTILATION
■ ATTIC INSULATION R-44   ■ 2" FOUNDATION INSULATION
■ AIR TIGHT CONSTRUCTION   ■ WINDOW GLASS LOW-E
■ INSULATED STEEL EXT. DOORS   ■ HIGH EFF. FURNACE/W. HEATER
■ INSULATED BAND JOIST R-19   ■ SETBACK THERMOSTAT
nh noah herman Sons/Builders 686-2230

Objectives

When you have finished reading this chapter, you should be able to do the following:

* Explain the difference between negotiating and bidding.
* Explain the four main steps in the bidding process.
* Describe four types of contracts.
* Explain how bonds protect the owner of a construction project.
* Describe two types of construction schedules.
* Describe project control procedures.

1. Resources:
* Chapter 8 Lesson Plan in the Teacher's Manual in this Teacher's Annotated Edition and in the Teacher's Resource Guide.
* Chapter 8 Study Guide in the Student Workbook.
* Chapter 8 Visual Master in the Teacher's Resource Guide.

$\mathbf{C}$onstruction companies get most of their business in one of two ways. Sometimes the owner of a project approaches a construction company and asks for an estimate on the project. Fig. 8-1. The owner and the construction company **negotiate**, or discuss the terms of, a contract for the company to do the project. A contract is needed to spell out the responsibilities of both the builder and the owner. The cost of the project and the finish date are also negotiated. When both parties agree on the terms, the contract is signed and construction is started.

The other way for a construction company to get business is to compete with other construction companies for a particular job. In this case, each company **bids**, or quotes a price for which it will do the job. Construction companies obtain most of their work through this competitive bidding process.

THE BIDDING PROCESS

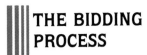

The bidding process is begun by the owner after the designing and engineering work on a project is finished. The owner sends out invitations to bid on the project. The bid invitation lets the construction companies know about the proposed project so they can decide whether they are interested. There are several ways of inviting companies to bid on a project. One way is to contact several companies individually and ask them to bid. Another popular way is to issue a public invitation. A series of advertisements is placed in newspapers and construction industry magazines. Fig. 8-2. Each advertisement states

- the type of work.
- the location of the project.
- where to get plans and specifications.
- the time and place of the bid opening.

Preparing a Bid

First a construction company must decide whether it has the staff, time, and resources to do the job. If so, office personnel prepare a bid. A key person in preparing the bid is the *estimator*. The estimator must be very careful when he or she prepares the bid. If the bid is too high, the company will not get the job. If the bid is too low, the company may get the job, but it will not make any profit on the project.

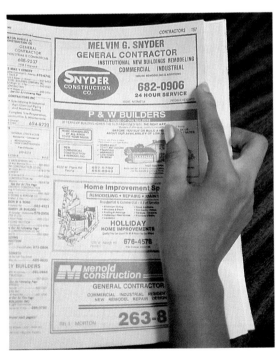

Fig. 8-1. Many contractors are listed in the Yellow Pages of the telephone book.

1. Under what circumstances might a negotiated contract be better for the owner than one that has been bid?
2. Explain why governmental projects are required to be advertised for bidding purposes?

3. Discuss the education and experience an estimator must have.
4. Emphasize that the best source of labor costs are records of past similar jobs. What does this tell us about the importance of accurate recordkeeping?

The Harbor Authority

Sealed proposals for the following contract will be received by the Chief Engineer, Room 32S Indiana Boulevard #1, Peoria, Massachusetts 10048, until 2:30 P.M. on the date indicated and will then be opened and read in Room N. 32E. Contract documents may be seen in Suite 5147 - 51st Floor and will be furnished upon request. Please call first for availability of Contracts. Questions by prospective bidders concerning any one of the contracts should be directed only to the person whose name and phone number is listed for the contract in question. No deposit is required.

Contract DAR-111-025 — Peoria International Airport — Terminal C — International Departures Facility - Bids Due Tuesday, December 11. Direct questions to Mr. Dennis Zempel.

The Harbor Authority

Fig. 8-2. The owner of a project may issue a public invitation to bid. This bid invitation was published in a construction magazine.

Estimating the Cost of Materials

The estimator studies the plans and specifications of the job carefully. Then he or she uses a special form to make a list of the materials needed. Fig. 8-3. The price of each material is found and multiplied by the amount of material needed. The resulting amounts are then added together to find the estimated cost of the materials.

Fig. 8-3. The estimator uses a form similar to this one to estimate the cost for the materials needed for each part of the project.

XYZ CONSTRUCTION COMPANY

ESTIMATE FOR _University Classroom Bldg._

ESTIMATOR _____ DATE _____

CHECKED BY _____ DATE _____

SEC/PROD	ITEM	QUANTITY	UNIT	MATERIAL	UNIT	EQUIP. OR SUB.	UNIT	LABOR	TOTAL
	Place wall footing	1825 cy	47¹⁰	860			5⁶⁰	101	962
	Place foundation walls	7900 cy	47¹⁰	3721			5⁶⁰	442	4163
	Place slab on grade	2650 cy	47¹⁰	1248			4⁶⁷	124	1372
	Cure and protect	9500 SF	0¹⁵	1425			0⁰³	224	1649
	Trowel finish	9500 SF					20	1900	1900
	Float finish	9500 SF					0¹⁸	1730	1730
	Expansion joints	196 LF	0⁴⁶	90			0³⁵	69	159
	Concrete pump					2800	128	1280	4080
	4 Power trowels	4 Days			100¹⁰	400		512	912
	Foreman	20 Days					128	2560	2560
				7344		3200		8943	19487
	Tax		5%	368					
	PT						23%	2057	2057
	FB						23%	2057	2057
									23969

_____ EXTENDED BY _____ DATE _____

_____ CHECKED BY _____ DATE _____

1. Get copies of pricing manuals that could be used by an estimator. Show the students the type of information available.

2. Mention that possible material price and labor cost increases must be factored into the bid.

Estimating the Cost of Labor

The cost of labor is estimated next. To determine labor costs, the estimator looks in labor reference books to find the standard amount of time needed to do certain jobs. In figuring labor costs, the contractor needs to take into consideration the number of workers needed, how long they will be needed, and the wage rate at which they will work. With this information, the estimator can estimate the total cost for labor for the job.

Estimating the Cost of Equipment

Equipment expenses must be estimated, too. Fig. 8-4. There are two kinds of equipment expenses. One kind of expense is the price or rental cost of the machines and equipment. The other is the cost to run and maintain the machines and equipment.

Getting Estimates from Subcontractors

Some of the special construction work may need to be subcontracted. The subcontractors will also need a set of plans and specifications to determine how much their part of the project will cost. The subcontractors figure out their own costs and profit. Then each subcontractor tells the general contractor his or her price for doing the work. The contractor has to include those prices in the bid.

Estimating Overhead Expenses

Another factor that must be considered is the company's overhead. **Overhead** is the cost of doing business. Costs for electricity, water, telephone service, office salaries, and postage are examples of overhead costs. Other overhead costs include the costs of advertising, insurance, and office rent. The estimator figures the approximate overhead for the project and includes it in the estimate.

Estimating Profit

The last figure that the estimator must calculate is the company's profit. This figure is difficult to estimate. If the profit is too high, the bid will be too high. This will eliminate the company from the competition. If the profit is too low, the job may not be worthwhile.

Fig. 8-4. The estimate includes rental or purchase costs as well as operating costs of all the equipment needed for a project.

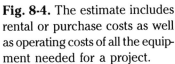

1. Explain how subcontractors can use plan rooms for getting the information that they need to prepare a bid to give the contractor.

2. Would the percentage of overhead vary for different construction companies? If so, what factors would cause this variance?

3. Discuss the circumstances in which a construction company might submit a bid that would not include any profit.

To put the bid together, the estimator adds the individual costs. He or she double-checks the figures for accuracy. A supervisor usually checks the figures also. Mathematical errors can cost the company a great amount of money. A large error might even bankrupt a company.

Analyzing the Bids

The bids from the contractors are submitted to the owner in sealed envelopes. At a specified time, the owner holds a *bid opening*. Each company that submits a bid sends a representative to the bid opening to hear all the bid prices. The sealed bids are opened one at a time. As each bid is opened, the bid price is read aloud so everyone can hear it. Fig. 8-5.

The contract is not usually awarded at the bid opening. The owner takes the time to analyze all the bids before he or she decides which construction company to hire. The analysis is done by the owner or by the architect or engineer for the project. All the bids are studied very carefully and are compared to one another. Those that do not meet the specifications are eliminated. The reputation of each of the remaining contractors is checked thoroughly to see that the company has been reliable on other jobs. Finally the owner decides which company will get the work. If more than one company qualifies, the one with the lowest bid is usually chosen.

Fig. 8-5. Sealed bids are opened and read aloud at a bid opening.

1. Might some subcontractors submit bids to several contractors on the same job? What happens if two bids are exactly the same?

2. Discuss the circumstances that would cause an owner to reject all bids and open the job for bids a second time.

For Discussion

By opening a job to bids by various companies, the owner helps to make sure that the project is built at the lowest possible price. Can you think of any circumstances in which the owner might now award the contract to the company with the lowest bid?

CONTRACTS AND LEGAL RESPONSIBILITIES

Once a builder has been selected, either by negotiation or by competitive bidding, a con-
1 tract is prepared. The **contract** is a written agreement between the owner and the contractor. The owner and the contractor are known as the *parties* to the contract. The responsibilities and rights of each party are stated in the contract. The contract contains information about the amount of work to be done, the price to be paid, and the method of payment. Both parties sign the contracts. Fig. 8-6. The contract
2 is a legal document. If one of the parties does not keep his or her part of the contract, he or she can be taken to court. The dispute will be settled there.

Did You Know?

Contracts arose because people in business needed a way to make sure that a promise could be enforced by law. The Romans had developed a system of law dealing with contracts. During the Dark Ages, from the fall of Rome (476 A.D.) to about 1000 A.D., society became more agricultural and town life decreased. At this time, contracts became less important. Around 1100 A.D., however, economic life began to flourish again. Then contract law became more important.

Fig. 8-6. The contract is signed by representatives of the owner and contractor.

1. Obtain a sample contract to show the students. Point out some interesting parts of the contract.

2. Why might a large construction firm have a lawyer on the staff? Why should a smaller contractor hire a lawyer to at least review any contract before it is signed?

Kinds of Contracts

There are four basic kinds of contracts. Each one is suitable for a particular type of job. The owner and the contractor must choose the right contract for each job.

Lump-Sum Contracts

A **lump-sum contract** is sometimes called a *fixed-price contract*. It is, as the name implies, a contract in which a lump sum (fixed price) is paid for the work to be done. The fixed price is agreed upon before the work begins. The sum may be paid in several payments. The final payment is made when the work is completed satisfactorily.

The advantage of the lump-sum contract is that all the parties know what to expect. The owner knows how much the project will cost. The construction company knows how much money it will receive.

Cost-Plus Contracts

In a **cost-plus contract**, the owner agrees to pay all the costs of construction, including materials and labor. In addition, the owner agrees to pay the contractor an extra amount to cover the contractor's overhead and profit. There are two types of cost-plus contracts. One is cost plus a fixed fee. The other is cost plus a percentage of the cost.

The *cost-plus-fixed-fee* contract states that the owner will reimburse, or pay back, the contractor for all the expenses of construction and will add a specific amount of money to that. The extra amount is agreed upon before the contract is signed. For example, suppose you agree to paint a neighbor's garage. Your neighbor promises to reimburse you for the paint and to pay you $20 extra. You know before you begin that your profit will be $20.

The *cost-plus-percent* contract is similar to the cost-plus-fixed-fee contract. The difference is that the extra amount is a percentage of the total cost

rather than a fixed amount. Using the same garage-painting example, suppose your neighbor agrees to reimburse you for the cost of the paint and pay you an extra 20 percent. If the paint cost $105, your neighbor will owe you $105 for the paint, plus 20 percent of $105, or $21. Thus, your neighbor will owe you $126. How much would the neighbor owe if the paint cost $85.

Incentive Contracts

An **incentive contract** is designed to reward or penalize the contractor, depending on when the job is completed. If the job is finished before the agreed-upon date, the contractor is rewarded with an amount of money that is specified in the contract. Generally, under this type of contract, the contractor gets to keep part of the savings if the company can keep costs lower than the original estimate. If the job is not done by the specified date, the contractor is penalized a certain amount of money.

Unit-Price Contracts

Sometimes it is difficult to estimate the amount of work that needs to be done on a project. A **unit-price contract** is good for that kind of job. The contractor gives the owner a unit price. The contractor will charge by the unit of work. Consider the garage-painting example again. Suppose you agree to paint the garage for $.50 per square foot. The unit is 1 square foot and the price per unit is $.50. Thus for every square foot you paint, your neighbor will pay you $.50. If you paint one 8-foot-by-20-foot wall, the neighbor will owe you $80 (8 ft. × 20 ft. = 160 sq. ft.; 160 sq. ft. × $.50 = $80). This kind of contract is often used for paving and highway repair work.

Bonds

The owner of a project has the right to expect the construction company to do the job well, complete the project on time, and pay its work-

1. You are a contractor. How would you bid on a job that has some unknown conditions? The owner insists on a fixed-price contract. Why would it be wise for the owner to place the unknown conditions under a separate contract?

2. Discuss the risks to the owner of a cost-plus contract. Would the cost-plus-fixed-fee or cost-plus-percent contract be most open to abuse by the contractor? Do cost-plus contracts have any disadvantages to the contractor?

ers. The owner depends on bonds to help make sure all these requirements are met. A **bond** is similar to an insurance policy. Bonds are meant to provide protection for the owner in the event the contractor does not follow the terms of the contract. To get a bond, a construction company must have a good reputation and financial dependability. The contractor pays a fee to the bonding company. In return for the fee, the bonding company issues the bond. Depending on the contractor's needs, the bond may be either a performance bond or a payment bond.

Performance Bonds

A **performance bond** guarantees that the
1 contractor will build the project according to the agreement. If for some reason the contractor is unable to finish the job, the bonding company is responsible for seeing that the rest of the work is done. This kind of bond guarantees that the owner will not have to pay additional money to another contractor to have the job completed.

It is very unusual for a bonding company to have to take over a project to finish it. Bonding companies are careful about the contractors to whom they give bonds. Since most contractors want to stay in business, they work to protect their reputation.

Payment Bonds

A **payment bond** is a guarantee that the contractor will pay his employees, subcontractors, and suppliers. This kind of bond is important because if someone is not paid, he or she can file a legal claim against the owner. This means that the unpaid party can claim ownership of the new structure. A payment bond prevents situations such as this from happening. If the contractor fails to pay a subcontractor, for example, the bonding company makes the payment. Thus, the owner is protected.

1. Explain that because a job is covered by a bond does not mean that the contractor has no responsibility. If the bonding company has to pay part of the bond amount, it will try to collect this from the contractor.

Safety and Liability

The construction company must also meet certain other legal obligations. The contractor must keep the site as safe as possible for the workers. The company may also be liable for 2 any accident that happens on the site. To be **liable** is to be legally responsible. Most construction companies are therefore very concerned about safety and liability. The safety and protection of their workers, the general public, the site, and the property close to the site are important considerations.

HEALTH & SAFETY

For someone not familiar with them, construction sites can be dangerous places. There may be deep holes for building foundations. There may be a variety of building materials stored there. Accidents are possible. The workers on construction sites should be properly clothed. They should also be familiar with the safety practices that should be followed on a construction site. The contractor does not like to have others on the site. For this reason, most large construction sites are fenced in. Nearby walkways may be covered. Don't trespass on a construction site.

Protecting the Workers

Construction work can be dangerous. Precautions must be taken to avoid as many accidents as possible. Workers in certain areas, called *hard hat areas*, wear hard hats to protect them from falling objects. Fig. 8-7. Other examples of personal protection include safety glasses and

2. According to the law, a construction site is classed as an "attractive nuisance." This means that the contractor could be liable for children injured on the site even if they are trespassing. What might a contractor do to minimize the liability?

Fig. 8-7. Hard hats help protect workers from falling objects.

gloves, which must be worn for certain operations. Safety glasses prevent flying objects such as slivers of metal or wood from getting into the workers' eyes. Gloves protect the workers' skin from exposure to harmful or irritating chemicals.

Keeping tools and equipment in good condition is another way to prevent accidents. Ladders must be sturdy and in good condition. The railings that are provided around scaffolds, or high platforms, to keep workers from falling must be solid. Fig. 8-8. It is common for a construction company to have weekly safety meetings to help the workers be more alert and aware of safety. Inspections may also be held periodically to identify unsafe conditions. Once they are identified, the problem areas should be corrected immediately.

Fig. 8-8. Railings are used to prevent workers from falling when they are working above the ground.

1. Explain the difference between safety glasses and regular plastic or hardened lenses in regular frames. Also explain the difference between safety glasses and light plastic visitor's glasses.
2. If possible, show a film on eye safety. There are several very effective ones available.

The Occupational Safety and Health Administration (OSHA) is an agency of the federal government. It is responsible for making sure that workers have a safe place to work. OSHA ¹ inspectors can visit a job site and perform a safety inspection. Fig. 8-9. If there is an unsafe condition, the inspector can shut down the job until the problem is corrected.

The government also requires that a company carry a special kind of insurance called *workman's compensation*. This insurance pays the medical expenses of a worker who is injured on the job.

Protecting the Public

The contractor is also responsible for making sure the public is not endangered by the construction. For example, the construction ² company may build a fence around the site to prevent people from coming too close. Fig. 8-10. If work is going on overhead, a special tunnel or canopy is built to prevent things from falling on passersby. Barricades may be used to block off a road or to redirect traffic. Sometimes a flag-³ person may be used to direct traffic around a dangerous condition. Fig. 8-11.

Fig. 8-9. OSHA inspectors check the site to make sure that safety laws are being obeyed.

Fig. 8-10. A fence around the job site keeps unauthorized persons out of the site and away from danger.

1. Ask each student to write a report on OSHA scaffolding standards. These can be found in the OSHA Construction Safety Standards.
2. If a construction site cannot be fenced, how can the contractor make it safer for the public and the workers?

3. Emphasize the need for drivers to slow down around construction sites and be alert for flagpersons' signals. Construction workers are sometimes killed on the job because of thoughtless motorists.

Fig. 8-11. A flagperson controls the traffic on a road construction project.

For Discussion

You have probably seen construction sites in your city or town. On these sites, what measures have the contractors taken to protect the public?

Protecting the Surroundings

The construction company must also provide protection for the area near the job site. Many times there are trees or other buildings near the site of the proposed structure. These must not be damaged while the new structure is being built. If the property around the site is damaged, the contractor is responsible for making the necessary repairs.

ORGANIZING THE JOB

Once a construction company gets a contract for a job, it must begin organizing for that job. A **project manager** is appointed to coordinate the money, workers, equipment, and materials for the job. He or she develops a schedule and plans for the storage of goods at the job site. A

1. Discuss steps that the students have seen taken on a construction site to protect existing trees and other features of the environment.

2. Point out that much work on a construction site requires that other jobs have already been done. Point out also that subcontractors must know ahead of time when they will be needed.

method of keeping track of all construction activities must be devised. Without organization, the work cannot be done efficiently.

Scheduling

The schedule of work tells what tasks must be done and when they must be completed. Two methods of scheduling are commonly used by contractors. With either method, the project manager can estimate the amount of time it will take to do each part of the job.

Bar Charts

The **bar chart** is easy to read and interpret. Figure 8-12 shows an example of a bar chart. The months are listed across the top of the chart. All the major jobs are listed down the side of the chart. A bar is used to show the starting and completion dates for each job.

Critical Path Method

The **critical path method (CPM) chart** is a diagram made of circles and lines. Fig. 8-13.

Fig. 8-12. A bar chart is used to show a construction schedule.

Project: _____

Date: _____ By: _____

OWEN CONSTRUCTION
CONSTRUCTION SCHEDULE

	July	August	September	October	November	December	January	February	March	April
Excavation and grading										
Foundations - formwork - walls										
Rebar										
Concrete										
Suspended slabs										
Slab on grade										
Plumbing underground										
Plumbing above ground										
Electrical underground										
Electrical above ground										
Mechanical - air conditioning										
Roofing										
Lath and plaster										
Millwork - doors - windows										
Painting										
Paving and landscaping - parking										
Hardware										
Final inspection - pick up comp.										

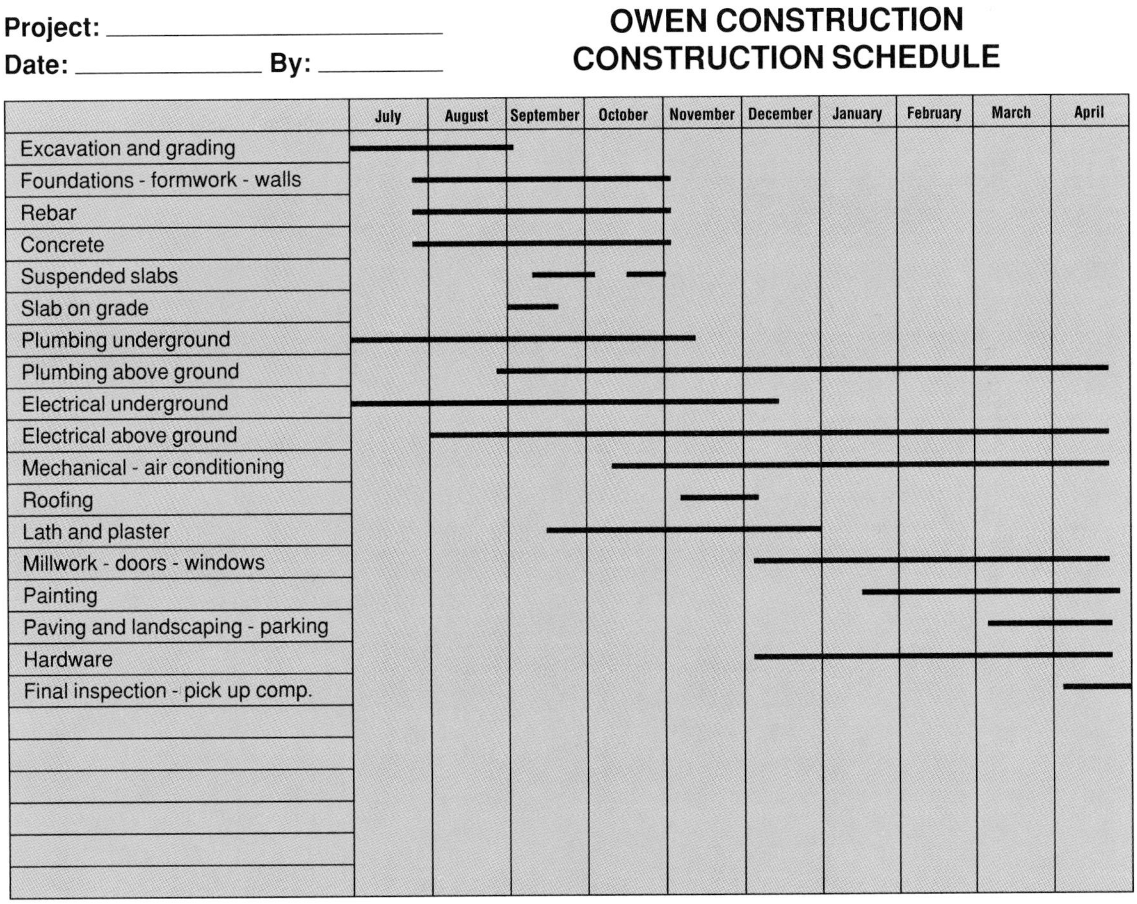

1. Emphasize that a schedule is no better than the person who has developed it. Allowances should be made for unexpected events.

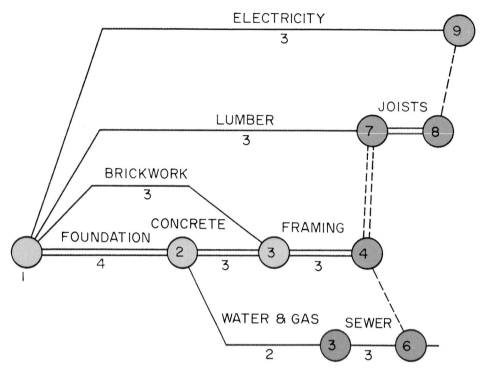

Fig. 8-13. A critical path method (CPM) chart.

Each line and circle has a meaning. This kind of schedule is useful because it shows the critical parts of the job clearly. Certain parts of a project have to be done before other parts. For example, the concrete cannot be poured until the reinforcing steel has been set in place. In turn, the steel cannot be placed until the concrete forms are built. Therefore, building the forms is a critical task.

Organizing the Job Site

The construction company must also have a plan for doing the work efficiently. One of the first steps in organizing the work site is to gain access to it. Usually streets already provide access to the site, but sometimes a *haul road* must be built to reach the site. Fig. 8-14.

1. Point out that a material shortage or the unavailability of a subcontractor in an area outside the critical path could create a problem.

Once access is established, several kinds of temporary structures are set up at the site. In many cases, the construction company brings in a trailer to be used as an office. Fig. 8-15. This will be the field office headquarters for the company. Portable restrooms are brought in. Sheds are built or trailers are brought in for storing materials. Some materials, such as insulation, must be protected from the weather. Other materials, such as pipe valves, are expensive and must be protected from damage and theft.

Utilities are needed temporarily at the job site during construction. Electricity is needed for power saws and other power tools. Telephones are necessary at the field office. Water is needed for drinking and washing. A waste container is needed for waste and scrap materials. Fig. 8-16.

2. Develop a site plan. Give each student a copy and have him or her organize the location of the items mentioned in "Organizing the Job Site." Efficiency should be emphasized.

Fig. 8-14. This haul road provides access to the construction site. It will be removed after the job is finished.

Fig. 8-15. A trailer is usually brought to the site to serve as an office.

1. What effect would a very small job site have on the contractor's bid? How would a small site affect job site organization?

Fig. 8-16. Even the location of waste disposal containers must be planned.

Ordering Materials

If materials are not at the site when they are needed, the job will be delayed. Ordering the materials at the right time is therefore an important job. The construction company's purchasing agent orders the materials according to the estimate that was prepared for the bid. He or she works to get the best price and delivery on the correct materials. The purchasing agent must be familiar with the delivery times for different materials. It may take a long time for some materials to be delivered. Other materials can be brought quickly to the site. Materials are ordered according to the estimate that was prepared for the bid.

For Discussion

You may have noticed certain temporary buildings at construction sites in your town or city. From what you have read in the text, can you identify the uses for these temporary buildings?

1. Get copies of purchase orders and invoices for several materials. Show the class what must be done with each. Explain who would be involved in their processing.

Fig. 8-17. A construction superintendent gives directions to the construction workers.

CONTROLLING THE JOB

Construction must be carefully controlled if the project is to be done well and on schedule. No matter how well a project has been planned, problems can arise. The person who controls all activity at the site is the **construction superintendent**. He or she must be aware of any problems and make corrections when they are needed. At the same time, he or she must keep a close watch on the materials that are bought and how much they cost. The cost of materials is checked through an accounting system.

Did You Know?

For centuries, accounting entries were made using pen and ink. Now, several accounting programs are available for computers. However, the computer has not changed the basic rules of accounting. Accounting rules remain the same. Computer accounting programs have, though, made accounting easier. They have made it easier especially for those who are not accountants. Computer accounting programs allow many small businesses to keep careful track of income and expenses. They could, of course, have done this without using a computer accounting program. In some cases, however, it might not have been as easy.

Project Control

Project control is the process of giving directions and making sure the job is done properly and on time. The construction superintendent is responsible for directing and monitoring the workers. He or she is almost always on the site to perform these functions. Fig. 8-17.

Another aspect of project control is monitoring the work. The construction superintendent sees that the working drawings are followed and that the correct materials are being used. He or she also checks the progress of each step to keep the project on schedule.

Project Accounting

The contractor must account for the progress made at the job site. To keep track of the progress, the contractor must keep accurate records of what has been done. This is known as **project accounting**. The contractor keeps track of how many carpenters are working, how much concrete has been used, and how close to schedule the project is progressing. Daily reports are turned in by the foreman for each type of worker, or *trade*. For example, the foreman for the bricklayers is responsible for a daily report of the number of workers and how much work is accomplished. Fig. 8-18. Weekly reports are sent to the home office. From these reports the master schedule is updated. The date on which the work is completed is checked against the schedule. The contractor meets periodically with the owner, architect, and engineer to report on the progress of the project. Such meetings are scheduled weekly or monthly, but they may be held whenever they are needed. Fig. 8-19.

Cost Accounting

When the construction company made its bid, it had to make an estimate of what it would cost to build the project. If the company uses more than the estimated amount of materials the costs will rise and the company will lose money. **Cost accounting** is the procedure by which the company keeps track of the costs of the project. The people who do the accounting for the company are very thorough. They check carefully all the

1. On a job of any size the superintendent will have one or more field engineers to assist in quality control. They will check the accuracy of subcontractors' work. The job of field engineer is for college or technical school graduates.

2. Provide an example of cost accounting for a construction job. Point out the amount budgeted for each division, the amount spent to date, and the amount left to spend or the amount overspent.

CARLSON CONSTRUCTION COMPANY, INC.

PRODUCTION SUMMARY REPORT

Job Name _Westside Hospital_   Job No. _84-163_

Foreman's Name _Fred Smith_   Clock No. _1508_

Late _May 1_

Breakdown Number

	Mon.	Tues.	Wed.	Thurs.	Fri.	Other	TOTAL
455.01 Pipe	102'	56'	101'	75'			334'
455.03 Pipe	30'		54'				84'
455.05 Elbow	6		8	2			16
455.06 Tee	1	1	1				3
455.09 Valve		1		2			3

Fig. 8-18. This report was submitted by the plumbing foreman. It gives a summary of the materials used on the project on May 1.

bills for materials and labor. If more money is being spent than was estimated, they notify the company managers so that corrections can be made.

The overall progress chart helps the contractor keep track of the job costs. As the work progresses, the appropriate changes are made in the cost of the project. This chart helps control the total cost of the project. Keeping good records of the costs also helps the company on its next bid. It can bid more accurately the next time because the estimator knows how much time and material it took to do the last job.

Fig. 8-19. At a progress meeting, the architect or engineer and the contractor discuss the progress of the job with the owner.

Did You Know?

Bookkeeping is the record-keeping part of accounting. Bookkeeping has been practiced for hundreds of years. In the 1400s, the Italians developed several manuals for bookkeeping. In fact, the modern system of bookkeeping developed in Italy in the 1200s. There still exist a set of bookkeeping records from the year 1340. All of the entries in the records were made correctly.

For Discussion

In this section, you have read about several methods used to keep track of the progress and cost of a project. What advantages are there in being able to keep careful track of the work being done on a project and the money being spent?

1. What would happen if the amount of material ordered for a certain job was not sufficient to complete the job? How could the blame be ascertained?

Construction Facts

SUPER SCHEDULE SPEEDS STRUCTURE

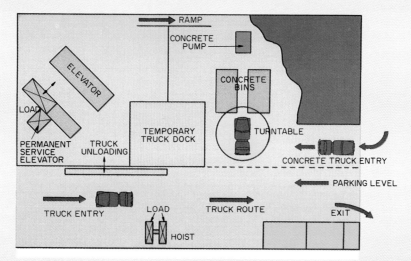

Careful planning by a Canadian firm, Olympia and York, helped speed up the construction of an 11-story Los Angeles high-rise building. The company developed a "super schedule"—a master plan for the construction site. Every detail of construction was carefully planned and scheduled. The plan included many advanced techniques, all planned to work together to save time and money. Some of the timesavers included using more and larger cranes and elevators, fine-tuning delivery schedules, controlling movement of all materials from a "command center," and systematizing storage.

Materials were delivered daily as they were needed. Few materials needed to be stored on the site. Companies delivering the materials had to sign up to reserve unloading positions and hoisting times. Each type of material, including drywall and glass windows, was stored in the same designated location on each floor. This reduced handling, congestion, and confusion.

One of the unique ideas was the use of a one-way delivery lane with a rotating turntable. Trucks drove onto the turntable, which was rotated half a turn. Then the truck was unloaded. While that was happening, another truck was driving onto the turntable. This allowed deliveries to be made twice as fast. This super schedule and advanced planning eliminated 152,000 hours of work time. It also shaved $3 million off the $96 million job.

1. What does the success of the scheduling in this example tell you about the capabilities of the schedulers? What did they have to know about the productivity of their workers and subcontractors?

2. Mention that the average profit on a large construction project may be around 4%. A saving of 3% would influence a company's overall profit. It would also influence its ability to bid on future similar projects.

Chapter Summary

Construction companies get their business by giving an estimate on a project or by bidding on a project. A bid must be carefully prepared. The cost of materials, labor, equipment, and overhead must be considered, among other expenses. A contract is prepared between the builder and the person hiring the builder. This contract outlines the rights and responsibilities of each party. There are lump-sum contracts, cost-plus contracts, incentive contracts, and unit-price contracts. A bond might also be required. This protects the owner if the builder does not follow the terms of the contract. There are performance bonds and payment bonds. The construction company is obligated to protect its workers and the public. A construction job is organized to coordinate money, workers, materials, and equipment. In controlling the construction project, the construction superintendent uses the practices of project control, cost accounting, and project accounting.

Test Your Knowledge

1. What are two ways in which a construction company can get business?
2. Name four types of information that should be included in a bid invitation.
3. Who is the key person in the bid preparation process?
4. Name five kinds of costs that an estimator must consider when preparing a bid.
5. In which type of contract is the total price agreed upon before construction begins?
6. What is the "'incentive" in an incentive contract?
7. How does a payment bond protect the owner of a project?
8. What are two safety precautions that construction workers can take?
9. What are the names of the two common methods of scheduling?
10. Who is responsible for controlling all the work at the site?

1. The answers to the Test Your Knowledge questions are in the Teacher's Manual at the front of this Teacher's Annotated Edition.

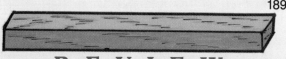

REVIEW

Activities

1. Look in the classified advertising section of your local newspaper. Find an advertisement that is an invitation to bid. Clip the bid invitation from the newspaper and attach it to a sheet of notebook paper. Beneath it, state in your own words what the invitation to bid is about.

2. Visit a construction site. Make a list of the safety and protective devices you see being used. Tell who the device is protecting (workers, the public, etc.).

3. Make a bar chart schedule of your daily activities. Across the top of the chart, list the hours of the day (7 A.M., 8 A.M., etc.). Down the left side, list the tasks you normally do (eat breakfast, ride the bus, etc.). Estimate the beginning and ending time for each task. Then draw the bar chart. Use the chart to check on your actual time use for one day.

Activity 1: Estimating Wall Construction Materials

Objective
After completing this activity, you will know how to calculate needed amounts of insulating materials.

Materials Needed
- Examples of various insulating materials. These examples include batts, blankets, reflective materials, a loose fill, and rigid materials.

Steps of Procedure
1. Measure the perimeter of the structure in Fig. A. The perimeter is the outside boundary of the structure. Also measure the ceiling height. Multiply the perimeter by the ceiling height.
2. Measure the area of the doors and windows. Multiply the width by the height.
3. Deduct the area for doors and windows. Many carpenters will deduct only the area of large windows and window-walls. They will disregard the area of doors and smaller openings. This allowance will make up for loss in cutting and fitting. It also will provide for additional material needed around plumbing pipes.
4. For an example, refer to Fig. A.
   Perimeter = 30′ + 40′ + 36′ + 20′ + 6′ + 20′
   Perimeter = 152′
   Ceiling height = 8′
   Area: perimeter × height = 152′ × 8′

Window wall = 12′ × 8′
Window wall = 96 sq. ft.
Net area = 1216 − 96
Net area = 1120 sq. ft.

5. Fill insulation comes in bags that usually contain 3 or 4 cu. ft. The number of cubic feet of fill insulation required can be calculated as follows:
   Area = 1200 sq. ft.
   Thickness = 4 in. = ⅓ ft.
   Cu. ft. required = 1200 × ⅓ = 400
   Less 10% (allowance for joists 16″ on center = 400 − 40)
   Net amount = 360
   Number of bags (4 cu. ft. = 90 bags)

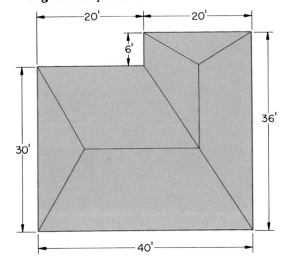

Fig. A. The perimeter dimensions of a house.

Activity 2: Conducting Soil Fracturing Tests

Objective

After completing this activity, you will be familiar with the concept of soil fracturing or shearing. Soil shearing is an important soil characteristic that must be tested before construction begins. By constructing the following apparatus, you will see the shearing characteristics of different soil samples. Testing soil by use of a soil fracturing test is one of many responsibilities of the engineers in charge of site preparation.

Materials Needed

- 1-4′ length of 2 × 4
- 2-8″ × 12″ × ½″ plywood sheets
- 32-1¼″ × #8 flathead wood screws
- 4-4″ × 8″ × ½″ plywood sheets
- 1-¾″ eyelet
- 1 pulley (½″ shaft)
- 1-3″ × ½″ metal rod (pulley shaft)
- work station with 2 vises
- drill and ⅛″ drill bit
- 10′ of string
- 25 lbs. of weight
- 1 stopwatch
- 2-12″ metal rules
- 1 roll of tape

Steps of Procedure

1. Cut the 2 × 4 into four 12″ lengths.
2. Fasten the 12″ pieces of 2 × 4 to the outer edges of one of the sheets of 8″ × 12″ × ½″ plywood. See Fig. A.

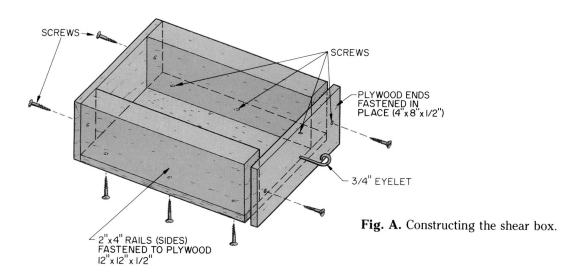

SCREWS

SCREWS

PLYWOOD ENDS
FASTENED IN
PLACE (4"x8"x1/2")

3/4" EYELET

2"x4" RAILS (SIDES)
FASTENED TO PLYWOOD
12"x12"x1/2"

Fig. A. Constructing the shear box.

ACTIVITIES

3. Repeat Step 2, with the second $8'' \times 12'' \times \frac{1}{2}''$ plywood.
4. Fasten the $4'' \times 8'' \times \frac{1}{2}''$ plywood sheets to the ends of each half of the shear box. See Fig. A.
5. Fasten the $\frac{3}{4}''$ eyelet to one-half of the shear box at the center of one end. See Fig. A.
6. Drill six moisture escape holes in the top and bottom plywood pieces at various locations.
7. Place the bottom half of the shear box in a vise. (The bottom half is the part without the eyelet.) Clamp the box between the $12''$ lengths.
8. Place the top half of the shear box on top of the bottom. The top half should slide easily on the bottom half. (The eyelet should be facing the second vise station.) Fig. B.

9. Tape each metal rule to the $12''$ side of the shear box. The edges of the rules should meet at the split line of the shear box.
10. Place the pulley on the metal shaft and fasten into the second vise station.
11. Fasten the string to the eyelet around the pulley. Let the free end hang toward the floor.
12. Remove the plywood top from the top half of the shear box. Fill the box with a soil sample. Pack the soil firmly into place.
13. Replace the plywood top.
14. Attach the weight to the free end of the string. Place a box beneath the weight. Start the stopwatch.

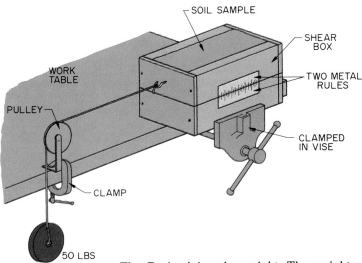

BOX BELOW

Fig. B. Applying the weight. The weight must be applied slowly and evenly.

BOX BELOW

15. Record the distance the top half moves in each minute. Continue to record these distances each minute until the stopwatch has run for ten minutes, or until a complete shear occurs. See Fig. C.
16. Now that you have collected all your data, construct a graph as shown in Fig. D.
17. Plot the shear value for each minute of testing.
18. Connect each of the plotted points in successive order to make a line graph.

SHEAR VALUE (in inches)	MINUTES
0.25	1
0.75	2
1.25	3
2.00	4
COMPLETE SHEAR	5
-	6
-	7
-	8
-	9
-	10

Fig. C. Recording the shear measurements.

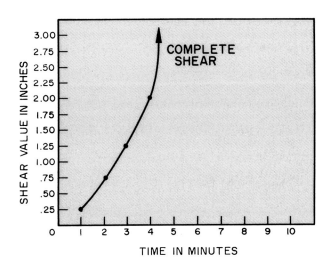

Fig. D. Plotting the shear values on a graph.

ACTIVITIES

194

Activity 3: Understanding the Systems Approach to Construction

Objective

After completing this activity, you will be able to identify the main parts of the construction industry when that industry is viewed as a system.

Materials Needed
- Paper (two 8½ " × 11" sheets per team)
- Pencil (one per team)
- Scissors (optional, one pair per team)

Steps of Procedure

1. Your teacher will organize the class into teams. There will be two persons to a team. He or she will then familiarize you with the following terms: system, input, resource, process, output, and feedback. Definitions for each of these terms follow.

   System: A whole made up of several different parts.

   Input: Something, such as information or energy, that is added to a system.

   Resource: An object or action that can be used to solve a problem.

   Process: A series of actions completed to reach a certain goal.

   Output: The amount of something produced.

   Feedback: The response of others to what has been done.

2. Refer to Fig. A. This shows the various parts of a system. It also shows the way in which the parts relate within a system.

3. Refer back to the sketch that accompanies Activity 3 in Section I (page 71). This sketch shows the way in which certain items were identified by the people as resources. These resources, along with certain construction processes, were then used to produce a certain output.

4. Take the two 8½ " × 11" sheets of paper. Fold each in half lengthwise. Then fold the paper in half widthwise. Fold the paper again widthwise. You will now have folded each sheet into eight panels. Cut or tear these panels apart.

5. On one side of each of the slips of paper, write one of the following terms. Each of these terms identifies one of the items shown in the drawings for Activity 3 of Section I.
   - Bridge
   - Column of rocks
   - The imagined bridge supported by a column of rocks
   - The imagined bridge (without the rock column support)
   - Horse and wagon
   - Hammers
   - Happy people
   - Rocks
   - Saws
   - Stream
   - Unhappy people
   - Wood

6. With your partner, study the drawings for Activity 3 in Section I.

7. Look carefully at each of the system terms just defined. Discuss the part that each of these plays in the story of the bridge-building.

8. Look at the slips of paper one by one. Discuss with your partner whether each of the

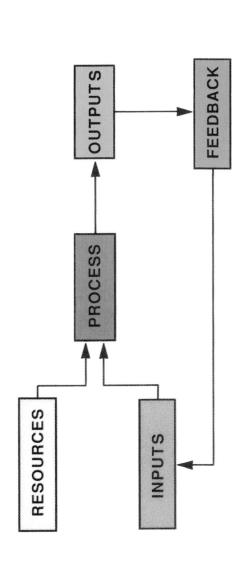

RESOURCES	INPUTS	FEEDBACK	OUTPUTS	PROCESSES
EXAMPLES: TOOLS MATERIALS INFORMATION PEOPLE	EXAMPLES: CUSTOMER NEEDS IDEAS	EXAMPLES: CUSTOMER RESPONSE PRODUCT QUALITY SALES	THE PRODUCT	EXAMPLES: WORK TECHNIQUES

Fig. A. The construction industry may be viewed as a system with various parts. These parts are shown here. Also shown are examples of each of the system parts.

items listed above is an input, a resource, a process, an output, or feedback. In identifying each item by one of these terms, ask yourself what part the item plays in the bridge-building story.

9. When you and your partner have decided on the term (input, resources, etc.) that best describes each of the items listed above, write that term on the back of the slip of paper. Each term may be used more than once. Some of the items shown in the story may not be used at all.

10. When all of the teams have finished, your teacher will discuss the correct answers. Compare your answers with the correct answers and the answers of other teams in the class.

Activity 4: Building a Wind-Powered Generator

Objective

After completing this activity, you will understand the construction and use of a windmill to generate alternating current (AC) electricity.

Materials Needed
- 1 6-volt bicycle light generator
- 4-4″ to 6″ plastic cups
- 1 wheel bearing with ¾″ opening
- 1-10″ × 10″ × ¾″ piece of plywood
- 4-24″ lengths of ¾″ metal conduit
- lengths of ¾″ metal conduit sufficient to construct a generator stand 5′ or taller.
- 15′ of No. 18 electrical wire
- 6-volt light bulb and receptacle
- enough ¾″ aluminum carriage bolts to assemble the generator stand.

Steps of Procedure
1. Figure A shows the general construction of the 6-volt, alternating current (AC) wind-powered generator. The generator used in this activity is available at most stores selling bicycles and bicycle parts. Your assignment

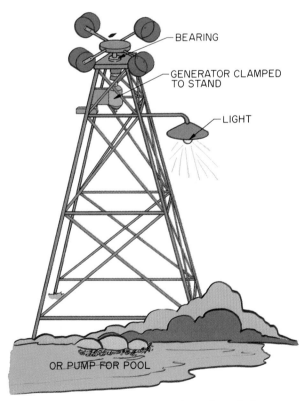

Fig. A. The general construction of a wind-driven generator.

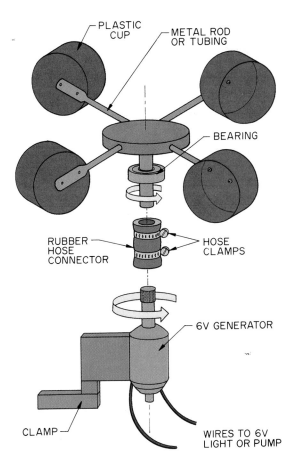

PLASTIC CUP — METAL ROD OR TUBING

BEARING

RUBBER HOSE CONNECTOR — HOSE CLAMPS

6V GENERATOR

CLAMP — WIRES TO 6V LIGHT OR PUMP

Fig. B. Attaching the generator to the wind-driven section.

is to build a small windmill to turn the bicycle generator. This generator can then be wired to a 6-volt light attached to the stand. It also could power a small 6-volt water pump for a fish pond in your back yard. Its uses are limited only by your imagination.

2. Figure B shows one method for attaching the generator to the wind-driven section of the generator system. The turning shaft of the windmill is attached to the generator with a rubber coupling and two hose clamps.

The bearing is mounted into the wood support of the windmill stand to allow free and easy turning of the windmill shaft. The generator must be clamped to the stand of the windmill so that only the generator shaft turns and not the entire generator.

3. Since the generator must operate outside in all kinds of weather, it is desirable to protect the generator. This can be done by constructing a small plastic shield around the generator. Do not seal it tightly or moisture can still accumulate around the generator and destroy it.

4. Select a location for your generator where there are frequent, steady winds. Since wind gusts can be quite strong, it is best to anchor your windmill stand into the ground or tightly onto the roof to prevent it from being blown over. Embedding the legs into coffee cans filled with cement is one good method of anchoring the stand into the ground.

5. Construction of the stand can be accomplished by flattening and drilling the ends of conduit to bolt the system together. The method you follow in your design may require the use of bolts, screws, and clamps not described in this activity. The main purpose of the stand is to raise the system high enough to expose it to a constant flow of air. At the same time, the stand must be strong enough to withstand heavy wind gusts.

Technical Considerations

- Consider a design large enough to drive a car generator to produce 12 volts of alternating current.
- Consider using a free-turning roof ventilator to generate electricity.

SECTION

IV

THE CONSTRUCTION PROJECT

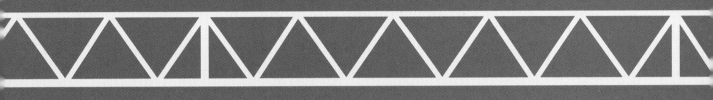

CHAPTER

9 TYPES OF CONSTRUCTION PROJECTS

Terms to Know

arch bridge
cantilever bridge
cofferdam
commercial
  buildings
dam

frame
  structures
highway
  construction
industrial buildings
mass structures

residential buildings
slab bridge
spillway
suspension bridges
truss bridges

Objectives

When you have completed reading this 1 **chapter, you should be able to do the following:**

- Describe the three basic types of buildings.
- Identify examples of light, heavy, industrial, and civil construction.
- Identify the basic types of structures.
- Explain the general procedure for constructing a highway.
- Describe the major construction tasks involved in building an airport.
- Explain two general procedures that can be used to construct a tunnel.
- Describe some special construction techniques needed to build a dam.
- Identify and describe five ways in which bridges can be constructed.

1. Resources:
- Chapter 9 Lesson Plan in the Teacher's Manual in this Teacher's Annotated Edition and in the Teacher's Resource Guide.
- Chapter 9 Study Guide in the Student Workbook.
- Chapter 9 Visual Master in the Teacher's Resource Guide.

any different types of construction projects are designed and built to meet specific needs in our communities. Houses and apartments, for example, are built to meet our need for shelter. Schools, offices, and stores, in addition to offering shelter, meet many of our cultural and economic needs. Highways, airports, bridges, and dams are built to meet still another need—transportation. In this chapter, you will learn more about various types of construction projects. Fig. 9-1.

TYPES OF STRUCTURES

Buildings can be classified by type. There are two basic types of structures: mass structures and frame structures. **Mass structures** use solid material, such as concrete, for the building's walls. These walls support the building. The weight of the building is carried to its foundation by the walls. **Frame structures** use a frame of metal, wood, or concrete to hold up the building. This frame carries the weight of the building to the foundation.

BUILDINGS

Buildings can be classified into three major types: residential, commercial, and industrial. **Residential buildings** are those in which people *reside*, or live. There are two basic kinds of residential buildings. Those designed to house one family are called *single-family units*. Those designed to house more than one family are called *multiple-family units*. Fig. 9-2. Residential buildings are usually constructed of wood framing or masonry. The foundation varies according to the location of the building. Most foundations are made of either poured concrete or concrete block. Most residential buildings are examples of *light construction*.

Fig. 9-1. Many different types of structures are constructed to meet the various needs of our society. The public transit system is an example of civil construction. The office buildings in the background are examples of heavy construction.

1. Ask each student to prepare a written description of a construction project that would meet more than one need. Ask the student to list and explain each need.

2. Have any commercial or industrial buildings in your community been converted to residential use? Discuss the construction techniques that have been used.

Fig. 9-2. Multiple-family units such as this apartment complex can provide living quarters for many people in a small amount of space.

Commercial buildings are those designed to accommodate businesses. Commercial buildings include buildings such as stores, office complexes, and many types of community service buildings. Fig. 9-3. Large businesses usually have steel-frame buildings on foundations of steel-reinforced concrete. Smaller businesses may have steel-frame, wood-frame, or masonry structures. In some cases, large wood-frame or masonry houses are converted to commercial buildings.

Some buildings are classified as commercial buildings even though they are not used for a specific business. Auditoriums, churches, convention centers, schools, libraries, and courthouses are commercial buildings. Such buildings are built in the same way as other commercial buildings from the same kinds of materials. Fig. 9-4. Some commercial buildings are examples of *heavy construction*.

Industrial buildings house the complex machinery that is used to manufacture goods. Industrial buildings are generally low buildings of only one or two stories. Nevertheless, this type of building can be huge, spreading out over a large amount of land. Some industrial buildings

Fig. 9-3. Some commercial buildings, such as the famous World Trade Center, provide offices for thousands of businesspeople.

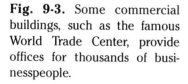
1. Discuss why large commercial buildings would be built with steel or steel-reinforced concrete framework.
2. Have the class contrast industrial buildings built in the early 1900s with those built today. What effect has the change from rail to highway transportation had on the location of industrial buildings?

Fig. 9-4. A school is considered a commercial building.

cover several acres of land. Industrial buildings are examples of *industrial construction.*

Processing industrial materials is a large-scale operation that requires special kinds of manufacturing facilities. In some respects, construction of these facilities is similar to other types of construction. The basic steel framework for industrial buildings must be erected. Both large and small buildings must be built, and utilities such as plumbing and wiring must be installed. However, in industrial plants, large machines and special equipment must be installed. Special foundations are required for the heavy machines and equipment.

Each different type of industrial plant has different construction needs. Fig. 9-5. For example, steel mills and petroleum refineries need

Fig. 9-5. A petroleum refinery is one example of an industrial building that has special construction requirements.

1. Obtain pictures of both commercial and industrial buildings under construction. Discuss their similarities and differences.
2. Discuss how a building for making furniture will differ from a steel mill.

special furnaces. Petroleum refineries also need complex fractionation towers to separate crude oil into its different components, such as gasoline and diesel fuel. Chemical processing plants also have special requirements. They need chemical baths and storage buildings that are highly resistant to chemical erosion.

For Discussion

This section describes the three types of buildings, residential, commercial, and industrial. In your town or city, do you see any examples of residential buildings that have been converted to a commercial use? What types of businesses do such buildings usually house?

 ## HIGHWAYS

Highways, airports, tunnels, bridges, and dams are discussed on the following pages. These are examples of *civil construction*.

Highways are constructed to give wheeled vehicles a proper surface on which to travel. 1 **Highway construction** is a general term used for the construction of any road or street. The basic steps of highway construction are preparing the soil, preparing the roadbed, and striping the finished road.

To prepare the soil for highway construction, trees, roots, and rocks must be removed. Then the ground must be leveled and graded to the proper elevation. Earth must be removed from 2 areas that are too high, and low spots must be filled in. Fig. 9-6.

Next the roadbed is prepared. There are two major types of roadbeds: flexible and rigid. A flexible roadbed requires a thick gravel subbase. The subbase spreads the load on the highway into the soil beneath the highway. It is usually covered with a concrete base. The top layer, a mixture of sand, asphalt, and either gravel or

Fig. 9-6. Building a road requires extensive earthworking.

1. Have a student or group of students study highway construction in greater detail. Ask them to explain where some of the heavy equipment described in Chapter 5 would be used.

2. Ask the class if they have observed any significant differences between the grade on a highway and that on a railroad. Why do you think there is that difference?

crushed rock, is designed to give slightly under a heavy load. This helps protect the surface of the highway from cracks and potholes due to stress.

A rigid roadbed consists of steel bars set on a sand base. Approximately 8 inches (20 cm) of concrete are poured over the bars. The resulting steel-reinforced concrete slab is capable of spreading the weight of traffic over a large area.

Before a new road can be used, it must be striped. Concrete pavement can be striped as soon as it hardens. Bituminous pavement has to cure for a week or two before it is ready to be striped.

For Discussion

This section describes two types of roadbeds: flexible and rigid. Based on what you have read in the book, what type of roadbed lies beneath the road that runs in front of your school?

AIRPORTS

The construction of an airport is actually a combination of road construction and building construction. The major road construction tasks for an airport include construction of the following:

• runways
• taxiways (the paths between the passenger terminals and the runways)
• aprons (the areas near the passenger terminals where planes park for boarding and deboarding)
• parking lots and roadways to handle the cars people drive to the airport

These four tasks may require many miles of road surfaces. For example, large international airports must have runways long enough to allow a Boeing 747 to land. Such a runway must be 13,000 to 14,000 feet (3,900 m to 4,200 m) long. The runways, taxiways, and aprons must also be strong enough to support the 350-ton aircraft. This requires a strong soil base and thick, steel-reinforced concrete. Fig. 9-7.

Fig. 9-7. The paved surfaces at airports must be made to be extra heavy-duty. The concrete for some runways is more than 10 feet (3 m) thick.

1. Discuss why weight limits are reduced on certain roads every spring while the frost comes out of the roadbed. Explain how this can affect a construction project located on one of these roads.

2. Obtain a layout drawing or aerial photo of your local airport. Ask the students to identify the components that make up the airport. Ask them what type of construction company would build each component.

HEALTH & SAFETY

There are types of pollution other than air pollution and water pollution. There is also noise pollution. Noise pollution can have a serious effect on health. It can, for example, contribute to stress. As air traffic has increased, the number of airports has grown. People living close to airports have been subjected to the sound of arriving and departing aircraft. A number of things have been done to reduce airport noise pollution. Many of these concern aircraft takeoff and landing procedures. New engine designs also have been introduced. These new designs have been able to cut some of the engine noise. Engineers are working on other ways to reduce aircraft engine noise.

Airports also need several kinds of buildings. Passenger terminals, freight terminals, hangars, control towers, maintenance buildings, and fire stations are all important to the operation of an airport. Each of these structures has special construction requirements. For example, a hangar must be large and strong enough to house one or more planes. It must be designed to give mechanics easy access to the planes. Fig. 9-8. A control tower must be designed to give air traffic controllers a clear view of the runways and all the air traffic in the area. Most control towers have huge windows on all sides to meet these needs.

Specially trained airport planners and engineers make the plans for most large airports. They work with city officials to find the best site for the airport. They study population trends to make sure the airport is built in a location that will be useful for many years. They determine the size of the airport according to the amount of air traffic it is expected to handle. Together with the city officials, they design an efficient system of buildings and runways. Because large airports require a long time to build, they are usually built in stages. As each stage is finished, it is opened for use by the public.

Fig. 9-8. Hangars are designed and constructed to give mechanics access to the planes for maintenance and repairs. This plane is being prepared for repainting.

1. Discuss with the students and list on the chalkboard sources of noise pollution other than aircraft. What solutions can be found for these?

2. Discuss why many airports are in highly populated areas. Were these areas like that when the airport was built? What happens when an airport is built away from populated areas?

Did You Know?

One of the major construction features of an airport is the runway. The earliest airports had only a single runway. Later, as air traffic increased, the number of runways also increased. Some airports had four and five runways. These various runways were needed because planes were relatively light. They could be affected by crosswinds on landing and takeoff. Thus, they needed to take off and land along runways that would minimize the effects of crosswinds. In the last twenty years, aircraft engines have become more powerful. Aircraft also have become heavier. This has meant that aircraft are not as affected by crosswinds. Many major international airports have only two main runways.

For Discussion

The text mentions several factors that must be considered in finding the best site for an airport. Can you list others not included in the text?

TUNNELS

Tunnels are constructed as underground passageways for roads and railroads. Their usual purpose is to streamline traffic or to route traffic around or through an obstacle. Figure 9-9 shows a modern rapid transit system that uses tunnels to route the tracks under parts of the city.

Fig. 9-9. Much of the Metro Rapid Transit System in Washington, D.C., is routed through tunnels under the city.

1. Ask a student or group of students to find out and explain to the class how runways are identified.

2. Have a student or group of students research and write a report on the history of tunneling. Ask the students to emphasize how tunneling was done before specialized machines were developed.

Sometimes tunnels are built under rivers. Such tunnels enable highway traffic to go under the rivers so that the rivers can stay open for ship traffic. Tunnels for roads and railroads are made through mountains because the route through the mountain is the shortest route to the other side.

Special tunnel-boring machines are used to create tunnels in soft rock such as limestone. Fig. 9-10. They use disk-shaped cutters to dig mud, cut through rock, and move loose earth out of the way. A steel *shield* is used to keep the earth around the tunnel from caving in until workers can stabilize it. Workers stabilize the walls of the tunnel by lining them with concrete or cast iron.

Sometimes tunnels must be built through hard, solid rock. In these cases, explosives are used to *blast*, or break up, the rock. Engineers must study the rock carefully to determine the proper amount of explosives. A small portion of rock is blasted at a time. Then the loose rock is removed and steel beams are inserted to support that portion while the next portion is blasted. Some tunnels built in hard rock are strong enough that they do not need iron or concrete supports. However, most are eventually lined to make them more durable.

Did You Know?

In 41 A.D., the Romans constructed a tunnel to drain a lake in central Italy. It was an enormous project, taking ten years and requiring the work of over 30,000 men. Today, tunnels are constructed using large tunneling systems. These tunneling systems consist of a large boring head, a power unit, and machinery for erecting the parts of the tunnel lining. There is also a conveyor for removing the material that has been cut away. These tunneling systems have allowed the construction of longer and larger tunnels. Such tunneling systems have also allowed tunnels to be completed more quickly.

Fig. 9-10. Special tunnel-boring machines use disk cutters to cut tunnels through soft rock.

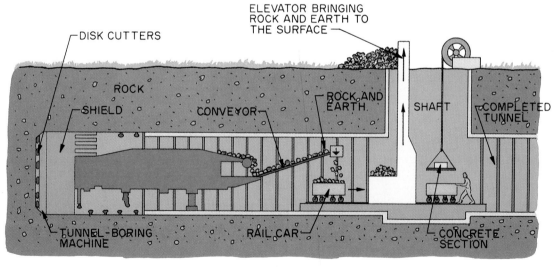

1. Explain how water is kept out of a tunnel that is being built under a body of water.
2. Ask students to tell the class about the tunnels that they have been through.

3. Discuss the relationship of techniques used in mining to those used in tunneling.

For Discussion

Tunnels are more common in regions where there are mountains and rivers. In or near your city or town, are there any tunnels that are used for traffic?

Fig. 9-11. This pedestrian bridge allows school children to cross a busy highway safely.

||| BRIDGES

A bridge is a structure that is built to span, or cross over, a river or a gap in the earth. A bridge provides a way for people and vehicles to cross from one side to the other. Bridges can also span other structures. A bridge on a highway might cross over railroad tracks or over another highway. Different types of bridges carry railroads, highway traffic, pipelines, and foot traffic. Fig. 9-11. Sometimes bridges are made with movable sections that can be raised or swung out of the way so that large boats can pass by. Fig. 9-12.

Bridges can be constructed in several different ways, depending on the required length of the bridge and on the weight it must support.

Fig. 9-12. This bridge can be raised to allow barges to pass through.

1. Ask a student or group of students to research and report on how bridge abutments are built under water.

2. Explain that concrete can be poured under water as long as it does not mix with the water. Concrete sets under water as well as in the air.

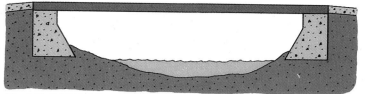

SLAB BRIDGE

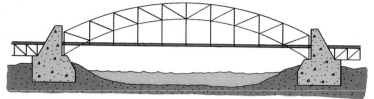

ARCH BRIDGE

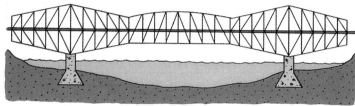

CANTILEVER BRIDGE

Fig. 9-13. Different kinds of bridges: slab, arch, truss (two types), cantilever, and suspension.

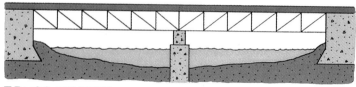

TRUSS BRIDGE

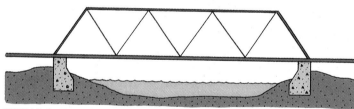

TRUSS BRIDGE

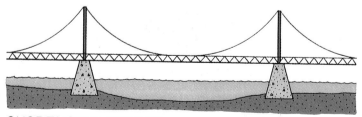

SUSPENSION BRIDGE

1. Discuss how a truss bridge differs from a cantilever bridge. Explain how a cantilever bridge is supported.

Fig. 9-13. Most bridges are anchored on each end by supports called abutments. The simplest type of bridge, the **slab bridge**, consists of a concrete slab supported by abutments. Some of the longer slab bridges are also supported by a pier, or beam, in the middle. This type of bridge is usually made of steel or steel-reinforced concrete and is used mostly for light loads and short spans.

Did You Know?

1 Computers are used to solve many design problems. This is especially true in the construction industry. For example, in designing suspension bridges, engineers have been able to calculate the shape of the suspension cables under changing loads.

An **arch bridge** is one in which an arch is used to carry the weight of the bridge. Arch 2 bridges are made of concrete or steel and are usually constructed over deep ravines. **Truss bridges** are supported by steel or wooden trusses, or beams that are put together to form triangular shapes. Triangles are used because the triangle is a particularly strong structural shape. Trusses are also used in combination with other bridges to give them additional support. One type of bridge that commonly uses trusses is a cantilever bridge. A **cantilever bridge** is used for fairly long spans. It has two beams, or cantilevers, that extend from the ends of the bridge. They are joined in the middle by a connecting section called a *suspended span*. The whole structure usually receives additional support from steel trusses.

The very longest crossings are spanned by suspension bridges. **Suspension bridges** are suspended from cables made of thousands of 3 steel wires wound together. One well-known example of a suspension bridge is the Golden Gate Bridge in San Francisco. Fig. 9-14.

Fig. 9-14. The Golden Gate Bridge in San Francisco is an example of a suspension bridge.

1. Ask each student to suggest an example of the use of the computer in the construction industry.
2. Explain why an arch is an effective means of carrying the weight of a long, heavy structure such as a bridge.

3. Explain to the class the directions of the various forces on the different parts of a suspension bridge.

Did You Know?

The ancient Romans were among the greatest bridge builders in history. They developed a type of natural cement that could be used to bond stones together. They also developed the cofferdam. This is a watertight enclosure in which the piers, which support the bridge, can be built. The Romans also took full advantage of the circular masonry arch. Examples of the skill of the Romans in building bridges can still be seen. Some of the bridges they built are still in use.

For Discussion

The text discusses the main types of bridges. Are there any bridges in your town or city? What types of bridges are they?

DAMS

A **dam** is a structure that is placed across a river to block the flow of water. This is usually done for one of two reasons. The most common reason for damming a river is to create a water reservoir for nearby communities. Fig. 9-15. Another important reason to dam a river is to collect water to power the water turbines in a hydroelectric power station.

Because a dam has a major effect on the surrounding environment, the site for the dam must be selected very carefully. Civil engineers typically spend years studying the characteristics of the land near a proposed dam site. The reservoir created by the dam may flood land that was previously inhabited or used for farming. Arrangements must be made to relocate people and structures that will be flooded. Fig. 9-16.

The construction of a dam is a major undertaking. A large dam may take ten years or longer to construct. A tremendous amount of earthworking must be done before construction on the dam can even be started. The soil must be made strong enough to hold both the dam and the weight of the water in the reservoir created by the dam. The earth must be built into an embankment to keep water from spilling around the dam. The dam itself must have a solid, strong foundation so that it will not wash away when the river swells. The dam must have strong gates to allow water to pass through the dam in controlled amounts.

A spillway must also be constructed. A **spillway** is a safety valve that allows excess water to bypass the dam. This is necessary because few dams are strong enough to withstand the force of floodwater. If the water could not bypass the dam, the dam would break.

Many underwater parts of the dam must be built on dry ground. To be able to work on dry ground, the construction workers must divert the river. This alone can be a major project if the river is a large one. A **cofferdam**, or watertight wall, must be built to keep water out of the worker's way. Fig. 9-17. This temporary wall can be made of timber, concrete, soil, or sheets of steel.

As work on the dam progresses, another cofferdam is built farther out in the river, and the first cofferdam is removed. This allows the water to flow around the sides of the construction site so that the river is not obstructed. After the workers finish the last underwater portion of the dam, the cofferdam is removed entirely.

1. Have a group of students research and present a written or oral report on dam collapses. Ask them to emphasize those points that would help in the design of future dams.

2. Explain that cofferdams are used for building the underwater parts of bridge abutments as well as parts of dams.